Things As They Are

THINGS AS THEY ARE

MISSION WORK
IN SOUTHERN INDIA

Old India. "You think you know us; you know nothing at all about us!" and the old eyes peer intently into yours, and the old head shakes and he smiles to himself as he moves off. Every bit of this picture is suggestive: the closed door behind,—only a Brahman may open that door; the mytho- logical carving,—only a Brahman has the right to understand it; the three-skein cord, —only a Brahman may touch it. Even the ragged old cloth is suggestive. In old India nothing but Caste counts for anything, and a reigning Prince lately gave his weight in gold to the Brahmans, as part payment for ceremonies which enabled him to eat with men of this old man's social position. Look at the marks on the baby's forehead; they are suggestive too.

AS THEY ARE

MISSION WORK

SOUTHERN INDIA

BY

AMY WILSON-CARMICHAEL

ZENANA MISSIONARY SOCIETY

AUTHOR OF
"FROM SUNRISE LAND" ETC.

WITH PREFACE BY
EUGENE STOCK

LONDON MORGAN AND SCOTT
Office of "The Christian"
12 PATERNOSTER BUILDINGS, E.C.
And may be ordered of any Bookseller
1905

Old rose. . . . . may have a. . . . . . the
. . . . suggestive. Would teeth
. . . . anything, and
. . . . gave his watch to
. . . . enabled him to see ani-
. . . . and men's moral qualities. Look-
logical carving,—only a Brahman had the   at the marks on the baby's forehead, they
right to understand it; the three-skein cord,   are suggestive too.

THINGS AS THEY ARE

MISSION WORK
IN SOUTHERN INDIA

BY

AMY WILSON-CARMICHAEL
KESWICK MISSIONARY C.E.Z.M.S.
AUTHOR OF
"FROM SUNRISE LAND," ETC.

WITH PREFACE BY
EUGENE STOCK

LONDON: MORGAN AND SCOTT
(OFFICE OF "The Christian".)
12, PATERNOSTER BUILDINGS, E.C.
And may be ordered of any Bookseller
1903

BY

FIRST EDITION . . *April* 1903
Reprinted . . *August* 1903

To the Memory of My Dear Friend,

ELEANOR CARR,

Whose last message to the Band, before her
translation on June 16, 1901, was:

"YOU WILL BE IN THE THICK OF THE FIGHT

BY THE TIME THIS REACHES YOU,

யுத்தம்கர்த்தருடை யது.

THE BATTLE IS THE LORD'S!"

Preface

———

THE writer of these thrilling chapters is a Keswick
missionary, well known to many friends as the
adopted daughter of Mr. Robert Wilson, the much-
respected chairman of the Keswick Convention. She
worked for a time with the Rev. Barclay Buxton in
Japan; and for the last few years she has been with the
Rev. T. Walker (also a C.M.S. Missionary) in Tinnevelly,
and is on the staff of the Church of England Zenana
Society.

I do not think the realities of Hindu life have ever
been portrayed with greater vividness than in this book;
and I know that the authoress's accuracy can be fully
relied upon. The picture is drawn without prejudice,
with all sympathy, with full recognition of what is
good, and yet with an unswerving determination to
tell the truth and let the facts be known,—that is, so
far as she dares to tell them. What she says is the
truth, and nothing but the truth; but it is not the
whole truth—*that* she could not tell. If she wrote it,
it could not be printed. If it were printed, it could not
be read. But if we read between the lines, we do just
catch glimpses of what she calls " the Actual."

It is evident that the authoress deeply felt the responsibility of writing such a book; and I too feel the

responsibility of recommending it. I do so with the prayer of my heart that God will use it to move many. It is not a book to be read with a lazy kind of sentimental " interest." It is a book to send the reader to his knees—still more to *her* knees.

Most of the chapters are concerned with the lives of Heathen men and women and children surrounded by the tremendous bars and gates of the Caste system. But one chapter, and not the least important one, tells of native Christians. It has long been one of my own objects to correct the curious general impression among people at home that native Christians, as a body, are—not indeed perfect,—no one thinks that, but—earnest and consistent followers of Christ. Narratives, true narratives, of true converts are read, and these are supposed to be specimens of the whole body. But (1) where there have been "mass movements" towards Christianity, where whole villages have put themselves under Christian instruction, mixed motives are certain; (2) where there have been two or three generations of Christians it is unreasonable to expect the descendants of men who may have been themselves most true converts to be necessarily like them. Hereditary Christianity in India is much like hereditary Christianity at home. The Church in Tinnevelly, of which this book incidentally tells a little, is marked by both these features. Whole families or even villages have " come over " at times; and the large majority of the Christians were (so to speak) born Christians, and were baptised in infancy. This is not in itself a result to be despised. " Christian England," unchristian as a great part of its population really is, is better than Heathen India; and in the chapter now referred to, Miss Carmichael herself notices the difference between a Hindu and a Christian

village. But the more widely Christianity spreads, the
more will there assuredly be of mere nominal profession.

Is the incorrect impression I allude to caused by
missionaries dwelling mostly on the brighter side of their
work? Here and there in the book there is just a
suggestion that they are wrong in doing so. But how
can they help it? What does a clergyman or an evangelist in England tell of? Does he tell of his many daily
disappointments, or of his occasional encouraging cases?
The latter are the events of his life, and he naturally
tells of them. The former he comprises in some general
statement. How can he do otherwise? And what can
the modern missionary do in the short reports he is able
to write? Fifty years ago missionary journals of immense length came home, and were duly published; and
then the details of Hindu idolatry and cruelty and
impurity, and the tremendous obstacles to the Gospel,
were better known by the few regular readers. Much
that Miss Carmichael tells was then told over and over
again, though not perhaps with a skilful pen like hers.
But the work has so greatly developed in each mission,
and the missions are so far more numerous and extended,
that neither can missionaries now write as their prede-
cessors did, nor, if they did, could all the missionary
periodicals together find space for their journals.

The fault of incorrect impressions lies mainly in the
want of knowledge and want of thought of home
speakers and preachers. I remember, thirty years ago,
an eloquent Bishop in Exeter Hall triumphantly flinging
in the face of critics of missions the question, "Is Tinnevelly a fiction?"—as if Tinnevelly had become a Christian
country, which apparently some people still suppose it to
be, notwithstanding the warning words to the contrary
which the C.M.S. publications have again and again

uttered. Even now, there are in Tinnevelly about twenty heathen to every one Christian; and of what sort the twenty are this book tells. Tinnevelly is indeed "no fiction," but in a very different sense from that of the good Bishop's speech. Again, a few months ago, I heard a preacher, not very favourable to the C.M.S., say that the C.M.S., despite its shortcomings, deserved well of the Church because it had "converted a nation" in Uganda! —as if the nation comprised only 30,000 souls. Some day the "Actual" of Uganda will be better understood, and the inevitable shortcomings of even its Christian population realised, and then we shall be told that we deceived the public—although we have warned them over and over again.

But the larger part of this book is a revelation—so far as is possible—of the "Actual" of Hinduism and Caste. God grant that its terrible facts and its burning words may sink into the hearts of its readers! Perhaps, when they have read it, they will at last agree that we have used no sensational and exaggerated language when we have said that the Church is only playing at missions! Service, and self-denial, and prayer, must be on a different scale indeed if we are ever—I do not say to convert the world—but even to evangelise it.

EUGENE STOCK.

Contents

————

xi

CONTENTS

Illustrations

xiii

Glossary

AGNI	God of Fire.
AIYO	Alas! "Ai" runs together almost like "eye." The word is repeated rapidly, Eye-eye Yō, Eye-eye Yō!
AMMA	Mother! (vocative case). "A" is pronounced like "u" in "up." The word is also used by all women and girls in speaking to each other, and it often means "Yes."
AMMAL	Lady or woman. "A" is pronounced like "u" in "up."
ANNA	One penny.
ARECA NUT	Nut "eaten" by the Indians with betel leaf or lime.
BETEL	Leaf of a creeper.
BANDY	A bullock cart.
BRAHMA	The first person in the Hindu Triad, regarded as the Creator.
BRAHMAN	The highest of the Hindu Castes.
BRAMO SAMĀJ	A sect of Hindu reformers who honour Christ as a man, but reject Him as a Saviour.
CHEE!	Exclamation of derision, disgust, or remonstrance.
COMPOUND	A piece of ground surrounding a house.
COOLIE	A paid labourer. "Coolie" is the Tamil word for pay.
CURRY	A preparation of meat or vegetables made by grinding various condiments and mixing them together.

xv

FAKEER	. .	Religious beggar.
GURU	. .	A religious teacher.
IYER	. .	Title given to Brahmans and Gurus.
PADDY	. .	Rice in the husk. Paddy fields=rice fields.
PARIAH	. .	A depressed class.
PÚJAH	. .	Worship. "U" is pronounced like "oo."
RUPEE	. .	Value 1s. 4d.
SAIVITE	. .	A worshipper of Siva.
SALAAM	. .	A salutation meaning "peace," used in greeting and farewell, and often in the sense of "thank you." The right hand is raised to the forehead as one says salaam.
SEELEY	. .	Tamil woman's dress of silk, muslin, or cotton.
SHANAR	. .	A Caste of Palmyra-palm climbers.
SIVA	. .	The third person in the Hindu Triad. The Destroyer.
TOM-TOM	. .	An Indian drum.
VAISHNAVITE	. .	A worshipper of Vishnu.
VELLALAR	. .	A Caste of landowners and cultivators.
VISHNU	. .	The second person in the Hindu Triad. The Preserver.

THINGS AS THEY ARE

MISSION WORK IN SOUTHERN INDIA

CHAPTER I

About the Book

"We can do nothing against the Truth, but for the Truth."
St. Paul, Asia and Europe.

"There is too little desire to know what is the actual state of mission work in India, and a regard to the showy and attractive rather than to the solid and practical. I will try, however, to avoid being carried away by the tide, and to set myself the task of giving as plain and unvarnished a statement as possible of what is actually being done or not done in the great field of our foreign labour."

Bishop French, India and Arabia.

THREE friends sat Native fashion on the floor of an Indian verandah. Two of the three had come out to India for a few months to see the fight as they saw it. They now proposed that the third should gather some letters written from the hot heart of things, and make them into a book, to the intent that others should see exactly what they had seen. The third was not sure. The world has many books. Does it want another, and especially another of the kind

this one would be? Brain and time are needed for all
that writing a book means. The third has not much of
either. But the two undertook to do all the most
burdensome part of the business. "Give us the letters,
we will make the book," and they urged reasons which
ended in—this.

This, the book, has tried to tell the Truth. That is all
it has to say about itself. The quotations which head the
chapters, and which are meant to be read, not skipped,
are more worthful than anything else in it. They are
chosen from the writings of missionaries, who saw the
Truth and who told it.

The story covers about two years. We had come
from the eastern side of this South Indian district, to
work for awhile in the south of the South, the farthest
southern outpost of the C.M.S. in India. Chapter II.
plunges into the middle of the beginning. The Band
Sisters are the members of a small Women's Itinerating
Band; the girls mentioned by translated names are the
young convert-girls who are with us; the Iyer is Rev. T.
Walker; the Ammal is Mrs. Walker; the Missie Ammal
explains itself.

The Picture-catching Missie Ammal is the friend who
proposed the book's making. This is her Tamil name,
given because it describes her as she struck the Tamil
mind. The pictures she caught were not easy to catch.
Reserved and conservative India considered the camera
intrusive, and we were often foiled in getting what we
most desired. Even where we were allowed to catch
our object peaceably, it was a case of working under
difficulties which would have daunted a less ardent

This photo was an exception. It was easy to catch. The man to the left is our house-boy; he is testing eggs. If the egg sinks, he buys it. The basket on the ground is made of palm leaf, and is used for drawing water from the well.

picture-catcher. Wherever the camera was set up, there swarms of children sprang into being, burrowed in and out like rabbits, and scuttled about over everything, to the confusion of the poor artist, who had to fix focus and look after the safety of her camera legs at the same time, while the second Missie Ammal held an umbrella over her head, and the third exhorted the picture, which speedily got restive, to sit still. So much for the mere mechanical.

Finally, I should explain the book's character. "Tell about things as they actually are"; so said the Two with emphasis. I tried, but the Actual eluded me. It was as if one painted smoke, and then, pointing to the feeble blur, said, "Look at the battle! 'the smoking hell of battle!' There is the smoke!" The Poet's thought was not this, I know, when she coined that suggestive phrase, "The Dust of the Actual," but it has been the predominating thought in my mind, for it holds that which defines the scope and expresses the purpose of the book, and I use it as the title of one of the chapters. It does not show the Actual. Principalities, Powers, Rulers of the Darkness, Potentialities unknown and unimagined, gathered up into one stupendous Force—we have never seen it. How can we describe it? What we have seen and tried to describe is only an indication of Something undescribed, and is as nothing in comparison with it—as Dust in comparison with the Actual. The book's scope, then, is bounded by this: it only touches the Dust; but its purpose goes deeper, stretches wider, has to do with the Actual and our relation to it.

But in touching the Dust we touch the outworkings

of an Energy so awful in operation that descriptive chapters are awful too. And such chapters are best read alone in some quiet place with God. For the book is a battle-book, written from a battle-field where the fighting is not pretty play but stern reality; and almost every page looks straight from the place where Charles Kingsley stood when he wrote—

> "God! fight we not within a cursèd world,
> Whose very air teems thick with leaguèd fiends—
> Each word we speak has infinite effects—
> Each soul we pass must go to heaven or hell—
> And this our one chance through eternity
> To drop and die, like dead leaves in the brake!
>
> .   .   .   .   .   .
>
> Be earnest, earnest, earnest; mad if thou wilt:
> Do what thou dost as if the stake were heaven,
> And that thy last deed ere the judgment day."

This is our bullock-bandy. The water was up to the top of the bank when we crossed last. The palms are cocoa-nuts.

CHAPTER II

Three Afternoons off the Track

"They are led captive by Satan at his will in the most quiescent manner." *David Brainerd, North America.*

"Oh that the Lord would pour out upon them a spirit of deep concern for their souls!" *Henry Martyn, India.*

"I ask you earnestly to pray that the Gospel may take saving and working effect." *James Gilmour, Mongolia.*

THE Western Ghauts sweep down to the sea in curves. Dohnavur is in one of the last of these curves. There are no proper roads running under the mountains, only rough country ruts crossing the plain. We were rolling along one of these at the rate of two miles an hour.

Crash and tumble went the bandy, a springless construction with a mat roof; bang over stones and slabs of rock, down on one side, up on the other; then both wheels were sharp aslant. But this is usual. On that particular First Afternoon the water was out, which is the South Indian way of saying that the tanks, great lake-like reservoirs, have overflowed and flooded the land. Once we went smoothly down a bank and into a shallow swollen pool, and the water swished in at the lower end and floated our books out quietly. So we had to stop, and fish them up; and then, huddled

5

close at the upper end we sat, somewhat damp, but happy.

At last we got to our destination, reached through a lane which then was a stream with quite a swift little current of its own. Cupid's Lake the place is called. We thought the name appropriate. Cupid's Lake is peopled by Castes of various persuasions; we made for the Robber quarter first. The Robber Caste is honourable here; it furnishes our watchmen and the coolies who carry our money. There is good stuff in the Robber Caste people: a valiant people are they, and though they were not prepared for the thing that was coming towards them, they met it with fortitude. A little girl saw it first. One glance at my hat through the end of the cart, and she flew to spread the news—

"Oh! everyone come running and see! A great white man is here! Oh what an appalling spectacle! A great white man!"

Then there was a general rush; children seemed to spring from the ground, all eyes and tongues and astonishment. "She isn't a man!" "He is!" "She isn't!" "He has got a man's turban!" "But look at her seeley!" (Tamil dress.) A *woman*, and white—it staggered them, till the assurances of the Band Sisters prevailed; and they let me into a neighbouring house, out of the sun which made that hat a necessity. Once it was off they lost all fear, and crowded round in the friendliest fashion; but later, one of the Band was amused by hearing me described in full: "Not a man, though great and white, and wearing a white man's turban, too! Was it not an appalling spectacle?" And the old body who was addressed held up both her hands amazed, and hastened off to investigate.

An English magazine told us lately exactly what these poor women think when they see, for the first time in their lives, the lady missionary. They greatly admire her, the article said, and consider her fairer and more divine than anything ever imagined before—which is very nice indeed to read; but here what they say is this: "Was it not an appalling spectacle? A great white man!"

And now that the spectacle was safe in the house, the instincts of hospitality urged clean mats and betel. Betel (pronounced *beetle*) is the leaf of a climbing plant, into which they roll a morsel of areca nut and lime. The whole is made up into a parcel and munched, but not swallowed. This does not sound elegant; neither is the thing. It is one of the minor trials of life to have to sit through the process.

We took a leaf or two, but explained that it was not our custom to eat it; and then we answered questions straight off for ten minutes. "What is your Caste?" "Chee!" in a tone of remonstrance, "don't you see she is *white*? Married or widow? Why no jewels? What relations? Where are they all? Why have you left them and come here? Whatever can be your business here? What does the Government give you for coming here?" These last questions gave us the chance we were watching for, and we began to explain.

Now what do these people do when, for the first time, they hear the Good Tidings? They simply stare.

In that house that day there was an old woman who

seemed to understand a little what it was all about.
She had probably heard before. But nobody else understood in the least; they did not understand enough to
make remarks. They sat round us on the floor and ate
betel, as everybody does here in all leisure moments, and
they stared.

The one old woman who seemed to understand followed
us out of the house, and remarked that it was a good
religion but a mistaken one, as it advocated, or resulted
in, the destruction of Caste.

In the next house we found several girls, and tried to
persuade the mothers to let them learn to read. If a
girl is learning regularly it gives one a sort of right of
entrance to the house. One's going there is not so much
observed and one gets good chances, but to all our persuasions they only said it was not their custom to allow
their girls to learn. Had *they* to do Government work?
Learning was for men who wanted to do Government
work. We explained a little, and mentioned the many
villages where girls are learning to read. They thought
it a wholly ridiculous idea. Then we told them as
much as we could in an hour about the great love of
Jesus Christ.

I was in the middle of it, and thinking only of it and
their souls, when an old lady with fluffy white hair
leaned forward and gazed at me with a beautiful, earnest
gaze. She did not speak; she just listened and gazed,
"drinking it all in." And then she raised a skeleton
claw, and grabbed her hair, and pointed to mine. "Are
you a widow too," she asked, "that you have no oil on
yours?" After a few such experiences that beautiful

gaze loses its charm. It really means nothing more nor less than the sweet expression sometimes observed in the eyes of a sorrowful animal.

But her question had set the ball rolling again. "Oil! no oil! Can't you even afford a halfpenny a month to buy good oil? It isn't your custom? Why not? Don't any white Ammals ever use oil? What sort of oil do the girls use? Do you *never* use castor oil for the hair? Oh, castor oil is excellent!" And they go into many details. The first thing they do when a baby is born is to swing it head downwards, holding its feet, and advise it not to sin; and the second thing is to feed it with castor oil, and put castor oil in its eyes. "Do we do none of these things?" We sang to them. They always like that, and sometimes it touches them: but the Tamils are not easily touched, and could never be described as unduly emotional.

All through there were constant and various interruptions. Two bulls sauntered in through the open door, and established themselves in their accustomed places; then a cow followed, and somebody went off to tie the animals up. Children came in and wanted attention, babies made their usual noises. We rarely had five consecutive quiet minutes.

When they seemed to be getting tired of us, we said the time was passing, to which they agreed, and, with a word about hoping to come again, to which they answered cordially, "Oh yes! Come to-morrow!" we went out into the street, and finished up in the open air. There is a tree at one end of the village; we stood under it and sang a chorus and taught the children who had followed us from house to house to sing it, and this attracted some passing grown-ups, who listened while we witnessed unto Jesus, Who had saved us and given us His joy. Nothing tells more than just this simple witness. To hear one of their own people saying, with evident sincerity, "One thing I know, that whereas I was blind now I see," makes them look at each other and nod their heads sympathetically. This is something that appeals, something they can appreciate; many a time it arrests attention when nothing else would.

We were thoroughly tired by this time, and could neither talk nor sing any more. The crowd melted—all but the children, who never melt—one by one going their respective ways, having heard, some of them, for the first time. What difference will it make in their lives? Did they understand it? None of them seemed specially interested, none of them said anything interesting. The last question I heard was about soap—"What sort of soap do you use to make your skin white?" Most of them would far prefer to be told that secret than how to get a white heart.

Afternoon Number Two found us in the Village of the Temple, a tumble-down little place, but a very citadel of pride and the arrogance of ignorance. We did not know that at first, of course, but we very soon found it out. There was the usual skirmish at the sight of a live white woman; no one there had seen such a curiosity. But even curiosity could not draw the Brahmans. They live in a single straggling street, and would not let us in. "Go!" said a fat old Brahman

We were not able to get the photo of that special girl in the blue seeley, but this girl is so like her that I put her here. She is a Vellalar. The jewels worn by a girl of this class run into thousands of rupees. They are part of the ordinary dress. This girl did not know we were coming, she was "caught" just as she was. She had a ball of pink oleander flowers in her hands and white flowers in her hair.

disdainfully; "no white man has ever trodden our street, and no white woman shall. As for that low-caste child with you"—Victory looked up in her gentle way, and he varied it to—"that child who eats with those low-caste people—she shall not speak to one of our women. Go by the way you have come!"

This was not encouraging. We salaamed and departed, and went to our bandy left outside ("low-caste bandies" are not allowed to drive down Brahman streets), and asked our Master to open another door. While we were waiting, a tall, fine-looking Hindu came and said, "Will you come to my house? I will show you the way." So we went.

He led us to the Vellala quarter next to the Brahmans, and we found his house was the great house of the place. The outer door opened into a large square inner courtyard. A wide verandah, supported by pillars quaintly carved, ran round it. The women's rooms, low and windowless, opened on either side; these are the rooms we rejoice to get into, and now we were led right in.

But first I had to talk to the men. They were regular Caste Hindus; courteous—for they have had no cause to fear the power of the Gospel—yet keen and argumentative. One of them had evidently read a good deal. He quoted from their classics; knew all about Mrs. Besant and the latest pervert to her views; and was up in the bewildering tangle of thought known as Hindu Philosophy. "Fog-wreaths of doubt, in blinding eddies drifted"—that is what it really is, but it is very difficult to prove it so.

One truth struck him especially—Christianity is the
only religion which provides a way by which there is
deliverance from sin *now*. There is a certain system of
philosophy which professes to provide deliverance in the
future, when the soul, having passed through the first
three stages of bliss, loses its identity and becomes
absorbed in God; but there is no way by which deliverance can be obtained here and now. "Sin shall not
have dominion over you"—there is no such line as this
in all the million stanzas of the Hindu classics. He
admitted this freely, admitted that this one tenet marked
out Christianity as a unique religion; but he did not go
on further; he showed no desire to prove the truth
of it.

After this they let us go to the women, who had all
this time been watching us, and discussing us with
interest.

Once safely into their inner room, we sat down on the
floor in the midst of them, and began to make friends.
There was a grandmother who had heard that white
people were not white all over, but piebald, so to speak;
might she examine me? There were several matronly
women who wanted to know what arrangements English
parents made concerning their daughters' marriages.
There were the usual widows of a large Indian household—one always looks at them with a special longing;
and there was a dear young girl, in a soft blue seeley
(Tamil dress), her ears clustered about with pearls, and
her neck laden with five or six necklets worth some
hundreds of rupees. She was going to be married;
and beyond the usual gentle courtesy of a well-brought-

The God King's Mountain. This is the story: Rama, king of Oudh, was banished from his kingdom, and Ravana, demon-king of Ceylon, carried off Sita, Rama's queen. The tribes of the South helped Rama to search for Sita. Their chief leaped from the mountain top over the sea to Ceylon and found the prisoned queen.

up Tamil girl, showed no interest in us. Almost all the
women had questions to ask. On the track it is different;
they have already satisfied their lawful curiosity concerning Missie Ammals; but here they have not had the
chance; and if we ignore their desires, we defeat our
own. They may seem to listen, but they are really
occupied in wondering about us. We got them to listen
finally, and left them, cheered by warm invitations to
return.

Then we thought of the poor proud Brahmans, and
hoping that, perhaps, in the interval they had inquired
about us, and would let us in, we went to them again.
We could see the fair faces and slender forms of the
younger Brahman women standing in the shadow behind
their verandah pillars, and some of them looked as if
they would like to let us in, but the street had not
relented; and a Brahman street is like a house—you
cannot go in unless you are allowed.

There was one kind-faced, courtly old man, and he
seemed to sympathise with us, for he left the mocking
group of men, and came to see us off; and then, as if to
divert us from the greater topic, he pointed to one of
the mountains, a spur of the God King's mountain,
famous in all South India, and volunteered to tell me its
story. We were glad to make friends with him even
over so small a thing as a mountain; but he would
speak of nothing else, and when he left us we felt baffled
and sorry, and tired with the tiredness that comes when
you cannot give your message; and we sat down on a
rock outside the Brahman street, to wait till the Band
Sisters gathered for the homeward walk.

It was sunset time, and the sky was overcast by dull grey clouds; but just over the Brahman quarter there was a rift in the grey, and the pent-up gold shone through. It seemed as if God were pouring out His beauty upon those Brahmans, trying to make them look up, and they would not. One by one we saw them go to their different courtyards, where the golden glow could not reach them, and we heard them shut their great heavy doors, as if they were shutting Him out.

In there it was dark; out here, out with God, it was light. The after-glow, that loveliest glow of the East, was shining through the rent of the clouds, and the red-tiled roofs and the scarlet flowers of the Flame of the Forest, and every tint and colour which would respond in any way, were aglow with the beauty of it. The Brahman quarter was set in the deep green of shadowy trees; just behind it the mountains rose outlined in mist, and out of the mist a waterfall gleamed white against blue.

We spent Afternoon Number Three in the Village of the Warrior, a lonely little place, left all by itself on a great rough moorland—if you can call a patch of bare land "moor" which is destitute of heather, and grows palms and scrub in clumps instead. It took us rather a long time to get to it, over very broken ground on a very hot day; but when we did get there we found such a good opening that we forgot about our feelings, and entered in rejoicing. There were some little children playing at the entrance to the village, and they led us straight to their own house, making friends in the most charming way as they trotted along beside us. They told us their family history, and we told them as much of ours as was necessary, and they introduced us to their mothers as old acquaintances. The mothers were indulgent, and let us have a room all to ourselves in the inner courtyard, where a dozen or more children gathered and listened with refreshing zest. *They* understood, dear little things, though so often their elders did not.

Then the mothers got interested, and sat about the door. The girls were with me. (We usually divide into two parties; the elder and more experienced Sisters go off in one direction, and the young convert-girls come with me.) And before long, Jewel of Victory was telling out of a full heart all about the great things God had done for her. She has a very sweet way with the women, and they listened fascinated. Then the others spoke, and still those women listened. They were more intelligent than our audience of yesterday; and though they did not follow nearly all, they listened splendidly to the story-part of our message. In the meaning, as is often the case, their interest was simply nil.

But we were sorry, and I think so were they, when a commotion outside disturbed us, and we were sorrier when we knew the cause. The village postman, who only visits these out-of-the-way places once a week, had appeared with a letter for the head of the house. One of the men folk had read it. It told of the death of the son in foreign parts—Madras, I think—and the poor old mother's one desire was to see us out of the room. She had not liked to turn us out; but, as the news spread, more women gathered clamouring round the door; and the

moment we left the room empty, in they rushed, with
the mother and the women who had listened to us,
and flinging themselves on the floor, cried the Tamil cry
of sorrow, full of a pathos of its own: "Ai-yō! Ai-yō!
Ai-Ai-yō!"

It was sad to leave them crying so, but at that
moment we were certainly better away. The children
came with us to the well outside the village, and we sat
on its wall and went on with our talk. They would
hardly let us go, and begged us to come back and "teach
them every day," not the Gospel—do not imagine their
little hearts craved for that—but reading and writing
and sums! As we drove off some of the villagers smiled
and salaamed, and the little children's last words followed
us as far as we could hear them: "Come back soon!"

Sometimes, as now, when we come to a new place, we
dream a dream, dream that perhaps at last it may be
possible to win souls peacefully. Perhaps these courteous,
kindly people will welcome the message we bring them
when they understand it better. Perhaps homes need
not be broken up, perhaps whole families will believe, or
individual members believing may still live in their own
homes and witness there. Perhaps—perhaps—! And
snatches of verse float through our dream—

> "Oh, might some sweet song Thy lips have taught us,
>   Some glad song, and sweet,
> Guide amidst the mist, and through the darkness,
>   Lost ones to Thy feet!"

It sounds so beautiful, so easy, singing souls to Jesus.
And we dream our dream.

Till suddenly and with violence we are awakened.

Someone—a mere girl, or a lad, or even a little child—
has believed, has confessed, wants to be a Christian. And
the whole Caste is roused, and the whole countryside
joins with the Caste; and the people we almost thought
loved us, hate us. And till we go to the next new
place we never dream that dream again.

CHAPTER III

Humdrum

"A missionary's life is more ordinary than is supposed. Plod rather than cleverness is often the best missionary equipment."
Rev. J. Heywood Horsburgh, China.

"Truly to understand the facts of work for Christ in any land, we must strip it of all romance, and of everything which is unreal." *Miss S. S. Hewlett, India.*

THERE have been times of late when I have had to hold on to one text with all my might: "It is required in stewards that a man be found *faithful*." Praise God, it does not say "successful."

One evening things came to a climax. We all spent a whole afternoon without getting one good listener. We separated as usual, going two and two to the different quarters of a big sleepy straggly village. Life and I went to the potters. Life spoke most earnestly and well to an uninterested group of women. After she had finished one of them pointed to my hat (the only foreign thing about me which was visible—oh that I could dispense with it!). "What is that?" she said. Not one bit did they care to hear. One by one they went back to their work, and we were left alone.

We went to another quarter. It was just the same. At a rest-house by the way I noticed a Brahman, and went to see if he would listen. He would if I would

Potters treading clay. They dig up the clay, tread it for an hour, and it is ready for use. The cord the men wear is the sign of their Caste. Artizans, weavers, potters, and fishermen wear a cord.

talk "about politics or education, but not if it was about religion." However, I did get a chance of pleading with him to consider the question of his soul's salvation, and he took a book and said he would read it at his leisure. And then he asked me how many persons I had succeeded in joining to my Way since I began to try. It was exactly the question, only asked in another form, which the devil had been pressing on me all the afternoon. After this he told me politely that we were knocking our heads against a rock; we might smash our heads, but we never would affect the rock.

"Rock! Rock! when wilt thou open?" It is an old cry; I cried it afresh. But the Brahman only smiled, and then with a gesture expressing at once his sense of his own condescension in speaking with me, and his utter contempt for the faith I held, motioned to me to go.

Outside in the road a number of Hindus were standing; some of them were his retainers and friends. I heard them say, as I passed through their midst, "Who will fall into the pit of the Christian Way!" And they laughed, and the Brahman laughed. "As the filth of the world, the offscouring of all things, unto this day."

We walked along the road bordered with beautiful banyan trees. We sat down under their shade, and waited for what would come. Some little children followed us, but before we could get a single idea clearly into their heads a man came and chased them away. "It is getting dark," he said. "They are only little green things; they must not be out late." It was broad daylight then, and would be for another hour. Some coolies

passing that way stopped to look at us; but before they
had time to get interested they too remarked that darkness was coming, and they must be off, and off they
went.

We were left alone after that. Within five minutes'
walk were at least five hundred souls, redeemed, but
they don't know it; redeemed, *but they don't want to
know it*. Sometimes they seem to want to know, but
however tenderly you tell it, the keen Hindu mind soon
perceives the drift of it all—Redemption must mean loss
of Caste. One day last week I was visiting in the
Village of the Red Lake. Standing in one of its courtyards you see the Western Ghauts rising straight up
behind. The Red Lake lies at the mountain foot; we
call it Derwentwater, but there are palms and bamboos,
and there is no Friar's Crag.

That afternoon I was bound for a house in the centre
of the village, when an old lady called me to come to
her house, and I followed her gladly. There were six
or eight women all more or less willing to listen; among
them were two who were very old. Old people in India
are usually too attached to their own faith, or too
utterly stupid and dull, to care to hear about another;
but this old lady had been stirred to something almost
like active thought by the recent death of a relative, and
she felt that she needed something more than she had to
make her ready for death. She was apparently devout.
Ashes were marked on her brow and arms, and she wore
a very large rosary. It is worn to accumulate merit. I
did not refer to it as I talked, but in some dim way she
seemed to feel it did not fit with what I was saying, for,

The Red Lake.   The palms are palmyras, the chief palm cultivated in these plains.

with trembling hands, she took it off and threw it to a child. I hoped this meant something definite, and tried to lead her to Jesus. But as soon as she understood Who He was, she drew back. "I cannot be a disciple of your Guru, here," she said; "would my relations bear such defilement?" Being a Christian really meant sooner or later leaving her home and all her people for ever. Can you wonder an old lady of perhaps seventy-five stopped at that?

The little children in the Village of the Warrior are not allowed to learn. The men of the place have consulted and come to the decision. The chill of it has struck the little ones, and they do not care to run the chance of the scolding they would receive if they showed too much interest in us. The mothers are as friendly as ever, but indifferent. "We hear this is a religion which spoils our Caste," they say, and that is the end of it. In the great house of the Temple Village they listened well for some weeks. Then, as it gradually opened to them that there is no Caste whatever in Christianity, their interest died.

How much one would like to tell a different story! But a made-up story is one thing and a story of facts is another. So far we have only found two genuine earnest souls there. But if those two go on—! Praise God for the joy on before!

We went again to the potters' village and sat on the narrow verandah and talked to a girl as she patted the pots into shape underneath where the wheel had left an open place. She listened for awhile; then she said, "If I come to your Way will you give me a new seeley

and good curry every day?" And back again we went
to the very beginning of things, while the old grandfather spinning his wheel chuckled at us for our folly
in wasting our time over potters. "As if *we* would
ever turn to your religion!" he said. "Have you ever
heard of a potter who changed his Caste?"

Caste and religion! They are so mixed up that we
do not know how to unmix them. His Caste to the
potter meant his trade, the trade of his clan for generations; it meant all the observances bound up with it;
it meant, in short, his life. It would never strike him
that he could be a Christian and a potter at the same
time, and very probably he could not; the feeling of the
Caste would be against it. Then what else could he be?
He does not argue all this out; he does not care enough
about the matter to take the trouble to think at all.
He has only one concern in life—he lives to make pots
and sell them, and make more and sell them, and so eat
and sleep in peace.

But the girl had the look of more possibility; she
asked questions and seemed interested, and finally suggested we should wait till she had finished her batch
of pots, and then she would "tell us all her mind." So
we waited and watched the deft brown hands as they
worked round the gaping hole till it grew together and
closed; and at last she had finished. Then she drew us
away from the group of curious children, and told us if
we would come in three days she would be prepared to
join our Way and come with us, for she had to work
very hard at home, and her food was poor and her seeley
old, and she thought it would be worth risking the wrath

There is always a hole left at the bottom of the vessel where it sat on the wheel. The women pat the edges gently with a wooden ladle till the hole is closed.

of her people to get all she knew we should give her if she came; and this was all her mind.

She had touched a great perplexity. How are we to live in India without raising desires of this sort? It is true the Brahmans look down upon us, and the higher Castes certainly do not look up, but to the greater number of the people we seem rich and grand and desirable to cultivate. The Ulterior-Object-Society is a fact in South India. We may banish expensive-looking things from our tables, and all pictures and ornaments from our walls, and confine ourselves to texts. This certainly helps; there is less to distract the attention of the people when they come to see us, and we have so many the fewer things to take care of—a very great advantage—but it does not go far towards disillusioning them as to what they imagine is our true position. We are still up above to them; not on a level, not one of themselves.

The houses we live in are airy and large, and they do not understand the need of protection from the sun. The food we eat is abundant and good, and to them it looks luxurious, for they live on rice and vegetable curry, at a cost of twopence a day. Our walls may be bare, but they are clean, and the texts aforesaid are not torn at the corners; so, whatever we say, we are rich.

Identification with the people whom we have come to win is the aim of many a missionary, but the difficulty always is the same—climate and customs are dead against it; how can we do it? George Bowen struck at English life and became a true Indian, so far as he could, but even he could not go all the way. No matter how far you may go, there is always a distance you cannot cover—yards or inches it may be, but always that fatal hiatus. We seem so undeniably up, far up above them in everything, and we want to get to the lowest step down, low enough down to lift lost souls up. On and on, if they will let us, time after time, by text and hymn and story, we have to explain what things really mean before they are able to understand even a fraction of the truth. The fact that this girl had thought enough to get her ideas into shape was encouraging, and with such slender cause for hope we still hoped. But when after some weeks' visiting she began to see that the question was not one of curries and seeleys but of inward invisible gifts, her interest died, and she was "out" when we went, or too busy patting her pots to have time to listen to us.

Humdrum we have called the work, and humdrum it is. There is nothing romantic about potters except in poetry, nor is there much of romance about missions except on platforms and in books. Yet "though it's dull at whiles," there is joy in the doing of it, there is joy in just obeying. He said "Go, tell," and we have come and are telling, and we meet Him as we "go and tell."

But, dear friends, do not, we entreat you, expect to hear of us doing great things, as an everyday matter of course. Our aim is great—it is *India for Christ!* and before the gods in possession here, we sing songs unto Him. But what we say to you is this: Do not expect every true story to dovetail into some other true story and end with some marvellous coincidence or miraculous conversion. Most days in real life end exactly as they

"I went down to the potter's house, and, behold, he wrought a work on the wheels." The vessel the potters are making here is worth about a halfpenny, but it is perfect of its kind. The moulder never lifts his hand from it from the moment he puts a lump of shapeless clay on the wheel till the moment he takes it off finished, so far as the wheel can finish it. If it is "marred," it is "marred in the *hand* of the potter," and instantly he makes it again another vessel as it seems good to him. He never wastes the clay.

began, so far as visible results are concerned. We do not find, as a rule, when we go to the houses—the literal little mud houses, I mean, of literal heathendom—that anyone inside has been praying we might come. I read a missionary story "founded on fact" the other day, and the things that happened in that story on these lines were most remarkable. They do not happen here. Practical missionary life is an unexciting thing. It is not sparkling all over with incident. It is very prosaic at times.

CHAPTER IV

Correspondences

"It is very pleasant when you are in England, and you see souls being saved, and you see the conviction of sin, and you see the power of the Gospel to bring new life and new joy and purity to hearts. But it is still more glorious amongst the heathen to see the same things, to see the Lord there working His own work of salvation, and to see the souls convicted and the hearts broken, and to see there the new life and the new joy coming out in the faces of those who have found the Lord Jesus."   *Rev. Barclay F. Buxton, Japan.*

BEFORE putting this chapter together, I have looked long at the photograph which fronts it. The longer one looks the more pitiful it seems. Perhaps one reads into it all that one knows of her, all one has done for her, how one has failed—and this makes it sadder than it may be to other eyes. And yet can it fail to be sad? Hood's lines reversed describe her—

"All that is left of her
Now is not womanly."

The day we took her photo she was returning from her morning worship at the shrine. She had poured her libation over the idol, walked round and round it, prostrated herself before it, gone through the prayers she had learned off by heart, and now was on her way home.

We had gone to her village to take photographs, and

A Saivite ascetic. Siva represents the severer side of Hinduism, the Powers of Nature which destroy. But as all disintegrated things are reintegrated in some other form, the two Powers, Destruction and Reconstruction, were united in the thought of the old Hindus, and Siva represents the double Power. The Saivite form of Hinduism is older than the Vaishnavite, and more widely spread over India. There are said to be 30,000,000 symbols of the god Siva scattered about the land. Saivites are instantly recognised by the mark of white ashes on their foreheads, and sometimes on the breast and arms, and often a necklet of berries is worn.

had just got the street scene in the morning light. The
crowd followed us, eager to see more of the doings of the
picture-catching box; and she, fearing the defiling touch
of the mixed Castes represented there, had climbed up
on a granite slab by the side of the road, and stood
waiting till we passed.

There we saw her, and there we took her,—for, to our
surprise, she did not object,—and now here she is, to
show with all the force of truth how far from ideal the
real may be. We looked at her as I look at her now,
stripped of all God meant her to have when He made
her, deep in the mire of the lowest form of idolatry, a
devotee of Siva. She had been to Benares and bathed
in the sacred Ganges, and therefore she is holy beyond
the reach of doubt. She has no room for any sense of
the need of Christ. She pities our ignorance when we
talk to her. Is she not a devotee? Has she not been
to Benares?

Often and often we meet her in the high-caste houses
of the place, where she is always an honoured guest
because of her wonderful sanctity. She watches keenly
then lest any of the younger members of the household
should incline to listen to us.

One of her relatives is an English-educated lawyer, a
bitter though covert foe, who not long ago stirred up
such opposition that we were warned not to go near the
place. Men had been hired "to fall upon us and beat
us." This because a girl, a connection of his, read her
Bible openly, instead of in secret as she had done before.
He connected this action on her part with a visit we had
paid to the house, and so induced certain of the baser

sort to do this thing. We went, however, just the same, as we had work we had promised to do, and saw the old gentleman sitting on the verandah reading his English newspaper in the most pacific fashion. He seemed surprised to see us as we passed with a salaam; we saw nothing of the beaters, and returned with whole bones, to the relief of the community at large. Only I remember one of our Band was woefully disappointed: "I thought, perhaps, we were going to be martyrs," she said.

And so we realise, as so often in India, the power of both extremes; the one with all the force of his education, and the other with all the force of her superstition, each uniting with the other in repelling the coming of the Saviour both equally need.

As one looks at the photograph, does it not help in the effort to realise the utter hopelessness, from every human point of view, of trying to win such a one, for example, to even care to think of Christ? There is, over and above the natural apathy common to all, an immense barrier of accumulated merit gained by pilgrimages, austerities, and religious observances, and the soul is perfectly satisfied, and has no desire whatever after God. It is just this self-satisfaction which makes it so hopeless to try to do anything with it.

And yet nothing is hopeless to God; "Set no borders to His strength," a Japanese missionary said. We say it over and over again to ourselves, in the face of some great hopelessness, like that photograph before us; and sometimes, as if to assure us it is so, God lifts some such soul into light. Just now we are rejoicing in

Street in the Red Lake Village. An ordinary typical village scene, except that just then there were more people than usual before the picture-catching box. The only way to keep them from crowding round it was to show them something else; this explains the group on the stones at the side.

a letter from the eastern side of the district, telling us of the growth in the new life of one who only a little while ago was a temple devotee.

One has often longed to see Him work as He worked of old, healing the sick by the word of His power, raising the dead. But when we see Him gathering one—and such a one!—from among the heathen to give thanks unto His holy Name and to triumph in His praise, one feels that indeed it is a miracle of miracles, and that greater than a miracle wrought on the body is a miracle wrought on the soul. But nothing I can write can show you the miracle it was. In that particular case it was like seeing a soul drawn out of the hand of the Ruler of Darkness. All salvation is that in reality, but sometimes, as in her case, when the whole environment of the soul has been strongly for evil in its most dangerous phase, then it is more evidently so.

Perhaps we should explain. We know that in its widest sense environment simply means "all that is." We know that "all that is" includes the existence of certain beings, described as " Powers " in Ephesians vi. 12. Some of us are more or less unconscious of this part of our environment. We have no conscious correspondence with it, but it is there. Others, again, seek and find such correspondence, to their certain and awful loss.

Such a subject can hardly bear handling in language. Thank God we know so little about it that we do not know how to speak of it accurately. Neither, indeed, do we wish to intrude into those things which we have not seen by any attempt at close definition; but we know there is this unhallowed correspondence between men and demons, which in old days drew down, as a lightning conductor, the flash of the wrath of God.

Here in India it exists; we often almost touch it, but not quite. We would not go where we knew we should see it, even if we might; so, unless we happen upon it, which is rare, we never see it at all. A year ago I saw it, and that one look made me realise, as no amount of explanations ever could, how absolutely out of reach of all human influence such souls are. *Nothing* can reach them, nothing but the might of the Holy Ghost.

So I close with this one look. Will you pray for those to whom in the moonless night, at the altar by the temple, there is the sudden coming of that which they have sought—the "possession," the "afflatus," which for ever after marks them out as those whose correspondences reach beyond mortal ken. All devotees have not received this awful baptism, but in this part of India many have.

We were visiting in a high-caste house. The walls were decorated with mythological devices, and even the old wood-carvings were full of idolatrous symbols. The women were listening well, asking questions and arguing, until one, an old lady, came in. Then they were silent. She sat down and discussed us. We thought we would change the subject, and we began to sing. She listened, as they always do, interrupting only to say, "That's true! that's true!" Till suddenly—I cannot describe what—something seemed to come over her, and she burst into a frenzy, exclaiming, "Let me sing! let me sing!" And then she sang as I never heard anyone sing before—the wildest, weirdest wail of a song all about idolatry, its uselessness and folly, its sorrow and sin.

So far I followed her, for I knew the poem well, but she soon turned off into regions of language and thought unreached as yet by me. Here she got madly excited, and, swaying herself to and fro, seemed lashing herself into fury. Nearer and nearer she drew to us (we were on the floor beside her); then she stretched out her arm with its clenched fist, and swung it straight for my eye. Within a hair's-breadth she drew back, and struck out for Victory's; but God helped her not to flinch.

Then I cannot tell what happened, only her form dilated, and she seemed as if she would spring upon us, but as if she were somehow held back. We dare not move for fear of exciting her more. There we sat for I know not how long, with this awful old woman's clenched fist circling round our heads, or all but striking into our eyes, while without intermission she crooned her song in that hollow hum that works upon the listener till the nerve of the soul is drawn out, as it were, to its very farthest stretch. It was quite dark by this time; only the yellow flicker of the wind-blown flame of the lamp made uncertain lights and shadows round the place where we were sitting, and an eerie influence fell on us all, almost mesmeric in effect. I did not need the awe-struck whispers round me to tell me what it was. But oh! I felt, as I never felt before, the reality of the presence of unseen powers, and I knew that the Actual itself was in the room with me.

At last she fell back exhausted, trembling in every limb. Her old head hit the wall as she fell, but I knew we must not help her; it would be pollution to her if we touched her. The people all round were too frightened

to move. So she fell and lay there quivering, her glitter-
ing eyes still fixed on us; and she tried to speak, but
could not.

Softly we stole away, and we felt we had been very
near where Satan's seat is.

Think of someone you love—as I did then—of someone whose hair is white like hers; but the face you
think of has peace in it, and God's light lightens it.
Then think of her as we saw her last—the old face torn
with the fear of hell, and for light the darkness thereof.

Oh, friends, do you care enough? Do we care enough
out here? God give us hearts that can care!

CHAPTER V

The Prey of the Terrible

"I believe we are in the midst of a great battle. We are not ourselves fighting, we are simply accepting everything that comes; but the Powers of Light are fighting against the Powers of Darkness, and they will certainly prevail. The Holy Spirit is working, but the people do not as yet know it is the Spirit."   *Hester Needham, Sumatra.*

THE devil's favourite device just now is to move interested people to far - away places. We have had several who seemed very near to the Kingdom. Then suddenly they have disappeared.

There was Wreath, of the Village of the Temple. She used to listen in the shadow of the door while we sat on the outside verandah. Then she got bolder, and openly asked to see Golden, and talk with her. One day, unexpectedly, Golden was led to the Red Lake Village, and to her surprise found Wreath there. She had been sent away from the Village of the Temple, and was now with some other relations, under even stricter guard. But God led Golden, all unknowingly, to go straight to the very house where she was. So she heard again.

Next time Golden went she could not see her alone, but somehow Wreath got her to understand that if she went to a certain tree near the women's bathing-place, at a certain time next week, she would try to meet her

3

there. Golden went, and they met. Wreath told her she believed it all, but she could not then face breaking Caste and destroying her family's name. They had been good to her, how could she disgrace them? Still, she eagerly wanted to go on hearing, and we felt that if she did, the love of God would win. So we were full of hope.

Next time Golden went she could find no trace of her. She has never seen her since. There is a rumour that she has been carried off over the mountains, hundreds of miles away.

In another village a bright, keen boy of seventeen listened one day when we taught the women, and, becoming greatly interested, openly took the Gospel's part when the village elders attacked it. After some weeks he gathered courage to come and see the Iyer. He was a very intelligent boy, well known all over the country-side, because he had studied the Tamil classics, and also because of his connection with one of the chief temples of the district.

A fortnight after his visit here, our Band went to his village. They heard that he was married and gone, where, no one would say. The relations must have heard of his coming to us (of course he was urged to tell them), and they rushed him through a marriage, and sent him off post haste. So now there is another key turned, locking him into Hinduism.

In the Village of the Wind a young girl became known as an inquirer. Her Caste passed the word along from village to village wherever its members were found, and all these relations and connections were speedily leagued in a compact to keep her from hearing more. When we

went to see her, we found she had been posted off somewhere else. When we went to the somewhere else
(always freely mentioned to us, with invitations to go),
we found she had been there, but had been forwarded
elsewhere. For weeks she was tossed about like this;
then we traced her, and found her. But she was
thoroughly cowed, and dared not show the least interest
in us. It is often like that. Just at the point where
the soul-poise is so delicate that the lightest touch affects
it, something, someone, pushes it roughly, and it trembles
a moment, then falls—on the wrong side.

The reason for all this alertness of opposition is, that
scattered about the five thousand square miles we call
our field, here and there seeds are beginning to grow.
Some of the sowers are in England now, and some are in
heaven—sowers and reapers, English and Tamil, rejoice
together! This is known everywhere, for the news
spreads from town to town, and then out to the villages,
and the result is opposition. Sometimes the little patch
of ground which looked so hopeful is trampled, and the
young seedlings killed; sometimes they seem to be
rooted up. When we go to our Master and tell Him,
He explains it: "An Enemy hath done this." But as
the measure of the Enemy's activity is in direct pro-
portion to the measure of God's working, we take it as
a sign of encouragement, however hindering it may be.
Satan would not trouble to fight if he saw nothing
worth attacking; he does not seem to mind the spread
of a head knowledge of the Doctrine, or even a cordial
appreciation of it. Often we hear the people say how
excellent it is, and how they never worship idols now,

but only the true God; and even a heathen mother will
make her child repeat its texts to you, and a father will
tell you how it tells him Bible stories; and if you are
quite new to the work you put it in the *Magazine*, and
at home it sounds like conversion. All this goes on
most peacefully; there is not the slightest stir, till something happens to show the people that the Doctrine is
not just a Creed, but contains a living Power. And
then, and not till then, there is opposition.

This opposition is sufficiently strong in the case of a
boy or young man (older Caste men and women rarely
"change their religion" in this part of South India), but
if a girl is in question, the Caste is touched at its most
sensitive point, and the feeling is simply intense. Men
and demons seem to conspire to hold such a one in the
clutch of the Terrible.

There is a young girl in Cupid's Lake Village whose
heart the Lord opened some weeks ago. She is a gentle,
timid girl, and devoted to her mother. "Can it be right
to break my mother's heart?" she used to ask us pitifully. We urged her to try to win her mother, but the
mother was just furious. The moment she understood
that her daughter wanted to follow Jesus, or "join the
Way," as she would express it, she gathered the girl's
books and burnt them, and forbade her ever to mention
the subject; and she went all round the villages trying to
stop our work.

At last things came to a crisis. The girl was told to
do what she felt would be sin against God. She refused.
They tried force, sheer brute force. She nerved herself
for the leap in the dark, and tried to escape to us. But

in the dark night she lost the way, and had to run back
to her home. Next morning the village priest spread a
story to the effect that his god had appeared to him, told
him of her attempt to escape, and that she would try
twice again, "but each time I will stand in the way and
turn her back," he said.

This naturally startled the girl. "Is his god stronger
than Jesus?" she asked in real perplexity. We told her
we thought the tale was concocted to frighten her; the
priest had seen her, and made up the rest. But twice
since then, driven by dire danger, that girl has tried to
get to us, and each time she has been turned back. And
now she is kept in rigorous guard, as her determination
to be a Christian is well known to all in the place.

Do you say, "Tell her to stay at home and bear it
patiently"? We do tell her so, when we can see her, but
we add, "till God makes a way of escape"; and if you
knew all there is to be known about a Hindu home, and
what may happen in it, you would not tell her otherwise.

But supposing there is nothing more than negative
difficulty to be feared, have you ever tried in thought to
change places with such a girl? Have you ever considered how impossible it is for such a one to grow?
The simple grace of continuance is in danger of wither-
ing when all help of every sort is absolutely cut off, and
the soul is, to begin with, not deeply rooted in God.
Plants, even when they have life, need water and
sunshine and air. Babes need milk.

You find it hard enough to grow, if one may judge
from the constant wails about "leanness," and yet you
are surrounded by every possible help to growth. You

have a whole Bible, not just a scrap of it; and you can read it all, and understand at least most of it. You have endless good books, hymn-books, and spiritual papers; you have sermons every week, numerous meetings for edification, and perhaps an annual Convention. Now strip yourself of all this. Shut your Bible, and forget as completely as if you had never known it all you ever read or heard, except the main facts of the Gospel. Forget all those strengthening verses, all those beautiful hymns, all those inspiring addresses. Likewise, of course, entirely forget all the loving dealings of God with your-self and with others—a Hindu has no such memories to help her. Then go and live in a devil's den and develop saintliness. The truth is, even you would find it difficult; but this Hindu girl's case is worse than that, a million times worse. Think of the life, and then, if you can, tell her she must be quite satisfied with it, that it is the will of God. You could not say that it is His will! It is the will of the Terrible, who holds on to his prey, and would rather rend it limb from limb than ever let it go.

We are often asked to tell converts' stories; and certainly they would thrill, for the way of escape God opens sometimes is, like Peter's from prison, miraculous; and truth is stranger than fiction, and far more interest-ing. But we who work in the Terrible's lair, and know how he fights to get back his prey, even after it has escaped from him, are afraid to tell these stories too much, and feel that silence is safest, and, strange as it may seem to some, for the present most glorifies God.

For a certain connection has been observed between publicity and peril. And we have learned by experience to fear any attempt to photograph spiritual fruit. The old Greek artist turned away the face that held too much for him to paint; and that turned-away face had power in it, they say, to touch men's hearts. We turn these faces away from you; may the very fact that we do it teach some at home to realise how much more lies in each of them than we can say, how great a need there is to pray that each may be kept safe. The names of one and another occur, because they came in the letters so often that I could not cross them all out without altering the character of the whole; they are part of one's very life.

But as even a passing mention may mean danger, unless a counteracting influence of real prayer protects them, we ask you to pray that the tender protection of God may be folded round each one of them; and then when we meet where no sin can creep into the telling, and no harm can follow it, they will tell you their stories themselves, and God will give you your share in the joy, comrades by prayer at home! But let us press it on you now—pray, oh, pray for the converts! Pray that they may grow in Christ. Pray that He may see of the travail of His soul, and be satisfied with each of them. And pray that we may enter into that travail of soul with Him. Nothing less is any good. Spiritual children mean travail of soul—spiritual agony. I wonder who among those who read this will realise what I mean. Some will, I think; so I write it. It is a solemn thing to find oneself drawn out in prayer which knows no relief till the soul it is burdened with is born. It is no less solemn afterwards, until Christ is formed in them. Converts are a responsible joy.

And now we have told you a little of what is going
on. There are days when nothing seems to be done, and
then again there are days when the Terrible seems almost
visible, as he gathers up his strength, and tears and mauls
his prey. And so it is true we have to fight a separate
fight for each soul. But another view of the case is a
strength to us many a time. "We are not ourselves
fighting, but the Powers of Light are fighting against the
Powers of Darkness," and the coming of the victory
is only a question of time. "Shall the prey be taken
from the Mighty or the captives of the Terrible be
delivered? But thus saith the Lord, **Even the captives
of the Mighty shall be taken away and the prey of
the Terrible shall be delivered.**"

CHAPTER VI

Missed Ends

"If you could only know what one feels on finding oneself . . . where the least ray of the Gospel has not penetrated! If those friends who blame . . . could see from afar what we see, and feel what we feel, they would be the first to wonder that those redeemed by Christ should be so backward in devotion and know so little of the spirit of self-sacrifice. They would be ashamed of the hesitations that hinder us . . . *We must remember that it was not by interceding for the world in glory that Jesus saved it. He gave Himself. Our prayers for the evangelisation of the world are but a bitter irony so long as we only give of our superfluity, and draw back before the sacrifice of ourselves.*" *M. François Coillard, Africa.*

"Someone must go, and if no one else will go, he who hears the call must go; I hear the call, for indeed God has brought it before me on every side, and go I must."
Rev. Henry Watson Fox, India.

THE tom-toms thumped straight on all night, and the darkness shuddered round me like a living, feeling thing. I could not go to sleep, so I lay awake and looked; and I saw, as it seemed, this:

That I stood on a grassy sward, and at my feet a precipice broke sheer down into infinite space. I looked, but saw no bottom; only cloud shapes, black and furiously coiled, and great shadow-shrouded hollows, and unfathomable depths. Back I drew, dizzy at the depth.

Then I saw forms of people moving single file along

the grass. They were making for the edge. There
was a woman with a baby in her arms and another
little child holding on to her dress. She was on the
very verge. Then I saw that she was blind. She lifted
her foot for the next step . . . it trod air. She was
over, and the children over with her. Oh, the cry as
they went over!

Then I saw more streams of people flowing from all
quarters. All were blind, stone blind; all made straight
for the precipice edge. There were shrieks as they
suddenly knew themselves falling, and a tossing up of
helpless arms, catching, clutching at empty air. But
some went over quietly, and fell without a sound.

Then I wondered, with a wonder that was simply
agony, why no one stopped them at the edge. I could
not. I was glued to the ground, and I could not call;
though I strained and tried, only a whisper would
come.

Then I saw that along the edge there were sentries
set at intervals. But the intervals were far too great;
there were wide, unguarded gaps between. And over
these gaps the people fell in their blindness, quite
unwarned; and the green grass seemed blood-red to me,
and the gulf yawned like the mouth of hell.

Then I saw, like a little picture of peace, a group of
people under some trees, with their backs turned towards
the gulf. They were making daisy chains. Sometimes
when a piercing shriek cut the quiet air and reached
them it disturbed them, and they thought it a rather
vulgar noise. And if one of their number started up
and wanted to go and do something to help, then all

the others would pull that one down. " Why should
you get so excited about it ? You must wait for a definite
call to go ! You haven't finished your daisy chains yet.
It would be really selfish," they said, " to leave us to finish
the work alone."

There was another group. It was made up of people
whose great desire was to get more sentries out; but
they found that very few wanted to go, and sometimes
there were no sentries set for miles and miles of the edge.

Once a girl stood alone in her place, waving the
people back; but her mother and other relations called,
and reminded her that her furlough was due; she must
not break the rules. And being tired and needing a
change, she had to go and rest for awhile; but no one
was sent to guard her gap, and over and over the people
fell, like a waterfall of souls.

Once a child caught at a tuft of grass that grew
at the very brink of the gulf; it clung convulsively,
and it called—but nobody seemed to hear. Then the roots
of the grass gave way, and with a cry the child went
over, its two little hands still holding tight to the torn-
off bunch of grass. And the girl who longed to be back
in her gap thought she heard the little one cry, and
she sprang up and wanted to go; at which they reproved
her, reminding her that no one is necessary anywhere;
the gap would be well taken care of, they knew. And
then they sang a hymn.

Then through the hymn came another sound like the
pain of a million broken hearts wrung out in one full
drop, one sob. And a horror of great darkness was upon
me, for I knew what it was—the Cry of the Blood.

Then thundered a Voice, the Voice of the Lord: "And He said, What hast thou done? The voice of thy brothers' blood crieth unto Me from the ground."

.   .   .   .   .

The tom-toms still beat heavily, the darkness still shuddered and shivered about me; I heard the yells of the devil-dancers and the weird wild shriek of the devil-possessed just outside the gate.

What does it matter, after all? It has gone on for years; it will go on for years. Why make such a fuss about it?

God forgive us! God arouse us! Shame us out of our callousness! Shame us out of our sin!

One afternoon, a few weeks after that night at the precipice edge, Victory and I were visiting in the Red Lake Village, when we heard the death-beat of the tom-tom and the shriek of the conch shell, and we knew that another had gone beyond our reach. One can never get accustomed to this. We stopped for a moment and listened.

The women we were teaching broke in with eager explanations. "Oh, he was such a great one! He had received the Initiation. There will be a grand ceremonial, grander than ever you have!" Then they told us how this great one had been initiated into the Hindu mysteries by his family priest, and that the mystical benefits accruing from this initiation were to be caused to revert to the priest. This Reverting of the Initiation was to be one of the ceremonies. We watched the procession pass down the street. They were going for water from a

sacred stream for the bathing of purification. When
they return, said the women, the ceremonies will begin.

A little later we passed the house, and stood looking
in through the doorway. There was the usual large
square courtyard, with the verandah running round three
sides. The verandah was full of women. We longed
to go in, but did not think they would let us. The
courtyard was rather confused; men were rushing about,
putting up arches and decorating them; servants were
sweeping, and cooking, and shouting to one another; the
women were talking and laughing. And all the time
from within the house came the sound of the dirge
for the dead, and the laugh and the wail struck against
each other, and jarred. No one noticed us for awhile,
but at last a woman saw us, and beckoned us to come.
"We are all defiled to-day; you may sit with us," they
said; and yielding to the instincts of their kindly Tamil
nature, they crushed closer together to make room for
us beside them. How I did enjoy being squeezed up
there among them. But to appreciate that in the least
you would have to work in a caste-bound part of
old India; you can have no idea, until you try, how
hard it is to refrain from touching those whom you
love.

The house door opened upon the verandah, and we
could hear the moan of the dirge. "There is sorrow
on the sea; it cannot be quiet." There was no quietness,
only the ceaseless moan, that kept rising into a wail;
there were tears in the sound of the wail, and I felt
like a sort of living harp with all its strings drawn
tight.

But the women outside cared nothing at all. It was strange to see how callous they were. It was not their *own* who had died, so they chatted and laughed and watched the proceedings—the tying of the garlands round the arches, the arrangement of offerings for the Brahmans. It was all full of interest to them. We tried to turn their thoughts to the Powers of the World to Come. But no. They did not care.

Presently there was a stir. "The men are coming!" they said. "Run! there is a shady corner under those palms on the far verandah! Run and hide! They are here!" And, even as they spoke, in streamed the men, each with his brass water-vessel poised on his head, and they saw us standing there. We thought they would turn us out, and were quite prepared to go at a sign from the head of the clan. But he was a friend of ours, and he smiled as we salaamed, and pointed to a quiet corner, out of the way, where we could see it all without being too much seen.

To understand this, which to me was a surprise, one must remember that by nature the Indian is most courteous, and if it were not for Caste rules we should be allowed to come much closer to them than is possible now. To-day they were all ceremonially unclean, so our presence was not considered polluting. Also the Indian loves a function; sad or glad, it matters little. Life is a bubble on the water; enjoy it while you may. And they sympathised with what they thought was our desire to see the show. This was human; they could understand it. So they let us stay; and we stayed, hoping for a chance later on.

Then the ceremonies began. They carried the dead man out and laid him in the courtyard under the arch of palms. He was old and worn and thin. One could see the fine old face, with the marks of the Hindu trident painted down the forehead. He had been a most earnest Hindu; all the rites were duly performed, and morning and night for many years he had marked those marks on his brow. Had he ever once listened to the Truth? I do not know. He must have heard about it, but he had not received it. He died, they told us, "not knowing what lay on the other side."

The water-bearers laid their vessels on the ground. Each had a leaf across its mouth. The priest was crowned with a chaplet of flowers. Then came the bathing. They threw up a shelter, and carried him there. It was reverently done. There was a touch of refinement in the thought which banished the women and children before the bathing began. Tamils bathe in the open air, and always clothed, but always apart. And as the women's verandah overlooked the screened enclosure, they were all ordered off. They went and waited, silent now, awed by the presence of the men. While the bathing was going on the priests chanted and muttered incantations, and now and again a bell was rung, and incense waved, and tapers lighted. Now they were causing that mysterious Something which still hovered round the lifeless form to leave it and return to them, and when the bathing was over they signified that all was done; the Influence had departed, descended; the funeral ceremonies might proceed.

And all this time, without a break, the dirge was

being sung by the mourners in the house. It was a
sort of undernote to all the sounds outside. Then the
old man, robed in white and crowned and wreathed with
flowers, was carried round to the other side; and oh,
the pitifulness of it all! St. Paul must have been
thinking of some such scene when he wrote to the
converts, "That ye sorrow not even as others which
have no hope." And I thought how strangely callous
we were, how superficial our sympathy. The Lord's command does not stir us, the sorrow of those we neglect
does not touch us; we think so much more of ourselves
and our own selfish pleasure than we think of the purpose for which we were saved—and at such a tremendous
cost! Oh for a baptism of reality and obedience to
sweep over us! Oh to be true to the hymns we sing
and the vows we make! *God make us true.*

Forgive all this. It was burnt into me afresh that
day as I sat there watching the things they did and
listening to what they said. We had come too late for
that old dead man, too late for most of the living ones
too. Can you wonder if at such solemn times one yields
oneself afresh and for ever to obey?

Rice was prepared for the dead man's use, and balls of
rice were ready to be offered to his spirit after his crema-
tion; for the Hindus think that an intermediate body
must be formed and nourished, which on the thirteenth
day after death is conducted to either heaven or hell,
according to the deeds done on earth. The ceremonies
were all characterised by a belief in some future state.
The spirit was somewhere—in the dark—so they tried
to light the way for him. This reminds me of one

ceremony especially suggestive. All the little grandchildren were brought, and lighted tapers given to them;
then they processioned round the bier, round and round
many times, holding the tapers steadily, and looking
serious and impressed.

Then the widow came out with a woman on either
side supporting her. And she walked round and round
her husband, with the tears rolling down her face, and
she wailed the widow's wail, with her very heart in it.
Why had he gone away and left her desolate? His
was the spirit of fragrance like the scented sandal-wood;
his was the arm of strength like the lock that barred
the door. Gone was the scent of the sandal, broken and
open the door; why had the bird flown and left but the
empty cage? Gone! was he gone? Was he really
gone? Was it certain he was dead? He who had
tossed and turned on the softest bed they could make,
must he lie on the bed of his funeral pyre? Must he
burn upon logs of wood? Say, was there no way to reach
him, no way to help him now? "I have searched for
thee, but I find thee not." And so the dirge moaned on.

I could not hear all this then; Victory told it to me,
and much more, afterwards. "Last time I heard it," she
said, "I was *inside*, wailing too."

As the poor widow went round and round she stopped
each time she got to the feet, and embraced them
fervently. Sometimes she broke through all restraint,
and clasped him in her arms.

After many ceremonies had been performed, the men
all went away, and the women were left to bid farewell to
the form soon to be carried out. Then the men came back

4

and bore him across the courtyard, and paused under the
arch outside, while the women all rushed out, tearing
their hair and beating themselves and wailing wildly.
As they were lifting the bier to depart the cry was,
"Stop! stop! Will he not speak?" And this, chanted
again and again, would have made the coldest care.
Then when all was over, and the long procession, headed
by the tom-toms and conch shells, had passed out of
sight, the women pressed in again, and each first let down
her hair, and seized her nearest neighbour, and they all
flung themselves on the ground and knocked their heads
against it, and then, rising to a sitting posture, they held
on to one another, swaying backwards and forwards and
chanting in time to the swaying, in chorus and antiphone.
All this, even to the hair-tearing and head-knocking,
was copied by the children who were present with
terrible fidelity.

We sat down among them. They took our hands and
rocked us in the orthodox way. But we did not wail
and we did not undo our hair. We tried to speak
comforting words to those who were really in grief, but
we found it was not the time. A fortnight later we
went again, and found the house door open because we
had been with them that day.

But we could not help them then, so we rose and
were going away, when, held by the power of that dirge
of theirs, I turned to look again. The last rays of the
afternoon sun were lighting up the courtyard, and shining
on the masses of black hair and grey. As I looked
they got up one by one, and put their disordered dress
to rights, and shook out the dust from their glossy hair,

A photo rarely possible. The dead woman lies in her bier; the white on her eyes and brow is the mask of Siva's ashes. Some of the mourners are so marked, so they are all Saivites. The fire is lighted from the pot of fire to the right. Just before it is lighted, the chief mourner takes a vessel of water, pierces a hole in it, walks round the dead, letting the water trickle out, pierces another hole and repeats the walk. After the third piercing and walk, he throws the pot backwards over his shoulder, and so it smashes, the water all splashes out. This is to refresh the spirit if it should be thirsty while its body is being burned.

and did it up again. And one by one, without farewell
of any sort, they went away. An hour later we met
groups of them coming home from bathing. They would
not touch us then. Afterwards the chief mourners came
out and bathed, and went all round the village wailing.
And the last thing I saw, as the sun set over the hills
and the place grew chill and dark, was the old widow,
worn out now, returning home in her wet things, wailing still.

I write this under a sense of the solemnity of being
"a servant . . . separated unto the Gospel." I would
not write one word lightly. But oh! may I ask you to
face it? Are we honest towards God? If we were,
would these people be left to die as they are being left
to die?

We feel for them. *But feelings will not save souls; it
cost God Calvary to win us.*

*It will cost us as much as we may know of the fellowship
of His sufferings, if those for whom He died that day are
ever to be won.*

 .   .   .   .   .   .

I am writing in the midst of the sights and the sounds
of life. There is life in the group of women at the
well; life in the voices, in the splash of the water, in
the cry of a child, in the call of the mother; life in
the flight of the parrots as they flock from tree to tree;
life in their chatter as they quarrel and scream; life,
everywhere life. How can I think out of all this, back
into death again?

But I want to, for you may live for many a year in
India without being allowed to see once what we have

seen twice within two months, and it cannot be for
nothing that we saw it. We must be meant to show it
to you.

The Picture-catching Missie and I were in the Village
of the Tamarind Tree, when for the second time I saw
it. They are very friendly there, and just as in the Red
Lake Village they let us look behind the curtain, so here
again they pushed it back, and let us in, and went on
with their business, not minding us. We crouched up
close together on the only scrap of empty space, and
watched.

Everything was less intense; the dead was only a poor
and very old widow who had lived her life out, and was
not wanted. There were no near kindred, only relations
by marriage; it was evident everyone went through the
form without emotion of any sort.

The woman lay on a rough bier on the floor, and
round her crowded a dozen old women. At her head
there was a brass vessel of water, a lamp-stand, some
uncooked rice, and some broken cocoanuts. Just before
we came in they had filled a little brass vessel from the
larger one. Now one of the old hags walked round the
dead three times, pouring the water out as she walked.
Then another fed her—fed that poor dead mouth, stuffed
it in so roughly it made us sick and faint. There were
other things done hurriedly, carelessly; we could not
follow them. The last was the rubbing on of ashes—she
had been a worshipper of Siva—also they covered the
closed eyes with ashes and patted them down flat. And
all the time the gabble of the women mocked at the
silence of death. There was no reverence, no sense of

This needs to be looked into. Gradually the middle closes. The women are holding each other's hands preparatory to swaying backwards and forwards as they chant the dirge for the dead. The lamp (you see in top near the vessel on the right) was lighted as soon as the old woman died, and placed at her head on the floor. So bitterly they show their sense of the darkness of death. The brass water vessel, with the leaves laid across its mouth, was filled with the water of purification. This was poured in a circle on the floor round the body. The bits of grass are the sacred Kusa grass used in many religious ceremonies.

solemnity; the ceremonial so full of symbol to its makers, the thinkers of Védic times, was to them simply a custom, a set of customs, to be followed and got through as quickly as might be by heedless hands. And yet they faithfully carried out every detail they knew, and they finished their heartless work and called to the men to come. The men were waiting outside. They came in and carried her out.

It seemed impossible to think of a photograph then; it was most unlikely they would let us take one, and we hardly felt in the spirit of picture-catching. Yet we thought of you, and of how you certainly could never see it unless we could show it to you; and we wanted to show it to you, so we asked them if we might. Of course if there had been real grief, as in the other I had seen, we could not have asked it, it would have been intrusion; but here there was none—*that* was the pathos of it. And they were very friendly, so they put their burden on the ground, and waited.

There it is. To the right the barber stands with his fire-bowl hanging from a chain; this is to light the funeral pyre. The smoke interfered with the photo, but then it is true to life. To the left stands the man with the shell ready to blow. At the back, with the sacred ashes rubbed on forehead and breast and arms, stand the two nearest relatives, who to-morrow will gather the ashes and throw them into the stream.

The picture was caught. The man with the shell blew it, the man with the fire came in front, the bearers lifted the bier; they went away with their dead.

Then the old women, who had been pressing through

the open door, rushed back in the usual way and began
the usual rock and dirge. These Comparison Songs are
always full of soul. They have sprung into being in
times of deepest feeling, taken shape when hearts were
as finely wrought moulds which left their impress upon
them. And to hear them chanted without any soul is
somehow a pitiful thing, a sort of profanation, like the
singing of sacred words for pay.

The photograph was not easy to take, the space was
so confined, the movement so continuous, the commotion
so confusing. *How* it was taken I know not; the women
massed on the floor were not still for more than a
moment. In that moment it was done. Then we persuaded three of them to risk the peril of being caught
alone. They would not move farther than the wall of
the house, and as it was in a narrow street, again there
were difficulties. But the crowning perplexity was at the
water-side. It was windy, and our calls were blown away,
so they did not hear what we wanted them to do, and
they splashed too vigorously. Their only idea just then
was to get themselves and their garments ceremonially
clean, defiled as they were by contact with the dead.

But let those six whom you can partly see stand for
the thousands upon thousands whom you cannot see at
all. Those thousands are standing in water to-day from
the North to the uttermost South, as the last act in the
drama which they have played in the presence of the dead.

    .   .   .   .   .

The women have gone from the well. The parrots
have flown to other trees. The Tamils say the body is
the sheath of the soul. I think of that empty sheath

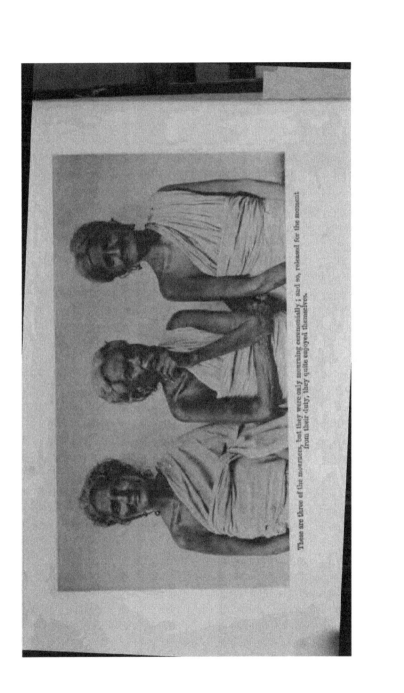

These are three of the mourners, but they were only mourning ceremonially; and so, released for the moment from their duty, they quite enjoyed themselves.

I saw, and wonder where the soul has flown. It has gone—but where? Has it gone home, like the women from the well? Has it flown far, like the birds among the trees? It has gone, it has gone, that is all we know. *It has gone.*

Then I read these words from Conybeare and Howson's translation: "If the tent which is my earthly house be destroyed I have a mansion built by God . . . eternal in the heavens. And herein I groan with earnest longings, desiring to cover my earthly raiment with the robes of my heavenly mansion. . . . *And He who has prepared me for this very end is God.*"

The dead man missed his End. That old dead woman missed it too. And the millions around us still alive are missing their End to-day. "This very End"—think of it—Mortality swallowed up in Life—Death only an absence, Life for ever a presence—Present with the Lord who has prepared us "for this very End."

Can we enjoy it all by ourselves? Will there be no sense of incompleteness if the many are outside, missing it all because they missed their End? Will the glory make us glad if they are somewhere far away from it and God? Will not heaven be almost an empty place to one who has never tried to fill it? Yet there is room, oh so much room, for those we are meant to bring in with us!

And there is room, oh so much room, along the edge of the precipice. There are gaps left all unguarded. Can it be that you are meant to guard one of those gaps? If so, it will always remain as it is, a falling-point for those rivers of souls, unless you come.

Are these things truth or are they imagination? If they are imagination—then let the paper on which they are written be burnt, burnt till it curls up and the words fall into dust. But if they are true—then what are we going to do? Not what are we going to say or sing, or even feel or pray—*but what are we going to do!*

The ceremonial bathing. They are all old women, but the very oldest old woman in India bathes most vigorously. After this bathing is over, they are purified from the defilement contracted by going to the house of the dead.

CHAPTER VII

"The Dust of the Actual"

"This may be counted as our richest gain, to have learned afresh one's utter impotency so completely that the past axiom of service, 'I can no more convert a soul than create a star,' comes to be an awful revelation, so that God alone may be exalted in that day." *Rev. Walter Searle, Africa.*

WE have just come back from a Pariah village. Now see it all with me. Such a curious little collection of huts, thrown down anywhere; such half-frightened, half-friendly faces; such a scurrying in of some and out of others; and we wonder which house we had better make for. We stop before one a shade cleaner than most, and larger and more open.

"May we come in?" Chorus, "Come in! oh, come in!" and in we go. It is a tiny, narrow slip of a room. At one end there is a fire burning on the ground; the smoke finds its way out through the roof, and a pot of rice set on three stones is bubbling cheerfully. No fear of defilement here. They would not like us to touch their rice or to see them eating it, but they do not mind our being in the room where it is being cooked.

At the other end of the narrow slip there is a goat-pen, not very clean; and down one side there is a raised mud place where the family apparently sleep. This side

and the two ends are roofed by palmyra palm. It is
dry and crackles at a touch, and you touch it every
time you stand up, so bits of it are constantly falling
and helping to litter the open space below.

Five babies at different stages of refractoriness are
sprawling about on this strip of floor; they make noises
all the time. Half a dozen imbecile-looking old women
crowd in through the low door, and stare and exchange
observations. Three young men with nothing particular
to do lounge at the far end of the platform near the
goats. A bright girl, with more jewellery on than is
usual among Pariahs, is tending the fire at the end near
the door; she throws a stick or two on as we enter, and
hurries forward to get a mat. We sit down on the mat,
and she sits beside us; and the usual questions are
asked and answered by way of introduction. There is a
not very clean old woman diligently devouring betel;
another with an enormous mouth, which she always holds
wide open; another with a very loud voice and a shock
of unspeakable hair. But they listen fairly well till
a goat creates a diversion by making a remark, and a
baby—a jolly little scrap in its nice brown skin and
a bangle—yells, and everyone's attention concentrates
upon it.

The goat subsides, the baby is now in its mother's
arms; so we go on where we left off, and I watch the
bright young girl, and notice that she listens as one who
understands. She looks rather superior; her rose-coloured
seeley is clean, and two large gold jewels are in each
ear; she has a little gold necklet round her throat,
and silver bangles and toe rings. All the others are

An ancient Pariah, but the baby in her arms is a son of the Caste of Palmyra Climbers. Both faces—the old crone's and the baby boy's—are very typical. The baby is a "Christian," I should explain, and his parents are true Christians, otherwise the Pariah woman would not have been allowed to touch him.

hopelessly grubby and very unenlightened, but they
listen just as most people listen in church, with a sort
of patient expression. It is the proper thing to do.

I am talking to them now, and till I am half-way
through nobody says anything, when suddenly the girl
remarks, "We have ten fingers, not just one!" which
is so astonishing that I stop and wonder what she can be
thinking of. I was talking about the one sheep lost out
of one hundred. What has that got to do with one
finger and ten? She goes on to explain, "I have heard
all this before. I have a sister who is a Christian, and
once I stayed with her, and I heard all about your
religion, and I felt in my heart it was good. But then
I was married" ("tied," she said), "and of course I forgot
about it; but now I remember, and I say if ten of our
people will join and go over to your Way, that will be
well, but what would be the use of one going? What is
the use of one finger moving by itself? It takes ten to
do the day's work."

"If ten of you had cholera, and I brought you cholera
medicine, would you say, 'I won't take it unless nine
others take it too'?" I replied. She laughs and the
others laugh, but a little uneasily. They hardly like this
reference to the dreaded cholera; death of the body is
so much more tremendous in prospect than death of
the soul. "You would take it, and then the others,
seeing it do you good, would perhaps take it too"; and
we try to press home the point of the illustration. But
a point pricks, and pricking is uncomfortable.

The three men begin to shuffle their feet and talk
about other things; the old mother-in-law proposes

betel all round, and hands us some grimy-looking leaves
with a pressing invitation to partake. The various
onlookers make remarks, and the girl devotes herself to
her baby. But she is thinking; one can see old memories
are stirred. At last with a sigh she gets up, looks round
the little indifferent group, goes over to the fireplace,
and blows up the fire. This means we had better say
salaam; so we say it and they say it, adding the usual
"Go and come."

It will be easier to help these people out of their low
levels than it will be to help their masters of the higher
walks of life. But to do anything genuine or radical
among either set of people is never really easy.

**"It takes the Ideal to blow a hair's-breadth off
the Dust of the Actual."**

It takes more. It takes **God**. It takes **God** to do
anything anywhere. Yesterday we were visiting in one
of the Caste villages, and one old lady, who really seems
to care for us, said she would greatly like to take my
hand in hers; "but," she explained, "this morning one
of the children of the place leaned over the edge of the
tank to drink, and he fell in and was drowned; so I have
been to condole with his people, and I have now returned
from bathing, and do not feel equal to bathing again."
If she touched me she would have to bathe to get rid of
the defilement. Of course I assured her I quite understood, but as she sat there within two inches of me, yet
so carefully preserving inviolate those two inches of
clear space, I felt what a small thing this caste-created
distance was, the merest "Dust of the Actual" on the
surface of the system of her life; and yet, "to blow a

hair's-breadth of it off, nothing less is needed than the
breath of the power of God. "Come, O Breath, and
breathe!" we cry. Nothing else will do.

Something in our talk led to a question about the
character of Jesus, and, as we tried to describe a little of
the loveliness of our dear Lord to her, her dark eyes
kindled. "How beautiful it is!" she said; "how beautiful
He must be!" She seemed "almost persuaded," but
we knew it was only almost, not quite; for she does not
yet know her need of a Saviour, she has no sense of sin.
Sometimes, it is true, that comes later; but we find that
if the soul is to resist the tremendous opposing forces
which will instantly be brought to bear upon it if it
turns in the least towards Christ, there must be a
conviction wrought within it; nothing so superficial as a
feeling, be it ever so appreciative or hopeful or loving,
will stand that strain.

So, though the eyes of this dear woman fill with tears
as she hears of the price of pain He paid, and though
she gladly listens as we read and talk with her and pray,
yet we know the work has not gone deep, and we make
our "petitions deep" for her, and go on.

In India men must work among men, and women
among women, but sometimes, in new places, as I have
told before, we have to stop and talk with the men
before they will let us pass. For example, one afternoon I was waylaid on my way to the women by the
head of the household I was visiting, a fine old man of
the usual type, courteous but opposed. He asked to look
at my books. I had a Bible, a lyric book, and a book of
stanzas bearing upon the Truth, copied from the old

Tamil classics. He pounced upon this. Then he began
to chant the stanzas in their inimitable way, and at the
sound several other old men drew round the verandah,
till soon a dozen or more were listening with that
appreciative expression they seem to reserve for their
own beloved poetry.

After the reader had chanted through a dozen or
more stanzas, he stopped abruptly and asked me if I
really cared for it. Of course I said I did immensely,
and only wished I knew more, for the Tamil classics are
a study in themselves, and these beautiful ancient verses
I had copied out were only gleanings from two large
volumes, full of the wisdom of the East.

They were all thoroughly friendly now, and we got
into conversation. One of the group held that there are
three co-eternal substances—God, the Soul, and Sin. Sin
is eternally bound up in the soul, as verdigris is inherent
in copper. It can be removed eventually by intense
meditation upon God, and by the performance of arduous
works of merit. But these exercises they all admitted
were incompatible with the ordinary life of most people,
and generally impracticable. And so the fact is, the
verdigris of sin remains.

I remember the delight with which I discovered that
Isaiah i. 25 uses this very illustration; for the word translated "dross" in English is the colloquial word for
verdigris in Tamil; so the verse reads, "I will turn My
hand to thee, and thoroughly purify thee, *so as to remove
thy verdigris.*"

Most of the others held a diametrically opposite view.
So far from Soul and Sin being co-eternal with God,

they are not really existent at all. Both are illusory.
There is only one existent entity. It is the Divine
Spirit, and it has neither personality nor any personal
qualities. All apparent separate existences are delusive.
Meditation, of the same absorbing type held necessary by
the other, is the only way to reach the stage of enlightenment which leads to reabsorption into the Divine
essence, in which we finally merge, and lose what
appeared to be our separate identity. We are lost in
God, as a drop is lost in the ocean.

Some of the men advocated a phase of truth which
reminds one of Calvinism gone mad, and others exactly
opposite are extravagantly Arminian. The Calvinists
illustrate their belief by a single illuminating word, *Cat-
hold*, and the Arminians by another, *Monkey-hold*. Could
you find better illustrations ? The cat takes up the
kitten and carries it in its mouth; the kitten is passive,
the cat does everything. But the little monkey holds
on to its mother, and clings with might and main.
Those who have watched the "cat-hold" in the house,
and the "monkey-hold" out in the jungle, can appreciate
the accuracy of these two illustrations.

But running through every form of Hinduism, however contradictory each to the other may be, there is the
underlying thought of pure and simple Pantheism. And
this explains many of the aforesaid contradictions, and
many of the incongruities which are constantly cropping
up and bewildering one who is trying to understand the
Hindu trend of thought. So, though those men all
affirmed that there is only one God, they admitted that
they each worshipped several. They saw nothing incon-

sistent in this. Just as the air is in everything, so God
is in everything, therefore in the various symbols. And
as our King has divers representative Viceroys and
Governors to rule over his dominions in his name, so the
Supreme has these sub-deities, less in power and only
existing by force of Himself, and He, being all-pervasive,
can be worshipped under their forms.

This argument they all unitedly pressed upon me that
afternoon, and though capital answers probably present
themselves to your mind, you might not find they
satisfied the Hindu who argues along lines of logic
peculiar to the East, and subtle enough to mystify the
practical Western brain; and then—for we are conceited
as well as practical—we are apt to pity the poor Hindu
for being so unlike ourselves; and if we are wholly
unsympathetic, we growl that there is nothing in the
argument, whereas there is a good deal in it, only we
do not see it, because we have never thought out the
difficulty in question. Quite opposite, sometimes we
have to meet a type of mind like that of MacDonald's
student of Shakespeare, who "missed a plain point from
his eyes being so sharp that they looked through it
without seeing it, having focussed themselves beyond it."
Assuredly there is much to learn before one can hope to
understand the winding of the thread of thought which
must be traced if one would follow the working of the
Hindu mind. Let no one with a facility for untying
mental knots think that his gift would be wasted in
India!

The word that struck those men that afternoon was
1 John v. 11 and 12: "God hath given us eternal life,

and this life is in His Son. He that hath the Son hath
life, and he that hath not the Son of God hath not life."
I was longing to get to the women, but when they began
to read those verses and ask about the meaning, I could
not go without trying to tell them. Oh, how one needed
at that moment Christ to become to us Wisdom, for it is
just here one may so easily make mistakes. Put the
truth of God's relation to the soul subjectively—" He
that hath the Son hath life "—before thoughtful Hindus
such as these men were, and they will be perfectly
enchanted ; for the Incarnation presents no difficulty to
them, as it would to a Mohammedan ; and perhaps, to
your sudden surprise and joy, they will say, that is
exactly what they are prepared to believe. " Christ in
me "—this is comprehensible. " The indwelling of the
Spirit of God "—this is analogous to their own phrase :
" The indwelling of the Deity in the lotus of the heart."
But probably by trading on words and expressions which
are already part of the Hindu terminology, and which
suggest to them materialistic ideas, we may seriously
mislead and be misled. We need to understand not only
what the Hindu says, but also what his words mean to
himself, a very different thing.

That talk ended in a promise from the men that they
would arrange a meeting of Hindus for the Iyer, if he
would come and take it, which of course he did. I
should like to finish up by saying, " and several were
converted," but as yet that would not be true. These
deep-rooted ancient and strong philosophies are formidable enough, when rightly understood, to make us feel
how little we can do to overturn them ; but they are

5

just as "Dust" in comparison with the force of the
"Actual" entrenched behind them. Only superficial
Dust; and yet, as in every other case, nothing but the
Breath of God can blow this Dust away.

We left the old men to their books and endless dis-
quisitions, and went on to the women's quarter. There
we saw a young child-widow, very fair and sweet and
gentle, but quieter than a child should be; for she is a
widow accursed. Her mind is keen—she wants to learn;
but why should a widow learn, they say, why should her
mind break bounds? She lives in a tiny mud-built
house, in a tiny mud-walled yard; she may not go out
beyond those walls, then why should she *think* beyond?
But she is better off than most, for she lives with her
mother, who loves her, and her father makes a pet of her,
and so she is sheltered more or less from the cruel
scourge of the tongue.

There is another in the next courtyard; she is not
sheltered so. She lives with her mother-in-law, and the
world has lashed her heart for years; it is simply callous
now. There she sits with her chin in her hand, just
hard. Years ago they married her, an innocent, playful
little child, to a man who died when she was nine years
old. Then they tore her jewels from her, all but two
little ear-rings, which they left in pity to her; and this
poor little scrap of jewellery was her one little bit of joy.
She could not understand it at first, and when her pretty
coloured seeleys were taken away, and she had to wear
the coarse white cloth she hated so, she cried with
impotent childish wrath; and then she was punished, and
called bitter names,—the very word *widow* means bitter-

Another widow. She was never a wife; and, moved by some sort of pity, they let her keep a jewel in each ear. She is a Vellalar; her people are wealthy landowners. She was ashamed of having yielded to the weakness of letting us take her photo; and when we went to show it to her, she would not look at it. She has no desire whatever to hear; and she and the young girl on the step at her feet are resolute in opposing the teaching.

ness,— and gradually she understood that there was something the matter with her. She was not like other little girls. She had brought ill-fortune to the home. She was accursed.

It is true that some are more gently dealt with, and many belong to Castes where the yoke of Custom lies lighter; for these the point of the curse is blunted, there is only a dull sense of wrong. But in all the upper Castes the pressure is heavy, and there are those who feel intensely, feel to the centre of their soul, the sting of the shame of the curse.

"It is fate," says the troubled mother; "who can escape his fate?" "It is sin," says the mother-in-law; and the rest of the world agrees. "'Where the bull goes, there goes its rope.' 'Deeds done in a former birth, in this birth burn.'"

Much of the working of the curse is hidden behind shut doors. I saw a young widow last week whose mind is becoming deranged in consequence of the severity of the penance she is compelled to perform. When, as they put it, "the god of ill-fortune seizes her," that is, when she becomes violent, she is quietly "removed to another place." No one sees what is done to her there, but I know that part of the treatment consists in scratching her head with thorns, and then rubbing raw lime juice in—lime juice is like lemon juice, only more acid. When the paroxysm passes she reappears, and does penance till the next fit comes. This has been repeated three times within the last few months.

I was visiting in a Hindu house for two years before

I found out that all that time a girl of seventeen was kept alone in an upper room. " Let her weep," they said, quoting a proverb; "'though she weeps, will a widow's sorrow pass?'" Once a day, after dark, she was brought downstairs for a few minutes, and once a day, at noon, some coarse food was taken up to her. She is allowed downstairs now, but only in the back part of the house ; she never thinks of resisting this decree —it, and all it stands for, is her fate. Sometimes the glad girl-life reasserts itself, and she plays and laughs with her sister-in-law's pretty baby boy; but if she hears a man's voice she disappears upstairs. There are proverbs in the language which tell why.

I sat on the verandah of a well-to-do Hindu house one day, and talked to the bright-looking women in their jewels and silks. And all the time, though little I knew it, a widow was tied up in a sack in one of the inner rooms. This wrong is a hidden wrong.

I do not think that anyone would call the Hindus distinctively cruel ; in comparison with most other Asiatics their instincts are kind. A custom so merciless as this custom, which punishes the innocent with so grievous a punishment, does not seem to us to be natural to them. It seems like a parasite custom, which has struck its roots deep into the tree of Hindu social life, but is not part of it. Think of the power which must have been exerted somewhere by someone before the disposition of a nation could be changed.

This custom as it stands is formidable enough. Many a man, Indian and foreign, has fought it and failed. It is a huge and most rigorous system of tyrannical oppression, a very pyramid to look at, old, immovable. But there is Something greater behind it. It is only the effect of a Cause—the Dust of the Actual.

What can alter the custom? Strong writing or speaking, agitations, Acts of Parliament? All these surely have their part. They raise the question, stir the Dust—but blow it off? Oh no! nothing can touch the conscience of the people, and utterly reverse their view of things, and radically alter them, but God.

Yes, it is true, we may make the most of what has been done by Government, by missionaries and reformers, but there are times in the heart histories of all who look far enough down to see what goes on under the surface of things, when the sorrow takes shape in the Prophet's cry, "We have not wrought any deliverance in the earth!"

It is true. *We* have not. We cannot even estimate the real weight of the lightest speck of the Dust that has settled on the life of this people. But we believe that our God, Who comprehended the dust of the earth in a measure, comprehends to the uttermost the Dust of the Actual, and we believe to see Him work, with Whom is strength and effectual working.

We believe to see, and believing even now we see; and when we see anything, be it ever so little, when the Breath breathes, and even "a hair's-breadth" of that Dust is blown away, then, with an intensity I cannot describe, we feel the presence of the Lord our God among us, and look up in the silence of joy and expectation for the coming of the Day when all rule, and all authority and power, yea, the power of the very Actual itself, shall be put down, that God may be all in all.

So again and yet again we ask you to pray not less for the Reform movement, and the Educational movement, and the Civilising movement of India, but far more for the Movement of the Breath of God, and far more for us His workers here, that we may abide in Him without Whom we can do nothing.

We wanted a dining-room photo, which is very difficult to get because of Caste rules; this being only cold rice and water, not hot rice and curry, was after some deliberation allowed. It would have been out of the question in a high-caste house.

CHAPTER VIII

Roots

"It is not an easy thing in England to lead an old man or woman to Christ, even though the only 'root' which holds them from Him is love of the world. As the Tamil proverb says, 'That which did not bend at five will not be bent at fifty,' still less at sixty or seventy. When a soul in India is held down, not by one root only, but by a myriad roots, who is sufficient to deliver it? Only He who overturneth the mountains by the roots. 'This kind goeth not out but by prayer and fasting.'"
An Indian Missionary.

"AMMA, you are getting old."

"Yes (grunt), yes."

"When we are old then death is near."

"Yes (grunt), yes."

"Then we must leave our bodies and go somewhere else." Three more grunts.

"Amma, do you know where you are going?"

Then the old woman wakes up a little, grunts a little more, "Who knows where she is going?" she mumbles, and relapses into grunts.

"I know where I am going," the girl answers. "Amma, don't you want to know?"

"Don't I want to know what?"

"Where you are going."

"Why do I want to know what?"

The girl goes over it again. The old woman turns to

her daughter-in-law. "Is the rice ready?" she says. The
girl tries again. The old woman agrees we all must
die. Death is near to the ancient; she is ancient, therefore death is near to her, she must go somewhere after
death. It would be well to know where she is going.
She does not know where she is going. Then she gazes
and grunts.

The girl tries on different lines. Whom is the old
woman looking to, to help her when death comes?

"God."

"What God?"

"The great God." And rousing herself to express
herself she declares that He is her constant meditation,
therefore all is well. "Is the rice ready?"

"No."

"Then give me some betel leaf," and she settles down to
roll small pieces of lime into little balls, and these balls
she rolls up in a betel leaf, with a bit of areca nut for
taste, and this betel leaf she puts into her mouth—all
this very slowly, and with many inarticulate sounds,
which I have translated "grunts." And this is all she
does. She does not want to listen or talk, she only
wants to scrunch betel, and grunt.

This is not a touching tale. It is only true. It
happened this evening exactly as I have told it, and the
girl, a distant connection of the old woman, who had
come with me so delightedly, eager to tell the Good
Tidings, had to give it up. She had begun by speaking
about the love of Jesus, but that had fallen perfectly
flat; so she had tried the more startling form of address,
with this result—grunts.

Enlargement of one of the old dames seen in chapter vi. A capital typical face. We have a number of these keen, interesting old people, but very rarely find they have any desire to "change their religion." They are "rooted."

I spent an afternoon not long ago with a more intelligent specimen. Here she is, a fine sturdy old character, one of the three you saw before. She was immensely interested with her photo, which I showed her, and she could not understand at all how, in the one moment when she stood against a wall, her face "had been caught on a piece of white paper." A little explanation opened the way for the greater thing I had come about. We were sitting on a mud verandah, opening on to a square courtyard; two women pounding rice, two more grinding it, another sweeping, a cow, some fowls, a great many children, and several babies, made it exceedingly difficult to concentrate one's attention on anything, and still more difficult to get the wandering brains of an old woman to concentrate on a subject in which she had no interest. She had been interested in the photograph, but that was different.

The conversation ended by her remarking that it was getting dark, ought I not to be going home? It was not getting dark yet, but it meant that she had had enough, so I salaamed and went, hoping for a better chance again. Next time we visited the Village of the Tamarind she was nowhere to be seen; she had gone to her own village, she had only come here for the funeral. Would she return, we asked? Not probable, they said, "she had come and gone." "Come and gone." As they said it, one felt how true it was. Come, for that one short afternoon within our reach; gone, out of it now for ever.

In that same village there is one who more than any other drew one's heart out in affection and longing, but so far all in vain.

I first saw her in the evening as we were returning
home. She was sitting on her verandah, giving orders
to the servants as they stood in the courtyard below.
Then she turned and saw us. We were standing in the
street, looking through the open door. The old lady, in
her white garments, with her white hair, sat among a
group of women in vivid shades of red, behind her the
dark wood of the pillar and door, and above the carved
verandah roof.

The men were fresh from the fields, and stood with
their rough-looking husbandry implements slung across
their shoulders; the oxen, great meek-eyed beasts, were
munching their straw and swishing their tails as they
stood in their places in the courtyard, where some little
children played.

The paddy-birds, which are small white storks, were
flying about from frond to frond of the cocoanut palms
that hung over the wall, and the sunset light, striking
slanting up, caught the underside of their wings, and
made them shine with a clear pale gold, gold birds in a
darkness of green. A broken mud wall ran round one
end, and the sunset colour painted it too till all the red
in it glowed; and then it came softly through the palms,
and touched the white head with a sort of sheen, and lit
up the brow of the fine old face as, bending forward, she
beckoned to us. "Come in! come in!" she said.

We soon made friends with her. She was a Saivite,
and we heard afterwards had received the Initiation; the
golden symbol of her god had been branded upon her
shoulder, and she was sworn to lifelong devotion to
Siva; but she had found that he was vain, and she never

worshipped him, she worshipped God alone, "and at night, when the household is sleeping, I go up alone to an upper room, and stretch out my hands to the God of all, and cry with a long, loud cry." Then she suddenly turned and faced me full. "Tell me, is that enough?" she said. "Is it all I must do for salvation? Say!"

I did not feel she was ready for a plunge into the deep sea of full knowledge yet, and I tried to persuade her to leave that question, telling her that if she believed what we told her of Jesus our Lord, she would soon know Him well enough to ask Him direct what she wanted to know, and He Himself would explain to her all that it meant to follow Him. But she was determined to hear it then, and, as she insisted, I read her a little of what He says about it Himself. She knew quite enough to understand and take in the force of the forceful words. She would not consent to be led gently on. "No, I must know it now," she said; and as verse by verse we read to her, her face settled sorrowfully. "So far must I follow, so far?" she said. "*I cannot follow so far.*"

It was too late for much talk then, but she promised to listen if we would come and read to her. She could not read, but she seemed to know a great deal about the Bible.

For some weeks one of us went once a week; sometimes the men of the house were in, and then we could not read to her, as they seemed to object; but oftener no one was about, and she had her way, and we read.

She told us her story one afternoon. She was the head of a famous old house; her husband had died many years ago; she had brought up her children successfully, and now they were settled in life. She had a Christian relation, but she had never seen him; she thought he had a son studying in a large school in England—Cambridge, I knew, when I heard the name; the father is one of our true friends.

All her sons are greatly opposed, but one of her little girls learnt for a time, and so the mother heard the Truth, and, being convinced that it was true, greatly desired to hear more.

But the child was married, and went away, and she feared to ask the Missie Ammal to come again, lest people should notice it and talk. So the years passed emptily, "and oh, my heart was an empty place, a void as empty as air!" And she stretched out her arms, and clasping her hands she looked at the empty space between, and then at me with inquiring eyes, to see if I understood.

How well one understood!

> "I am an emptiness for Thee to fill,
> My soul a cavern for Thy sea, . . .
> I have done nought for Thee, am but a Want."

She had never heard it, but she had said it. We do not often hear it said, and when we do our whole heart goes out to meet the heart of the one who says it; everything that is in us yearns with a yearning that cannot be told, to bring her to Him Who said " Come."

We were full of hope about her, and we wrote to her Christian relative, and he wrote back with joy. It seemed so likely then that she would decide for Christ.

But one day, for the first time, she did not care to

read. I remember that day so well; it was the time of
our monsoon, and the country was one great marsh. We
had promised to go that morning, but the night before
the rivers filled, and the pool between her and us was a
lake. We called the bandyman and explained the
situation. He debated a little, but at last—"Well, the
bulls can swim," he said, and they swam.

We need not have gone, she was "out." "Out," or
"not at home to-day," is a phrase not confined to Society
circles where courtesy counts for more than truth.
"I am in, but I do not want to see you," would have
been true, but rude.

This was the first chill, but she was in next time, and
continued to be in, until after a long talk we had, when
again the question rose and had to be faced, "Can I be a
Christian _here_?"

It was a quiet afternoon; we were alone, only the
little grandchildren were with her—innocent, fearless,
merry little creatures, running to her with their wants,
and pulling at her hands and dress as babies do at home.
Their grandmother took no notice of them beyond an
occasional pat or two, but the childish things, with their
bright brown eyes and little fat, soft, clinging hands went
into the photo one's memory took, and helped one the
better to understand and sympathise in the humanness
of the pretty home scene, that humanness which is so
natural, and which God meant to be. I think there is
nothing in all our work which so rends and tears at the
heart-strings within us, as seeing the spiritual clash with
the natural, and to know that while Caste and bigotry
reign it always must be so.

We had a good long talk. "I want to be a Christian," she said, and for a moment I hoped great things, for she as the mistress of the house was almost free to do as she chose. I thought of her influence over her sons and their wives, and the little grandchildren; and I think my face showed the hope I had, for she said, looking very direct at me, "By a Christian I mean one who worships your God, and ceases to worship all other gods; for He alone is the Living God, the Pervader of all and Provider. This I fully believe and affirm, but I cannot break my Caste."

"Would you continue to keep it in all ways?"

"How could I possibly break my Caste?"

"And continue to smear Siva's sign on your forehead?"

"That is indeed part of my Caste."

More especially part of it, I knew, since she had received the Initiation.

Then the disappointment got into my voice, and she felt it, and said, "Oh, do not be grieved! These things are external. How can mere ashes affect the internal, the real essential, the soul?"

It was such a plausible argument, and we hear it over and over again; for history repeats itself, there is nothing new under the sun.

I reminded her that ashes were sacred to Siva.

"I would not serve Siva," she answered me, "but the smearing of ashes on one's brow is the custom of my Caste, and I cannot break my Caste."

Then she looked at me very earnestly with her searching, beautiful, keen old eyes, and she went over ground she knew I knew. She reminded me what the require-

ments of her Caste had always been, that they must be
fulfilled by all who live in the house, and she told me in
measured words and slow that I knew she could not live
at home if she broke the laws of her Caste. But why
make so much of trifling things? For matter and spirit
are distinct, and when the hands are raised in prayer,
when the lamp is lighted and wreathed with flowers, the
outward observer may mistake and think the action is
pujah to Agni, but God who reads the heart understands, and judges the thought and not the act. "Yes,
my hand may smear on Siva's ashes, while at the same
moment my soul may commune with God the Eternal,
Who only is God."

I turned to verse after verse to show her this sort of
thing could never be, how it would mock at the love of
Christ and nullify His sacrifice. I urged upon her that
if she were true, and the central thought of her life were
towards God, all the outworkings would correspond,
creed fitting deed, and deed fitting creed without the
least shade of diversity. Faith and practice are not to
be confused, each is separate from the other; the two
may unite or the one may be divorced from the other
without the integrity of either being affected: this is the
unwritten Hindu code which she and hers had ever held;
and now, after years of belief in it, to face round suddenly
to its opposite—this was more than she could do. She
held, as it were, the Truth in her hand, and turned it
round and round and round, but she always ended where
she began; she would not, *could* not, see it as Truth, or
perhaps more truly, would not accept it. It meant too
much.

There she sat, queen of her home. The sons were
expected, and she had been making preparations for their
coming. Her little grandchildren played about her, each
one of them dear as the jewel of her eye. How could
she leave it all, how could she leave them all—home, all
that it stands for; children, all that they mean?

Then she looked at me again, and I shall never forget
the look. It seemed as if she were looking me through
and through, and forcing the answer to come. She spoke
in little short sentences, instinct with intensity. "I
cannot live here and break my Caste. If I break it
I must go. I *cannot* live here without keeping my
customs. If I break them I must go. You know all
this. I ask you, then, tell me yes or no. Can I live
here and keep my Caste, and at the same time follow
your God? Tell me yes or no!"

I did not tell her—how could I? But she read the
answer in my eyes, and she said, as she had said before,
"I cannot follow so far—so far, *I cannot follow so far!*"

"Reverence for opinions and practice held sacred by
his ancestors is ingrained in every fibre of a Hindu's
character, and is, so to speak, bred in the very bone of his
physical and moral constitution." So writes Sir Monier
Williams. It is absolutely true.

Oh, friends, is it easy work? My heart is sore as I
write, with the soreness that filled it that day. I would
have given anything to be able truthfully to say "yes"
to her question. But "across the will of nature leads on
the path of God" for them; and they have to follow so
very far, so very, very far!

All trees have roots. To tear up a full-grown tree by

the roots, and transplant it bodily, is never a simple process. But in India we have a tree with a double system of roots. The banyan tree drops roots from its boughs. These bough roots in time run as deep underground as the original root. And the tap root and its runners, and the branch roots and theirs, get knotted and knit into each other, till the whole forms one solid mass of roots, thousands of yards of a tangle of roots, sinuous and strong. Conceive the uprooting of such a tree, like the famous one of North India, for instance, which sheltered an army of seven thousand men. You cannot conceive it; it could not be done, the earthward hold is so strong.

The old in India are like these trees; they are doubly, inextricably rooted. There is the usual great tap root common to all human trees in all lands—faith in the creed of the race; there are the usual running roots too—devotion to family and home. All these hold the soul down.

But in India we have more—we have the branch-rooted system of Caste; Caste so intricate, so precise, that no Western lives who has traced it through its ramifications back to the bough from which it dropped in the olden days.

This Caste, then, these holding laws, which most would rather die than break, are like the branch roots of the banyan tree with their infinite strength of grip. But the strangest thing to us is this: the people love to have it so; they do not regard themselves as held, these roots are their pride and joy. Take a child of four or five, ask it a question concerning its Caste, and you will see how that baby tree has begun to drop branch rootlets

6

down. Sixty years afterwards look again, and every rootlet has grown a tree, each again sending rootlets down ; and so the system spreads.

But we look up from the banyan tree. God! what are these roots to Thee? These Caste-root systems are nothing to Thee! India is not too hard for Thee! O God, come !

CHAPTER IX

The Classes and the Masses

"We speak of work done against the force of gravitation. If the magnitude of a force can be estimated in any sense by the resistance which it has to overcome, then verily there is no land under the sun more calculated than India to display the Grand Forces of God's Omnipotent Grace. For here it has to face and overcome the *combined resistances* of the Caste system, entrenched heathenism, and deeply subtle philosophies. Praise God! it can and will be done. Thou, who alone doest wondrous things, work on. 'So will we sing and praise Thy power.'" *Rev. T. Walker, India.*

PERHAPS it would help towards the better understanding of these letters if we stopped and explained things a little. Some may have been wondering, as they read, how it is that while the South Indian fields are constantly quoted as among the most fruitful in the world, we seem to be dealing with a class where fruit is very rare, and so subject to blighting influences after it has appeared, that we hardly like to speak of it till it is ripe and reaped and safe in the heavenly garner. I think it will be easier to understand all this if we view Hindu Tamil South India (with which alone this book deals) from the outside, and let it fall into two divisions, the Classes and the Masses. There is, of course, the border line between, crossed over on either side by some who belong to the Classes but are almost of the Masses, and by some who belong to the Masses but are almost of the Classes. Broadly speaking, however, there is a distinct difference between the two. As to their attitude towards the Gospel, the Classes and the Masses unite; they are wholly indifferent to it.

In a paper read at the Student Volunteers' Conference in 1900, a South Indian missionary summed up the matter in a comprehensive sentence: "Shut in for millenniums by the gigantic wall of the Himalayas on the North, and by the impassable ocean on the South, they have lived in seclusion from the rest of the world, and have developed social institutions and conceptions of the universe, and of right and wrong, quite their own. Their own religion and traditionary customs are accepted as sufficiently meeting their needs, and they are not conscious of needing any teaching from foreigners. They will always listen courteously to what we say, and this constitutes an open door for the Gospel, but of conscious need and hungering for the Gospel there is little or none. So long as it is only a matter of preaching, there are in the world no more patient listeners than the Hindus. But as soon as a case arises of one of their number abandoning the Caste customs and traditionary worship, all their hostility is aroused, and the whole community feels it a duty of patriotism to do its utmost to deprive that individual of liberty of action, and to defend the vested rights of Hinduism."

For the true Hindu is fervently Hindu. His religion "may be described as bound up in the bundle of his everyday existence." His intense belief in it, and in his Caste, which is part of it, gives edge to the blade

with which he fights the entrance of a new religion to
his home. This new religion he conceives of as something inherently antagonistic to his Caste, and as Caste
is at every point connected with Hinduism, a thing interwoven with it, as if Hinduism were the warp and Caste
the woof of the fabric of Indian life, we cannot
say he is mistaken in regarding Christianity as a foe
to be fought if he would continue a Caste Hindu. So
far, in South Indian religious history, we have no example
on a large scale of anything approaching the Bramo
Samáj of the North. In the more conservative South
there is almost no compromise with, and little assimila-
tion of, the doctrine which makes all men one in Christ.

To return to the division—Classes and Masses—the
Classes comprise members of what are known as the
higher Castes, and in speaking of towns and villages
where these dwell, and of converts from among them,
the prefix "Caste" is sometimes used. Among the
Classes we find women of much tenderness of feeling
and a culture of their own, but their minds are narrowed
by the petty lives they live, lives in many instances
bounded by no wider horizon than thoughts concerning
their husbands and children and jewels and curries, and
always their next-door neighbour's squabbles and the
gossip of the place. Much of this gossip deals with
matters which are not of an elevating character. It
takes us years to understand it, because most of the
conversation is carried on in allusion or innuendo. But
it is understood by the children. One of our converts
told me that she often prays for power to forget the
words she heard, and the things she saw, and the games

she played, when she was a little child in her mother's room.

The young girls belonging to the higher Castes are kept in strict seclusion. During these formative years they are shut up within the courtyard walls to the dwarfing life within, and as a result they get dwarfed, and lose in resourcefulness and independence of mind, and above all in courage; and this tells terribly in our work, making it so difficult to persuade such a one to think for herself or dare to decide to believe. Such seclusion is not felt as imprisonment; a girl is trained to regard it as the proper thing, and we never find any desire among those so secluded to break bounds and rush out into the free, open air. They do not feel it cramped as we should; it is their custom.

It is this custom which makes work among girls exceedingly slow and unresultful. They have to be reached one by one, and it takes many months of teaching before the mind opens enough to understand that it may be free. The reaction of the physical upon the mental is never more clearly illustrated than in such cases. Sometimes it seems as if the mind *could* not go out beyond the cramping walls; but when it has, by God's illumination, received light enough to see into the darkness of the soul, and the glory that waits to shine in on it, conceive of the tremendous upheaval, the shock of finding solid ground sink, as gradually or suddenly the conviction comes upon such a one that if she acts upon this new knowledge there is no place for her at home. She must give everything up—*everything!*

Do you wonder that few are found willing to " follow

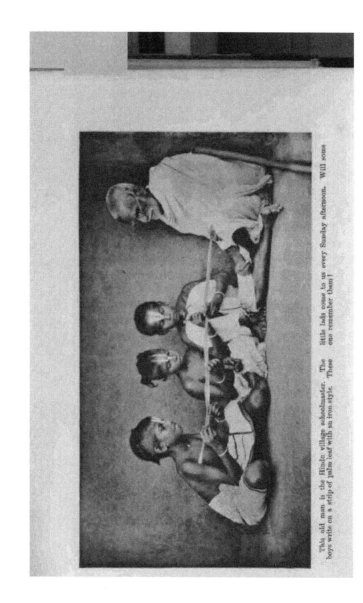

This old man is the Hindu village schoolmaster. The little lads come to us every Sunday afternoon. Will some boys write on a strip of palm leaf with an iron style. These one remember them?

so far"? Do you wonder that our hearts nearly break
sometimes, as we realise the cost for them? Do you
wonder that, knowing how each is set as a target for
the archer who shoots at souls, we fear to say much about
them, lest we should set the targets clearer in his sight?

The men and boys of the Classes live a more liberal
life, and here you find all varying shades of refinement.
There is education, too, and a great respect for learning,
and reverence for their classic literature and language,
a language so ancient that we find certain Tamil words
in the Hebrew Scriptures, and so rich, that while "nearly
all the vernaculars of India have been greatly enriched
from the Sanscrit, Sanscrit has borrowed from Tamil."
Almost every Caste village has its own little school, and
every town has many, where the boys are taught reading,
writing, poetry, and mental arithmetic.

There is not much education among the Masses.
Here and there a man stands out who has fought his
way through the ignorance of centuries, up into the light
of the knowledge of books. Such a man is greatly
respected by the whole community. The women have
the same kindly nature as the women of the Classes, and
there is surprising responsiveness sometimes, where one
would least expect it. We have known a Tamil woman,
distinctly of the Masses, never secluded in her girlhood,
but left to bloom as a wild flower in the field, as sensitive
in spirit as any lady born. The people are rough and
rustic in their ways, but there are certain laws observed
which show a spirit of refinement latent among them;
there are customs which compare favourably with the
customs of the masses at home. As a whole, they are like

the masses of other lands, with good points and bad points in strong relief, and just the same souls to be saved.

Converts from among the Masses, as a general rule, are able to live at home. There is persecution, but they are not turned out of village, street, or house. Often they come in groups, two or three families together perhaps, or a whole village led by its headman comes over. There is less of the single one-by-one conversion and confession, though there is an increasing number of such, and they are the best we have.

It is easy to understand how much more rapidly Christianity spreads under such conditions than among those prevailing among the Classes; we see it illustrated over and over again. For example, in a certain high-caste Hindu town some miles distant from our station on the Eastern side, a young man heard the Gospel preached at an open-air meeting; he believed, and confessed in baptism, thus breaking Caste and becoming an alien to his own people. He has never been able to live at home since, and so there has been no witness borne, no chance to let the life show out the love of God. The men of that household doubtless know something of the truth; they know enough, at least, to make them responsible for refusing it; but what can the women know? Only that the son of the house has disgraced his house and name; only that he has destroyed his Caste and broken his mother's heart. "Shame upon him," they cry with one voice, "and curses on the cause of the shame, the 'Way' of Jesus Christ!" It is useless to say they are merely women, and do not count; they *do* count. Their influence counts for a very great deal.

Theoretically, women in India are nothing where religion
is concerned; practically, they are the heart of the Hindu
religion, as the men are its sinew and brain. There has
never been a convert in that town since that young man
was banished from it, out-casted by his Caste.

But in a village only a few miles from that town a
heathen lad believed, and was baptised, and returned
home, not so welcome as before, but not considered too
defiled to be reckoned a son of the household still. His
father is dead, his mother is a bitter opponent, but his
brother has come since, and within a stone's - throw
another; and so it goes on: the life has a chance to tell.
Almost every time we have gone to that village we have
found some ready for baptism, and though none of the
mothers have been won, they witness to the change in
the life of their sons. "My boy's heart is as white as
milk now," said one, who had stood by and seen that
boy tied up and flogged for Christ's sake. They rarely
"change their religion," these staunch old souls; "let me go
where my husband is; he would have none of it!" said
one, and nothing seems to move them; but they let their
boys live at home, and perhaps, even yet, the love will
break down their resistance. They are giving it a chance.

I think this one illustration explains more than many
words would the difference between work among the
Classes and the Masses, and why it is that one form of
work is so much more fruitful than the other.

The Masses must not be understood as a vast casteless
Mass, out-casted by the Classes, for the Caste system
runs down to the very lowest stratum, but their Caste
rules allow of freer intercourse with others. We may visit

in their houses more freely, enter more freely into their thoughts, share more freely in the interests of their lives. We are less outside, as it were. But the main difference between the one set of people and the other lies deeper; it is a difference underground. It works out, however, into something all can see. Among the Masses, " mass movements" are of common occurrence; among the Classes, with rare exceptions, each one must come out alone.

This is often forgotten by observers of the Indian Field from the home side. There are parts of that field where the labourers seem to be always binding up sheaves and singing harvest songs; and from other parts come fewer songs, for the sheaves are fewer there, or it may be there are none at all, only a few poor ears of corn, and they had to be gathered one by one, and they do not show in the field.

A village woman of the Shanar Caste. This photo shows the baby's ears being prepared for the jewels her mother hopes will fill them by and by. Holes are made first and filled with cotton wool, graduated leaden weights are added till the lobes are long enough. This custom is hideous and heathenish, but is followed by the majority of Christians. Short ears are rare except among the Brahmans and Pariahs (extremes meet again)!

CHAPTER X

The Creed Chasm

"I have had to deal in the same afternoon's work, on the one hand with men of keen powers of intellect, whose subtle reasoning made one look to the foundations of one's own faith ; and on the other hand with ignorant crowds, whose conception of sin was that of a cubit measure, and to whom the terms 'faith' and 'love' were as absolutely unknown as though they had been born and bred in some undeveloped race of Anthropoids."   *Rev. T. Walker, India.*

IN writing about the Classes and the Masses of South India, one great difference which does not exist at home should be explained. In England a prince and a peasant may be divided by outward things—social position, style of life, and the duty of life—but in all inward things they may be one—one in faith, one in purpose, one in hope. The difference which divides them is only accidental, external; and the peasant, perhaps being in advance of the prince in these verities of existence, may be regarded by the prince as nobler than himself: there is no spiritual chasm between them. It is the same in the realm of scholarship. All true Christians, however learned or however unlearned, hold one and the same faith. But in India it is not so. The scholar would smile at the faith of the simple villagers, he would even teach them to believe that which he did not believe himself, holding that it was more suitable for them, and he would marvel at your ignorance if you confounded his creed with theirs; and yet in name both he and they are Hindus.

Sir Monier Williams explains the existence of this difference by describing the receptivity and all-comprehensiveness of Hinduism. " It has something to offer which is suited to all minds, its very strength lies in its infinite adaptability to the infinite diversity of human characters and human tendencies. It has its highly spiritual and abstract side, suited to the metaphysical philosopher; its practical and concrete side, suited to the man of affairs and the man of the world; its æsthetic and ceremonial side, suited to the man of poetic feeling and imagination; its quiescent and contemplative side, suited to the man of peace and lover of seclusion. Nay, it holds out the right hand of brotherhood to nature worshippers, demon worshippers, animal worshippers, tree worshippers, fetich worshippers. It does not scruple to permit the most grotesque forms of idolatry and the most degrading varieties of superstition, and it is to this latter fact that yet another remarkable peculiarity of Hinduism is mainly due—*namely, that in no other System of the world is the chasm more vast which separates the religion of the higher, cultured, and thoughtful Classes, from that of the lower, uncultured, and unthinking Masses.*"

Naturally, therefore, work among them is different; one almost needs a different vocabulary for each, and certainly one needs a different set of ideas. I remember how, in one afternoon's work, we saw the two types most perfectly. In thinking of it, it is as if one saw again the quiet face of the old scholar against a background

of confusion, the clear calm features carved as in ivory,
and set with a light upon it; chaotic darkness behind.
We were visiting his wife, when he came out from the
inner room, and asked if he might talk with us. Usually
to such a question I say no; we have come to the women,
who are far the more needy, the men can easily hear
if they will. But he was such an old man, I felt I
could not refuse; so he began to tell me what he held
as truth, which was, in brief, that there are two sets of
attachment, one outer, one inner; that deliverance from
these, and from Self, the Ego, which regards itself as
the doer, constitutes Holiness; that is, that one must be
completely disentangled and completely self-less. This
attained, the next is Bliss, which is progressive. First
comes existence in the same place as God. Second,
nearness to God. Third, likeness to God. Fourth,
identity with God. Then he quoted from a classic
beloved by all the old Tamil school, stanza after stanza,
to prove the truth of the above, ending with one which
Dr. Pope has thus translated—

> "*Cling thou to that which He to Whom nought clings hath bid
> thee cling,*
> *Cling to that bond, to get thee free from every clinging thing.*"

He knew Sanscrit, and read me strange-sounding passages
from a huge ancient book, and then, in return for a
booklet, he gave me one of Mrs. Besant's translations
from the *Bhagavad Gita*.

The talk ended in my quoting what he could not
deny was the true heart-cry of one of his greatest poets.
"I know nothing! nothing! I am in darkness! Lord,
is there no light for me!" And another, from the

poem he had quoted, which asks the question, "What is the use of knowledge, mere knowledge, if one does not draw near to the All-knowing, All-pure One?" And this led into what he would not listen to at first, a little reading from the Book of books, before whose light even these wonderful books pale as tapers in clear sunshine. The marvel of our Bible never shows more marvellous than at such times, when you see it in deed and in truth the Sword of the Spirit, and it *cuts*.

The old man asked me to come again, and I did, as the Iyer was away. He often got out of my depth, and I longed to know more; but I always found the Bible had the very word he needed, if he would only take it. So far as I know, he did not, and I left him—to quote his own words, though not spoken of himself, alas!—"bewildered by numerous thoughts, meshed in the web of delusion."

As we left our old scholar, we came upon a thing wholly foolish and brainless, animalism in force. It was the difference between the Classes and the Masses once for all painted in glare. A huge procession was tearing along the streets and roads, with all the usual uproar. They stopped when they got to a big thorn bush, and then danced round it, carrying their idols raised on platforms, and borne by two or three dozen to each. We passed, singing as hard as ever we could "Victory to Jesus' Name! Victory!" and when we got rather out of the stream, stopped, and sang most vigorously, till quite a little crowd gathered, and we had a chance to witness.

It was dark, and the flaming torches lit up the wildest, most barbaric bit of heathenism I have seen for a long time.

The great black moving mass seemed like some hellish sea which had burst its bounds, and the hundreds of red-fire torches moving up and down upon it like lights in infernal fishermen's boats, luring lost souls to their doom.

As we waited and spoke to those who would hear, a sudden rush from the centre of things warned us to go; but before we could get out of the way, a rough lad with a thorn-branch torch stuck it right into the bandy, and all but set fire to us. He ran on with a laugh, and another followed with an idol, a hideous creature, red and white, which he also pushed in upon us. Our bullocks trotted as fast as they could, and we soon got out of it all, and looking back saw the great square of the devil temple blazing with torches and firebrands, and heard the drummings and clangings and yells which announced the arrival of the procession.

All that night the riotous drumming continued, and, as one lay awake and listened, one pictured the old scholar sitting in the cool night air on his verandah, reading his ancient palm-leaf books by the light of the little lamp in the niche of his cottage wall.

CHAPTER XI

Caste viewed as a Doer

"It is matter for especial notice that in every department of applied science we have to deal with the unseen. All forces, whether in physics, mechanics, or electricity, are invisible."　　　　　*Alexander Mackay, Africa.*

THE division of the Tamil people, over fifteen million strong, into Classes and Masses, though convenient and simple, is far too simple to be of value in giving an accurate idea of the matter as it is understood from within. As we said, it is only an outside view of things. A study of Caste from an Indian point of view is a study from which you rise bewildered.

What is Caste? What is electricity? Lord Kelvin said, on the occasion of his jubilee, that he knew no more of electric and magnetic force . . . than he knew and tried to teach his students of natural philosophy fifty years ago in his first session as Professor. We know that electricity exists, we are conscious of its presence in the phenomena of light, heat, sound; but we do not know what it is.

Nothing could more perfectly illustrate Caste. You cannot live long in a conservative part of India, in close contact with its people, without being conscious of its presence; if you come into conflict with it, it manifests itself in a flash of opposition, hot rage of persecution, the roar of the tumult of the crowd. But try to define it, and you find you cannot do it. It is not merely birth, class, a code of rules, though it includes all these. It is a force, an energy; there is spirit in it, essence, hidden as the invisible essence which we call electricity.

Look at what it does. A few months ago a boy of twelve resolved to be a Christian. His clan, eight thousand strong, were enraged. There was a riot in the streets; in the house the poison cup was ready. Better death than loss of Caste.

In another town a boy took his stand, and was baptised, thus crossing the line that divides secret belief from open confession. His Caste men got hold of him afterwards; next time he was seen he was a raving lunatic. The Caste was avenged.

It may be someone will wonder if these things are confined to one part of the field, so I quote from another, working in a neighbouring field, Tamil, but not "ours."

She tells of a poor low-caste woman who learned in her home, and believed. Her husband also believed, and both thought of becoming Christians. The village soothsayer warned them that their father's god would be angry; they did not heed him, but went on, and suddenly their baby died. This was too much for their faith then, and they both went back to idolatry.

A few years afterwards their eldest child began to learn to read, and the mother's faith revived. The soothsayer and her husband reminded her of the infant's fate, but she was brave, and let her child learn. Then her cow suddenly died. "Did we not tell you so?" they

7

said, and for the moment she was staggered; but she
rallied, and only became more earnest in faith. So the
soothsayer threatened worse.

Then a Caste meeting was called to determine what
could be done with this woman. The husband attended
the meeting, and was treated to some rice and curry;
before he reached home he was taken violently ill, and in
three days he died. The relatives denounced the woman
as the cause of her husband's death, took her only son
from her, and entreated her to return to her father's gods
before they should all be annihilated. They gave her
"two weeks to fast and mourn for her husband, then
finding her mind as firmly fixed on Christ as before, they
sent her to Burmah."

This happened recently. It is told without any effort
to appeal to the sympathies of anyone, simply as a fact; a
witness, every line of it, to the power of Caste as a Doer.
But there is something in the tale, told so terribly quietly,
that makes one's heart burn with indignation at the
unrelenting cruelty which would hound a poor woman
down, and send her, bereft of all she loved, into exile,
such as a foreign land would be to one who knew only
her own little village. And when you remember the
Caste was "low," which they took such infinite pains to
guard, you can judge, perhaps, what the hate would be,
the concentration of scorn and hate, if the Caste were
higher or high.

But look at Caste in another way, in its power in the
commonplace phases of life. For example, take a kitchen
and cooking, and see how Caste rules there. For cooking
is not vulgar work, or *infra dig.* in any sense, in India;

Cooking in a house of the Shanar Caste, always the most accessible of all Castes here, but this is a specially friendly home, or we should not have been allowed to take the photo. The small girl who is grinding curry stuff on the stone is the "imp" of chapter xx.

all Caste women in good orthodox Hindu families either
do their own or superintend the doing of it by younger
members of the same family or servants of the same
Caste. "We Europeans cannot understand the extent to
which culinary operations may be associated with religion.
The kitchen in every Indian household is a kind of sanc-
tuary or holy ground. . . . The mere glance of a man of
inferior Caste makes the greatest delicacies uneatable, and
if such a glance happens to fall on the family supplies
during the cooking operations, when the ceremonial purity
of the water used is a matter of almost life and death to
every member of the household, the whole repast has to
be thrown away as if poisoned. The family is for that
day dinnerless. Food thus contaminated would, if eaten,
communicate a taint to the souls as well as bodies of the
eaters, a taint which could only be removed by long and
painful expiation." Thus far Sir Monier Williams (quoted
as a greater authority than any mere missionary !). Think
of the defilement which would be contracted if a member
of the household who had broken Caste in baptism took
any part in the cooking. It would never be allowed.
Such a woman could take no share in the family life.
Her presence, her shadow, above all her touch, would be
simply pollution. Therefore, and for many other reasons,
her life at home is impossible, and the Hindu, without
arguing about it, regards it as impossible. It does not
enter into the scheme of life as laid down by the rules of
his Caste. He never, if he is orthodox, contemplates it
for a moment as a thing to be even desired.

Cooking and kitchen work may seem small (though it
would not be easy for even the greatest to live without

reference to it), so let us look out on the world of trade, and see Caste again as a Doer there. If a merchant becomes a Christian, no one will buy his goods; if he is a weaver, no one will buy his cloth; if he is a dyer, no one will buy his thread; if he is a jeweller, no one will employ him. If it is remembered that every particular occupation in life represents a particular Caste, it will be easily understood how matters are complicated where converts from the great Trades Unions are concerned. Hence the need of Industrial Missions, and the fact that they exist.

A man wants to become a Christian, say, from the blacksmith or carpenter Caste. As a Christian he loses his trade, and he has been trained to no other. His forefathers worked in iron or wood, and he cannot attempt to learn other work. Let the Christians employ him, you say. Some do; but the question involves other questions far too involved for discussion here. And even if we discussed it, we should probably end where we began—facing a practical problem which no one can hope to solve while Caste is what it is.

Just now this system is in full operation in the case of a lad of the brassworker Caste. He is a thoughtful boy, and he has come to the conclusion that Christianity is the true religion; he would like to be a Christian; if the conditions were a little easier he would be enrolled as an inquirer to-morrow. But here is the difficulty. His father is not strong, his mother and little sisters and brothers are his care; if he were a Christian he could not support them; no one would sell him brass, no one would buy the vessels he makes. He knows only his inherited trade. He can make fine water-pots, lamps, vases, and vessels of all sorts, nothing else. He is too old to learn any other trade; but supposing such an arrangement could be made, who would support the family in the meantime? Perhaps we might do it; we certainly could not let them starve; but it would not do to tell him so, or to hold out hopes of earthly help, till we know beyond a doubt that he is true. This is what is holding him back. He reads over and over again, "He that loveth father or mother more than Me is not worthy of Me," and then he looks at his father and mother and the little children; and he reads the verse again, and he looks at them again. It is too hard.

It is easy enough to tell him that God would take care of them if he obeys. We do tell him so, but can we wonder at the boy for hesitating to take a step which will, so far as he can see, take house and food and all they need from his mother and those little children?

These are some of the things which make work in India what is simply called difficult. We do not want to exaggerate. We know all lands have their difficulties, but when being a Christian means all this, over and above what it means elsewhere, then the bonds which bind souls are visibly strengthened, and the work can never be described as other than very difficult.

Or take the power of Caste in another direction—its callous cruelty. I give one illustration from last year's life.

I was visiting in the house where the old lady lives upon whom the afflatus fell. The first time we went there we saw a little lad of three or four, who seemed to be suffering with his eyes. He lay in a swinging bag hung from the roof, and cried piteously all the time we were there. Now, two months afterwards, there he lay crying still, only his cries were so weary he had hardly strength to cry.

They lifted him out. I should not have known the child—the pretty face drawn and full of pain, the little hands pressed over the burning eyes. Only one who has had it knows the agony of ophthalmia. They told me he had not slept, "not even the measure of a rape-seed," for three months. Night and day he cried and cried; "but he does not make much noise now," they added. He couldn't, poor little lad!

I begged them to take him to the hospital, twenty-five miles away, but they said to go to a hospital was against their Caste. The child lay moaning so pitifully it wrung my heart, and I pleaded and pleaded with them to let me take him if they would not. Even if his sight could not be saved, something could be done to ease the pain, I knew. But no, he might die away from home, and that would disgrace their Caste.

"Then he is to suffer till he is blind or dead?" and I felt half wild with the cold cruelty of it.

"What can we do?" they asked; "can we destroy our Caste?"

Oh, I did blaze out for a moment! I really could not help it. And then I knelt down among them all, just broken with the pity of it, and prayed with all my heart and soul that the Good Shepherd would come and gather the lamb in His arms!

I wonder if you can bear to read it? I can hardly bear to write it. But you have not seen the little wasted hands pressed over the eyes, and then falling helplessly, too tired to hold up any longer; and you have not heard those weak little wails—and to think it need not have been!

But we could do nothing. We were leaving the place next day, and even if we could have helped him, they would not have let us. They had their own doctor, they said; the case was in his hands. As we came away they explained that one of the boy's distant relatives had died two years ago, and that this was what prevented any of them leaving the house, as some obscure Caste rule would be broken if they did; otherwise, *perhaps* they might have been able to take him somewhere for change of treatment. So there that child must lie in his pain, one more little living sacrifice on the altar of Caste.

The last thing I heard them say as we left the house was, " Cry softly, or we'll put more medicine in !" And the last thing I saw was the tightening of the little hands over the poor shut eyes, as he tried to stifle his sobs and " cry softly." *This told one what the " medicine" meant to him.* One of the things they had put in was raw pepper mixed with alum.

Is not Caste a cruel thing ? Those women were not heartless, but they would rather see that baby die in torture by inches, than dim with one breath the lustre of their brazen escutcheon of Caste !

This is one glimpse of one phase of a power which is only a name at home. It is its weakest phase; for the hold of Caste upon the body is as nothing to the hold it has upon the mind and soul. It yields to the touch of pain sometimes, as our medical missionaries know; but it

tightens again too often when the need for relief is past.
It is unspeakably strong, unmercifully cruel, and yet it
would seem as though the very blood of the people ran
red with it. *It is in them*, part of their very being.

This, then, is Caste viewed as a Doer. It does strange
things, hard things, things most cruel. It is, all who
fight it are agreed, the strongest foe to the Gospel of
Christ on the Hindu fields of South India.

A fairly typical Vellalar. "I determined not to laugh"! That was what she said when she saw it, and she was fairly satisfied with the result of her efforts. The jewels are gold, the seeley a rich red. A woman of this type makes a fine picture,—the strong intelligent face, the perfect arms and hands, the glistening gold on the clear brown, and the graceful dress harmonising so perfectly with the colour of eyes and hair. The one deformity is the ear, cut so as to hold the jewels, which are so heavy that one wonders the stretched lobes do not break.

CHAPTER XII

Petra

"This work in India . . . is one of the most crucial tests the Church of Christ has ever been put to. The people you think to measure your forces against are such as the giant races of Canaan are nothing to." *Bishop French, India and Arabia.*

IT was very hot, and we were tired, and the friendly voice calling "Come in! come in! Oh, come and rest!" was a welcome sound, and we went in.

She was a dear old friend of mine, the only real friend I have in that ancient Hindu town. Her house is always open to us, the upper room always empty—or said to be so—when we are needing a rest. But she is a Hindu of the Hindus, and though so enlightened that for love's sake she touches us freely, taking our hands in hers, and even kissing us, after we go there is a general purification; every scrap of clothing worn while we were in the house is carefully washed before sunset.

She insisted now upon feeding us, called for plantains and sugar, broke up the plantains, dabbed the pulp in the sugar, and commanded us to eat. Then she sat down satisfied, and was photographed.

This town, a little ancient Hindu town, is two hours' journey from Dohnavur. There are thirty-eight stone temples and shrines in and around it, and five hundred

altars. No one has counted the number of idols; there
are two hundred under a single tree near one of the smaller
shrines. Each of the larger temples has its attendant
temple-women; there are two hundred recognised Servants of the gods, and two hundred annual festivals.

Wonderful sums are being worked just now concerning
the progress of Christianity in India. A favourite sum
is stated thus: the number of Christians has increased
during the last decade at a certain ratio. Given the
continuance of this uniform rate of increase, it will follow
that within a computable period India will be a Christian
land. One flaw in this method of calculation is that it takes
for granted that Brahmans, high-caste Hindus, and Mohammedans will be Christianised at the same rate of progress
as prevails at present among the depressed classes.

There are sums less frequently stated. Here in the
heart of this Hindu town they come with force; one
such sum worked out carefully shows that, according
to the present rate of advance, it will be more than
twenty thousand years before the Hindu towns of this
district are even nominally Christian. Another still
more startling gives us this result: according to the
laws which govern statistics, thirteen hundred thousand
years must pass before the Brahmans in this one South
Indian district are Christianised. And if the sum is
worked so as to cover all India, the result is quite as
staggering to faith based on statistics.

Praise God, this is not His arithmetic! It is a purely
human invention. We believe in the Holy Ghost, the
Lord and Giver of Life; we believe in God, even God
Who calleth the things that are not as though they

were: therefore these sums prove nothing. But if such sums are worked at all, they ought to be worked on both sides, and not only on the side which yields the most encouraging results.

Two of us spent a morning in the Brahman street. In these old Hindu towns the Brahman street is built round the temple, and in large towns this street is a thoroughfare, and we are allowed in. The women stood in the shadow of the cool little dark verandahs, and we stood out in the sun and tried to make friends with them. Then some Mission College boys saw us and felt ashamed that we should stand in that blazing heat, and they offered us a verandah; but the women instantly cleared off, and the men came, and the boys besought us under their breath to say nothing about our religion.

We spoke for a few minutes, throwing our whole soul into the chance. We felt that our words were as feathers floating against rocks; but we witnessed, and they listened till, as one of them remarked, it was time to go for their noontide baths, and we knew they wished us to go. We went then, and found a wall at the head of the Brahman street, and we stood in its shadow and tried again. Crowds of men and lads gathered about us, but our College boys stood by our side and helped to quiet them. "Now you see," they said to us, as they walked with us down the outer street, "how quite impossible for us is Christianity."

It is good sometimes to take time to take in the might of the foe we fight. That evening two of us had a quiet few minutes under the temple walls. Those great walls, reaching so high above us, stretching so far beyond us, seemed a type of the wall Satan has built round these souls.

We could touch this visible wall, press against it, feel its solid strength. Run hard against it, and you would be hurt, you might fall back bleeding; it would not have yielded one inch.

And the other invisible wall? Oh, we can touch it too! Spirit-touch is a real thing. And so is spirit-pain. But the wall, it still stands strong.

It was moonlight. We had walked all round the great temple square, down the silent Brahman streets, and we had stood in the pillared hall, and looked across to the open door, and seen the light on the shrine.

Now we were out in God's clean light, looking up at the mass of the tower, as it rose pitch-black against the sky. And we felt how small we were.

Then the influences of the place began to take hold of us. It was not only masonry; it was mystery. "The Sovereigns of this present Darkness" were there.

How futile all of earth seemed then, against those tremendous forces and powers. What toy-swords seemed all weapons of the flesh. Praise God for the Holy Ghost!

While we were sitting there a Brahman came to see what we were doing, and we told him some of our thoughts. He asked us then if we would care to hear his. We told him, gladly. He pointed up to the temple tower. "That is my first step to God." We listened, and he unfolded, thought by thought, that strange old Védic philosophy, which holds that God, being omnipresent, reveals Himself in various ways, in visible forms, in incarnations, or in spirit. The visible-form method of revelation is the lowest; it is only, as it were, the first of a series of steps which lead up to the highest, intelligent adoration of and absorption into the One Supreme Spirit. " We are only little children yet. We take this small first step, it crumbles beneath us as we rise to the next, and so step by step we rise from the visible to the invisible, from matter to spirit—to God. But," he added courteously, " as my faith is good for me, so, doubtless, you find yours for you."

Next morning we went down to the river and had talks with the people who passed on their way to the town. It was all so pretty in the early morning light. Men were washing their bullocks, and children were scampering in and out of the water. Farther down-stream the women were bathing their babies and polish-ing their brass water-vessels. Trees met overhead, but the light broke through in places and made yellow patches on the water. Out in one of those reaches of yellow a girl stood bending to fill her vessel; she wore the common crimson of the South, but the light struck it, and struck the shining brass as she swung it up under her arm, and made her into a picture as she stood in her clinging wet red things against the brown and green of water and wood. Everywhere we looked there was something beautiful to look at, and all about us was the sound of voices and laughter, and the musical splashing of water; then, as we enjoyed it all, we saw this:

Under an ancient tree fifteen men were walking slowly round and round, following the course of the sun. Under the tree there were numbers of idols, and

piles of oleander and jessamin wreaths, brought fresh
that morning. The men were elderly, fine-looking men;
they were wholly engrossed in what they were doing.
It was no foolish farce to them; it was reality.

There is something in the sight of this ordinary,
evident dethronement of our God which stirs one to
one's inmost soul. We could not look at it.

Again and again we have gone to that town, but
to-day those men go round that tree, and to-day that
town is a fort unwon.

Petra, I have called it; the word stands for many a
town walled in as that one is. In Keith's *Evidence
of Prophecy* there is a map of Petra, the old strong
city of Edom, and in studying it a light fell upon
David's question concerning it, and his own triumphant
answer, "Who will lead me into the strong city?
Who will bring me into Edom? Wilt not Thou, O
God?" for the map shows the mountains all round,
except at the East, where they break into a single
narrow passage, the one way in. There was only one
way in, but there *was* that one way in!

Here is a town walled up to heaven by walls of
Caste and bigotry, but there must be one way in. Here
is a soul walled all round by utter indifference and
pride, but there must be one way in.

"Who will lead me into the strong city? Who will
bring me into Edom? Wilt not Thou, O God?"

CHAPTER XIII

Death by Disuse

"There is a strong tendency to look upon the Atonement of Christ as possessing some quality by virtue of which God can excuse and overlook sin in the Christian, a readiness to look upon sinning as the inevitable accompaniment of human nature 'until death do us part,' and to look upon Christianity as a substitute for rather than a cause of personal holiness of life."
Rev. I. W. Charlton, India.

"From many things I have heard I fancy many at home think of the mission as a sort of little heaven upon earth, but when one looks under the surface there is much to sadden one. . . . Oh, friends, much prayer is needed! Many of the agents know apparently nothing about conversion.

"You may not like my writing so plainly, but sometimes it seems as if only the bright side were given, and one feels that if God's praying people at home understood things more as they really are . . . more prayer for an outpouring of the Holy Spirit on our agents and converts would ascend to God. . . . We do long to see all our pastors and agents really converted men, men of prayer and faith, who, knowing that they themselves are saved, long with a great longing to see the heathen round them brought out of darkness into His light, and the Christians who form their congregations, earnest converted men and women." *A. J. Carr, India.*

"Fifty added to the Church sounds fine at home, but if only five of them are genuine what will it profit in the Great Day?"
David Livingstone, Africa.

"Oh for the Fire to set the whole alight, and melt us all into one mighty Holy-Ghost Church!" *Minnie Apperson, China.*

THE lamps were being lighted, the drums beaten, the cymbals struck, and the horns blown for evening pujah in all the larger temples and shrines of the "Strong City," when we turned out of it, and, crossing the stream that divides the two places, went to the Christian hamlet, which by contrast at that moment seemed like a little corner of the garden of the Lord. Behind was the heathenish clash and clang of every possible discord, and here the steady ringing of the bell for evening service; behind was all that ever was meant by the "mystery of iniquity," and here the purity and peace of Christianity. This is how it struck me at first; and even now, after a spell of work in the heart of heathendom, Christendom, or the bit of it lying alongside, is beautiful by contrast. There you have naked death, death unadorned, the corpse exhibited; here, if there is a corpse, at least it is decently dressed. And yet that evening it was forced upon me that death is death wherever found and however carefully covered.

The first of the Christians to welcome us was a bright-looking widow—this is her photograph. We soon made friends. She told us she had been "born in the Way"; her grandfather joined it, and none of the family had gone back, so she was sure that all was right. We were not so sure, and we tried to find out if she knew the difference between joining the Way and coming to Christ. This was only a poor little country hamlet, but everywhere we have travelled, among educated and uneducated alike, we have found much confusion of thought upon this subject.

"God knows my heart," she said, "God hears my prayers. If I see a bad dream in the night, I pray to God, and putting a Bible under my head, I sleep in perfect peace." Could anything be more conclusive?

There were numbers of other proofs forthcoming: If your grandfather gave six lamps to the church, value

"I do feel so shy!" she was just on the point of saying to me, by way of appeal to be released, when the camera clicked and she was caught. Widows do not wear jewels, as a rule, among the Hindus of the higher Castes, but Christians do as they like. She is a village woman of fairly good position.

three and a half rupees each (the lamps are hanging
to-day, and bear witness to the fact); if your father never
failed to pay his yearly dues, besides regular Sunday collec-
tions (his name is in the church report, and how much he
gave is printed); if you freely help the poor, and give
them paddy on Christmas Day (quite a sackful of it); if
you never offer to demons (no, not when your children
are sick, and the other faithless Christians advise you);
if you never tie on the cylinder (a charm frequently
though covertly worn by purely nominal Christians);
and finally, if you have been baptised and confirmed, and
"without a break join the Night-supper," surely no one
can reasonably doubt that you are a Christian of a very
proper sort? As to questions about change of heart, and
chronic indulgence in sins, such as lying—who in this
wicked world lives without lying? And when it pleases
God to do it He will change your heart.

We took the evening meeting for the villagers, who
meanwhile had gathered and were listening with
approval. Privacy, as we understand it, is a thing
unknown in India. "That is right," they remarked
cheerfully; "give her plenty of good advice!" And we
all trooped into the prayer-room.

Once in there, everyone put on a sort of church
expression, and each one took his or her accustomed seat
in decorous silence. The little school-children sat in rows
in front on the mats with arms demurely folded, and
sparkling eyes fixed solemnly; the grown-up people sat
on their mats on either side behind, and we sat on
ours facing them. We began with a chorus, which the
children picked up quickly and shouted lustily, the

8

grown-ups joining in with more reserve; and then we got to work.

Blessing spoke. She had once been a nominal Christian, and she knew exactly where these people were, and how they looked at things. Her heart was greatly moved as she spoke, and the tears were in her eyes, for she knew none of these friends had the joy of conscious salvation, and she told me afterwards she had thirst and hunger for them. But they listened unimpressed. Then we had prayer and a quiet time; sometimes the Spirit works most in quiet, and we rose expectantly; but there was no sign of life.

After the meeting was over they gathered round us again. They are always so loving and friendly in these little villages; but they could not understand what it was that troubled us. Were they not all *Christians*?

Shortly afterwards they came, as their kindly custom is, to bring us fruit and wreaths of flowers on New Year's Day. I missed my first friend of that evening, and asked for her. "That widow you talked to?" said the old catechist, "three days ago fever seized her, and"— He broke off and looked up. Then I longed to hear how she had died, but no one could tell me anything. Oh, the curtain of silence that covers the passing of souls!

We went soon afterwards to the village, sure that at last the people would be stirred; for she had been a leader among the women, and her call, even in this land of sudden calls, had been very sudden. But we did not find it had affected anyone. They all referred to her in the chastened tone adopted upon such occasions, and, sighing, reminded each other that God was merciful, and she had always been, up to the measure of her ability, a very good woman.

We felt as if we were standing with each one of those people separately, in the one little standing space we were sure of, before that curtain, and we spoke with them as you speak with those whom you know you may never see again on this side of it. But they looked at us, and wondered what was the matter with us. Were they not *Christians*? Did they not believe in God? Did they not pray regularly night and morning for forgiveness, protection, and blessing? So they could not understand.

Was it that the power to understand had been withered up within them? Was the soul God gave them dead—sentenced to death by disuse? Dead they are in apathy and ignorance and putrefying customs, and the false security that comes from adherence to the Christian creed without vital connection with Christ. These poor Christians are dead.

"Why should it be thought a thing incredible with you that God should raise the dead?" Lord, it is not a thing incredible. Thou hast done it before. Oh, do it again. Do it soon!

I have told you how much we need your help for the work among the heathen; but often we feel we need it almost as much for the work among the Christians. Over and over again it is told, but still it is hardly understood, that the Christians need to be converted; that the vast majority are not converted; that statistics may mislead, and do not stand for Eternity work; that many a pastor, catechist, teacher, has a name to live, but is dead; that the Church is very dead as a whole—thank God for every exception. We do not say this thoughtlessly; the words are a grief to write. We humble ourselves that it is so, and take to ourselves the blame. It is true that the corpse of the dead Church is dressed, just as it is at home, only here it is even more dressed; and because the spirit of the land is intensely religious, its grave-clothes are vestments. But dressed death is still death.

This will come as a shock to those who have read stories of this or that native Christian, and generalising from these stories, picture the Church as a company of saints. God has His saints in India, men and women hidden away in quiet places out of sight, and some few out in the front; but the cry of our hearts is for more. So we tell you the truth about things as they are, though we know it will not be acceptable, for the best is the thing that is best liked at home; so the best is most frequently written.

This may seem to cross out what was said before, about the darker side of the truth being often told. It does not cross it out: read through the magazines and reports, and you will find truth-revealing sentences, which show facts to those who have eyes to see; but though this is so, all will admit that the sanguine view, as it is called, is by far the most in evidence, for the sanguine man is by far the most popular writer, and so is more pressed to write. "People will read what is buoyant and bright; the more of that sort we have the better," wrote a Mission secretary out in the field not long ago, to a missionary who did not feel free to write in quite that way. Those who, to quote another secretary, "are afraid of writing at all, for fear of telling lies"—excuse the energetic language; I am quoting, not inventing—naturally write much less, and so the best gets known.

This is nobody's fault exactly. The home authorities

print for the most part what is sent to them. They
even call attention sometimes to the less cheerful view
of things; and if, yielding occasionally to the pressure
which is brought to bear upon them by a public which
loves to hear what it likes, they take the sting out of
some strong paragraph by adding an editorial " Neverthe-
less," is it very astonishing ?

Do you think we are writing like this because we are
discouraged ? No, we are not discouraged, except when
sometimes we fear lest you should grow weary in prayer
before the answer comes. This India is God's India.
This work is His. Oh, join with us then, as we join
with all our dear Indian brothers and sisters who are
alive in the Lord, in waiting upon Him in that intensest
form of waiting *which waits on till the answer comes*;
join with us as we pray to the mighty God of revivals,
" O Lord, revive Thy work ! Revive Thy work in the
midst of the years ! In the midst of the years make
known ! "

CHAPTER XIV

What Happened

"Some years ago England was stirred through and through by revelations which were made as to the 'Bitter Cry' of wronged womanhood. In India the bitter cry is far more bitter, but it is stifled and smothered by the cruel gag of Caste. Orthodox Hindus would rather see their girls betrayed, tortured, murdered, than suffer them to break through the trammels of Caste." *Rev. T. Walker, India.*

THERE is another ancient town near Dohnavur, and in that town another temple, and round the temple the usual Brahman square. In one of the streets of this square we saw the girl whose face looks out at you. It struck us as a typical face, not beautiful as many are, but characteristic in the latent power of eyes and brow, a face full of possibilities.

We were rarely able to get anything we specially wanted, but we got this. I look at it now, and wonder how it will develop as the soul behind it shapes and grows. That child is enfolded in influences which ward off the touch of the grace of life.

We saw numbers of women that day, but only at the distance of a street breadth; they would not come nearer, for the town is still a Petra to us, we are waiting to be led in.

But if we were able to get in enough to take a photograph, surely we were "in" enough to preach the Gospel?

Here is one who might be a queen. What she may be is very different. She is a Brahman girl; all her people are Hindus. She has never even felt a desire, or seen any one in her town who felt a desire, to "fall into the pit of Christianity."

Why not stop and there speak of more important matters? What was to hinder *then*?

Only this: in that town they have heard of converts coming out, and breaking Caste in baptism, and they have made a law that we (with whom they know some of these converts are) shall never be allowed to speak to any of their women. That hindered us there. But even supposing we had been free to speak, as we trust we shall be soon, and supposing she had wanted to hear, the barriers which lie between such a child and confession of Christ are so many and so great that when, as now, one wants to tell you about them, one hardly knows how to do it. Words seem like little feeble shadows of some grim rock, like little feeble shadows of the grasses growing on it, rather than of *it*, in its solidity; or, to revert to the old thought, all one can say is just pointing to the Dust as evidence of the Actual.

"What is to hinder high - caste women from being baptised, and living as Christians in their own homes?" The question was asked by an Englishman, a winter visitor, who, being interested in Missions, was gathering impressions. We told him no high-caste woman would be allowed to live as an open Christian in her own home; and we told him of some who, only because they were suspected of inclining towards Christianity, had been caused to disappear. "What do you suppose happened to them?" he asked, and we told him.

We were talking in the pleasant drawing-room of an Indian Hotel. Our friend smiled, and assured us we must be mistaken. We were under the English Government; such things could not be possible. We looked round the quiet room, with its air of English comfort

and English safety; we looked at the quiet faces, faces
that had never looked at fear, and we hardly wondered
that they could not understand.

Then in a moment, even as they talked, we were far
away in another room, looking at other faces, faces un-
quiet, very full of fear.   We knew that all round us, for
streets and streets, there were only the foes of our Lord;
we knew that a cry that was raised for help would be
drowned long before it could escape through those many
streets to the great English house outside.   There were
policemen, you say.   But policemen in India are not as
at home.   *Policemen can be bribed.*

And now we are looking in again.   There is a very dark
inner room, no window, one small door; the walls are solid,
so is the door.   If you cried in there, who would hear?

And now we are listening—someone is speaking: "Once
there was one; she cared for your God.   She was buried
into the wall in there, and that was the end of her." . . .

But we are back in the drawing-room, hearing them
tell us these things could never be. . . . Three years
passed, and a girl came for refuge to us.   She loved her
people well; she would never have come to us had they
let her live as a Christian at home.   But no, "Rather than
that she shall burn," they said.   We were doubtful about
her age, and we feared we should have to give her up if
the case came on in the courts.   And if we had to give
her up?   We looked at the gentle, trustful face, and we
could not bear the thought; and yet, according to our
friends, the Government made all safe.

About that time a paper came to the house; names, dates,
means of identification, all were given.   This was the story

in brief. A young Brahman girl in another South Indian
town wanted to be a Christian, and confessed Christ at
home. She earnestly wished to be baptised, but she was too
young then, and waited, learning steadily and continuing
faithful, though everything was done that could be done
to turn her from her purpose. She was betrothed against
her will to her cousin, and forbidden to have anything to
do with the Christians. "She was never allowed to go
out alone, and was practically a prisoner."

For three years that child held on, witnessing steadfastly
at home, and letting it be clearly known that she was and
would be a Christian. A Hindu ceremony of importance
in the family was held in her grandfather's house, and she
refused to go. This brought things to a crisis. Her people
appointed a council of five to investigate the matter. "She
maintained a glorious witness before them all," says the
missionary; "declared boldly that she was a Christian, and
intended to join us; and when challenged about the Bible,
she held it out, and read it to the assembled people."

For a time it seemed as if she had won the day, but fresh
attempts were made upon her constancy by certain religious
bigots of the town. They offered her jewels—that failed;
tried to get her to turn Mussulman, that being less disgraceful than to be a Christian; and last and worst, tried
to stain that white soul black—but, thank God! still
they failed.

At last the waiting time was over; she was of age to
be baptised, and she wrote to tell her missionary friend
about it. He sent her books to read, and promised to let
her know within two days what he could arrange to do.
"Her letter was dated from her grandfather's house," the

missionary writes, "to which she said she had been sent, and put in a room alone. "On the following day, hearing a rumour of her death, I went to N.'s house, and there found her body, outside the door. I caused it to be seized by the police, and the post-mortem has revealed the fact that the poor child was poisoned by arsenic. Bribes have been freely used and atrocious lies have been told, and the net result of all the police inquiries, so far, is that no charge can be brought against anyone."

Last year we met one of the missionaries from this Mission, on the hills, and we asked him if anyone had been convicted. He said no one had been convicted, "the Caste had seen to that."

Here, then, is a statement of facts, divested of all emotion or sensationalism. A child is shut up in a room alone, and poisoned; when she is dead, her body is thrown outside the door. It was found. *There have been bodies which have not been found*; but we are under the British Government—nothing can have happened to them !

The British Government does much, but it cannot do everything. It is notorious in India that false witnesses can be bought at so much a head, according to the nature of witness required. Bribery and corruption are not mere names here, but facts, most difficult for any straightforward official to trace and track and deal with. We know, and everyone knows, that the White Man's Government, though strong enough to win and rule this million-peopled Empire, is weak as a white child when it stands outside the door of an Indian house, and wants to know what has gone on inside, or proposes to regulate what shall go on. It cannot do it. The thought is vain.

" Why not have her put under surveillance ? " asked a
friend, a military man, about a certain girl who wanted
to be a Christian ; as if such surveillance were practicable,
or ever could be, under such conditions as obtain in
high - caste Hindu and Mohammedan circles, except in
places directly under the eye of Government.   We know
there are houses where, at an hour's notice, any kind and
any strength of poison can be prepared and administered :
quick poison to kill within a few minutes ; slow poisons
that undermine the constitution, and do their work
so safely that no one can find it out ; brain poisons,
worse than either, and perhaps more commonly used, as
they are as effective and much less dangerous.   But we
could not prove what we know, and knowledge without
proof is, legally speaking, valueless.

And yet we know these things, we have heard " a cry
of tears," we have heard " a cry of blood "—

> " Tears and blood have a cry that pierces heaven
> Through all its hallelujah swells of mirth ;
> God hears their cry, and though He tarry, yet
> He doth not forget."

CHAPTER XV

"Simply Murdered"

"'Agonia'—that word so often on St. Paul's lips, what did it mean? Did it not just mean the thousand wearinesses . . . and deeper, the strivings, the travailings, the bitter disappointments, the 'deaths oft' of a missionary's life?"
Rev. Robert Stewart, China.

THERE are worse things than martyrdom. There are some who are "simply murdered." There is one who belongs to a Caste which more than any other is considered tolerant and safe. Men converts from this Caste can live at home, and if a husband and wife believe, they may continue living in their own house, among the heathen. And yet this is what happened to a girl because it was known that she wanted to be a Christian.

First persecution. Treasure, as her name may be translated, had learnt as a child in the little mission school, and when we went to her village she responded, and took her stand. She refused to take part in a Hindu ceremony. She was beaten, at first slightly, then severely. This failed, so they sent her out of our reach to a heathen village miles away. This also failed, and she was brought home, and for some months went steadily on, reading and learning when she could, and all the time brightly witnessing. She was a joy to us.

She was very anxious to come out and be baptised, but her age was the difficulty. When a convert comes, the first thing to be done is to let the police authorities know. They send a constable, who takes down the convert's deposition, which is then forwarded to head-quarters. One of the first questions concerns age. In some cases a medical certificate is demanded, and the girl's fate turns on that; if we can get one for over sixteen we are safe from prosecution in the Criminal Courts, but eighteen is the safest age, as the Civil Courts, if the case were to proceed, would force us to give her up if she were under eighteen. The difficulty of proving the age, unless the girl is evidently well over it, is very serious. The medical certificate usually takes off a year from what we have every reason to believe is the true age.

One other proof remains—the horoscope. This is a Hindu document written on a palm leaf at the birth of the child; but it is always carefully kept by the head of the family, and so, as a rule, unobtainable. When a case comes on in Court a false horoscope may be produced by the relatives; this was done in a recent case tried in our Courts, so we cannot count upon that. In this girl's case we got the Government registers searched for birth-records of her village, but all such registers we found had been destroyed; none were kept of births sixteen years back. So, though she believed herself to be, and we believed her to be, and the Christians who had known her all her life were sure she was, "about sixteen," we knew it could not be proved. She was a very slight girl, delicate and small for her age. This

was against her, and there were other reasons against
her coming just then. She had to wait.

I shall never forget the day I had to tell her so.
She could not understand it. She knew that all the
higher Castes had threatened to combine, and back up
her father in a lawsuit, if she became a Christian; but
she thought it would be quite enough if she stood up
before the judge, and said she knew she was of age, and
she wanted to come to us. "I will not be afraid of the
people," she pleaded, "I will stand up straight before
them all, and speak without any fear!"

I remember how the tears filled her eyes as I explained things; it was so hard for her to understand
that we had no power whatever to protect her. It
would be worse for her if she came and had to be given
up. She was fully sensible of this, but "Would God
let them take me away? Would He not take care of
me?" she asked.

I suppose it is right to obey the laws. They are, on
the whole, righteous laws, made in the defence of these
very girls. It would never do if anyone could decoy
away a mere girl from her parents or natural guardians.
But the unrighteous thing, as it seems to us, is that the
whole burden of proof lies upon us, and that in these
country villages no facilities such as Government registers
of birth are to be had, by which we could hope legally to
prove a point about which we are morally sure. We
feel that as the burden of proof rests upon us, surely
facilities should be obtainable by which we could find
out a girl's age before she comes, so that we might
know whether or not we might legally protect her.

Still more strongly we feel it is strange justice which decrees that though a child of twelve may be legally held competent to undertake the responsibilities of wifehood, six years more must pass before she may be legally held free to obey her conscience. Free! She is never legally free! A widow may be legally free; a wife in India, never! Hardly a single Caste wife in all this Empire would be found in the little band of open Christians to-day, if the missionary concerned had not risked more than can be told here, and put God's law before man's. But oh, the number who have been turned back!

One stops, forces the words down—they come too hot and fast. There are reasons. As I write, a young wife dear to us is lying bruised and unconscious on the floor of the inner room of a Hindu house. Her husband, encouraged by her own mother, set himself to make her conform to a certain Caste custom. It was idolatrous. She refused. He beat her then, blow upon blow, till she fell senseless. They brought her round and began again. There is no satisfactory redress. She is his wife. She is not free to be a Christian. He knows it. Her relations know it. She knows it, poor child.

O God, forgive us if we are too hot, too sore at heart, for easy pleasantness! And, God, raise up in India Christian statesmen who will inquire into this matter, and refuse to be blindfolded and deceived. His laws and ours clash somewhere; the question is, where?

To return to Treasure, we left her waiting to come. A Christian teacher lived next door, and Treasure used to slip in sometimes, as the two courtyards adjoined. We had put up a text on the wall for her: "Fear not:

for I have redeemed thee, I have called thee by thy name; thou art Mine." This was her special text, and she looked at it now; and then she grew braver, and promised to be patient and try to win her mother, who was bitterly opposed.

But oh, how I remember the wistfulness of her face as I went out; and one's very heart can feel again the stab of pain, like a knife cutting deep, as I left her— to her fate.

You have seen a tree standing stark and bare, a bleak black thing, on a sunny day against a sky of blue. You have looked at it, fascinated by the silent horror of it, a distorted cinder, not a tree, and someone tells you it was struck in the last great thunderstorm.

Next time we saw Treasure she was like that. What happened between, so far as it is known, was this. They tried to persuade her, they tried to coerce her; she witnessed to Jesus, and never faltered, though once they dragged her out of the house by her hair, and holding her down against the wall, struck her hard with a leather strap. One of the Christians saw it, and heard the poor tortured child cry out, "I do not fear! I do not fear! It will only send me to Jesus!"

Then they tried threats. "We will take you out to the lake at night, and cut you in little pieces, and throw you into it." She fully believed them, but even so, we hear she did not flinch.

Then they did their worst to her.

It was a Sunday morning. The Saturday evening before she had managed to see the teacher. She told her hurriedly how one had come, "a bridegroom" she called him, a student from a Mission College; he was telling her all sorts of things—that Christianity was an exploded religion; and how a great and learned woman (Mrs. Besant) had exposed the missionaries and their ways, so that no thinking people had any excuse for being deceived by them.

Then she added earnestly, "It is the devil. Do pray for me. They want me to marry him secretly! Oh, I must go to the Missie Ammal!" And if we had only known, we would have risked anything, any breach of the law of the land, to save her from a breach of the law of heaven! For all this talk, between an Indian girl of good repute and her prospective husband, is utterly foreign to what is considered right in Old India. It in itself meant danger. But we knew nothing, and next day, all that Sunday, she was shut up, and no one knows what happened to her. On Monday she was seen again; but changed, so utterly changed!

We heard nothing of this till the following Wednesday. The Christians were honestly concerned, but the Tamil is ever casual, and they saw no reason for distressing us with bad news sooner than could be helped.

As soon as we heard, I sent two of the Sisters who knew her best, to try and see her if possible. They managed to see her for two or three minutes, but found her hopelessly hard. Every bit of care was gone. She laughed in a queer, strained way, they said. It was no use my trying to see her. But I determined to see her. I cannot go over it all again, it is like tearing the skin off a wound; so the letter written at the time may tell the rest of it.

"On Saturday I went. I went straight to the teacher's

9

house, and sent off the bandy at once, and by God's
special arrangement got in unnoticed. For hours we sat
in the little inner room, waiting; we could hear her
voice in the courtyard outside—a hard, changed voice.
The teacher tried to get her in, but no, she would not
come. Oh, how we held on to God! I could not bear
to go till I had seen her.

" At last we had to go. The cart came back for us,
thus proclaiming where we were, and the last human
chance was gone. And then, just then, like one walking
in a dream, Treasure wandered in and stood, startled.

" She did not know we were there. We were kneeling
with our backs to the door. I turned and saw her.

" I cannot write about the next five minutes; I thought
I realised something of what Satan could do in this land,
but I knew nothing about it. Oh, when will Jesus come
and end it all?

" Just once it seemed as if the spell were broken. My
arms were round her, though she had shrunk away at
first, and tried to push me from her; she was quiet now,
and seemed to understand a little how one cared. She
knelt down with me, and covered her eyes as if in
prayer, while I poured out my soul for her, and then we
were all very still, and the Lord seemed very near. But
she rose, unmoved, and looked at us. We were all quite
broken down, and she smiled in a strange, hard, foolish
way—that was all.

" The cause no one knows. There are only two possible
explanations. One is poison. There is some sort of
mind-bewildering medicine which it is known is given
in such cases. This is the view held by the Christians

on the spot. One of them says her cousin was dealt with in this way. He was keen to be a Christian, and was shut up for a day, and came out—dead. Dead, she means, to all which before had been life to him.

" The other, and worse, is sin. Has she been forced into some sin which to one so enlightened as she is must mean an awful darkness, the hiding of God's face ?

" I cannot tell you how bright this dear child was. Up till that Saturday evening her faith never wavered ; she was a living sign to all the town that the Lord is God. The heathen are triumphant now."

I have told you plainly what has happened. God's Truth needs no painting. I leave it with you. Do you believe it is perfectly true ? Then what are you going to do ?

CHAPTER XVI

Wanted, Volunteers

"We have a great and imposing War Office, but a very
small army. . . . While vast continents are shrouded in almost
utter darkness, and hundreds of millions suffer the horrors of
heathenism or of Islam, the burden of proof lies upon you to
show that the circumstances in which God has placed you
were meant by Him to keep you out of the foreign mission
field."   *Ion Keith Falconer, Arabia.*

IN one of the addresses delivered at the International
Student Missionary Conference, London, in January
1900, a South Indian missionary spoke of the
Brahman race as "the brain of India." "Their numbers are comparatively small—between ten and fifteen
millions—but though numerically few—only five per
cent. of the Hindu population—they hold all that
population in the hollow of their hand. They occupy
every position of influence in the land. They are
the statesmen and politicians, the judges, magistrates,
Government officials, and clerks of every grade. If
there is any position conferring influence over their
fellow-men, it will be held by a Brahman. Moreover, they are a sacred Caste, admitted by the people
to be gods upon earth—a rank supposed to have
been attained by worth maintained through many trans-
migrations."

Among the Petras of this district is a little old-

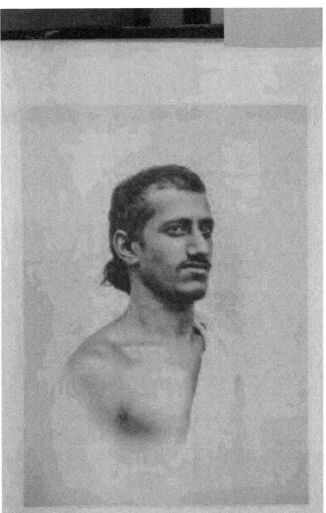

A typical Brahman face. It is keener than the photo shows, and has the cynical expression so many Brahman faces have. Such a man is hard to win.

fashioned country town, held in strength by the Brahmans. No convert has ever come from that town, and the town boasts that none ever shall. None of the houses are open yet to teaching, or even visiting, but we are making friends, and hope for an entrance soon. We spent a morning out in the street; they had no objection to that, and as the free young Brahmans gathered round us, or stood for a moment against a wall to be "caught," it was difficult, even for us who knew it, to realise how bound they were. "Bound, who should conquer; slaves, who should be kings." Bound, body and soul, in a bondage perfectly incomprehensible to the English mind.

Afterwards, when we saw the photographs, we recalled one and another who, while they were young students like these, dared to desire to escape from their bondage; but back they were dragged, and the chains were riveted faster than ever, and every link was tested again, and hammered down hard.

We wanted to be sure of our facts about each of them, that these facts may further answer that smile which assures us things are not as we imagine; so the Iyer wrote to a brother missionary who had known these lads well, and asked him to tell what happened to each of them. This morning the answer to that letter came, and was handed to me with "I hardly like to give it to you, but it tells the truth about what goes on." These boys were students in our C.M.S. College.

The first one mentioned in the letter is a young Brahman who confessed Christ in baptism, and bravely withstood the tremendous opposition raised by his friends,

who came in crowds for many weeks, and tried by every
argument to persuade him to return to Hinduism; but
he preached Christ to them. They brought his young
wife, and she tore her hair and wailed, and besought him
not to condemn her to the shame of a widow's life. This
was the hardest of all to withstand; he turned to the
missionary and said, "Oh my father, take her away! She
is tearing out my heart!"

Then came the baptism day of another Brahman
student, his friend, who previous to this had been seized
by his relatives, shut up and starved, and then fed with
poisoned food; but the poison was not strong enough to
kill, and he had escaped, and was now safe and ready for
baptism.

It was remembered afterwards how the friend of the
newly baptised stood and rejoiced, and praised God.
Then, the baptism over, fearing no danger in open day,
he went to the tank to bathe. He was never seen
again.

What happened exactly no one knows. It is thought
that men hired to watch him seized their opportunity,
and carried him off. What they did then has never
been told. Contradictory reports about the boy have
reached the missionaries. One, that he is still holding
on, another that he is now a priest in one of the great
Saivite temples of South India. Which is true, God
knows.

But we are under the English Government. Could
nothing be done? One of his near relatives is the
present Judge of the High Court of one of our Indian
cities. And among the crowd of Brahmans who came

Is not this a weak face! Dogged too with the doggedness of weakness, but far from being courageous.

during those weeks, there were influential men, graduates of colleges, members of the legal profession—a favourite profession in India. And yet this thing was done.

There was another; the means used to get hold of him cannot be written here. That is the difficulty which fronts us when we try to tell the truth as it really is. It simply cannot be told. The Dust may be shown—or a little of it; the whole of the Actual, never.

There were others near the Kingdom, but it is the same story over again. They were all spirited away from the college; the missionary writes, "*it makes one's heart sick to think of them, and the hellish means invented to turn them from Christ.*" These are not the words of sentimental imagination. They are the words of a man who gives evidence as a witness. But even a witness may *feel*.

He tells us of one, a bright, happy fellow, he says he was, whose friends made no objection to his returning home after his baptism, and he returned, thinking he would be able to live as a Christian with his wife. They drugged his food, then what they did has to be covered with silence again. . . . They did their worst. . . . When he awoke from that nightmare of sin, he sought out his missionary friend. Some of the Hindus even, "ashamed of the vile means used" to entice him and destroy him, would have wished him to be received again as a Christian, but his spirit was broken. He said he could not disgrace the cause of Christ by coming back; he would go away where he would not be known. He left his wife, and went. He has never been heard of since.

Our comrade tells of another, and again, in telling it, we have to leave it half untold. This one was eager to confess Christ in baptism; he was a student at college then, and very keen. His father knew of his son's desire, and he did what few Hindu fathers would do, *he turned his home into a hell, in order to ruin his boy.* The infernal plot succeeded. God only knows how far the soul is responsible when the mind is dazed and then inflamed by those fearful drugs. But we do know that the soul He meant should rise and shine, sinks, weighted down by the unspeakable shame of some awful memory, darkened, as by some dark dye that has stained it through and through.

I think of others as I write: one was a boy we knew well, a splendid, earnest lad, keen to witness for Christ. He told us one evening how he had been delivered from those who were plotting his destruction. For several months after his decision to be a Christian, he lived at home and tried to win his people; but they were incensed against him for even thinking of breaking Caste, and would not listen to him. Still he waited, and witnessed to them, not fearing anything. Then one day, suddenly some men rushed into the room where he was sitting, seized and bound and gagged him. They forced something into his mouth as he lay on the floor at their mercy; he feared it was a drug, but it was only some disgusting stuff which, to a Hindu, meant unutterable defilement. Then they left him bound alone, and at night he managed to escape. A few months after he told us this, we heard he had been seized again, and this time " drugged and done for."

In South India baptism does not prevent the Caste from using every possible means to get the convert back; once back, certain ceremonies are performed, after which he is regarded as purified, and reinstated in his Caste. The policy of the whole Caste confederation is this: get him back unbaptised if you can, but anyhow *get him back*. Two Brahman lads belonging to different parts of this district decided for Christ, went through all that is involved in open confession, and were baptised. One of the two was sent North for safety; his people traced him, followed him, turned up unexpectedly at a wayside station in Central India, and forced him back to his home in the South. Once there, they took their own measures to keep him. The other lad was sent to Madras. The Brahmans found out where he was, broke into the house at night, overpowered the boy's protectors, and carried him off. They too did what seemed good to them there, and they too succeeded. No one outside could interfere. The Caste guards its own concerns.

"O Lord Jesus Christ!" wrote one, a Hindu still, " who knowest us to be placed in such danger that it is as if we were within some magical circle drawn round us, and Satan standing with his wand without, keeping us in terror, break the spell of Satan, and set us free to serve Thee!"

All this may be easy reading to those who are far away from the place where it happened. Distance has a way of softening too distinct an outline; but it is not easy to write, it comes so close to us. Why write it, then? We write it because it seems to us it should be more fully known, so that men and women who know our

God, and the secret of how to lay hold upon Him, should lay hold, and hold on for the winning of the Castes for Christ.

Surely the very hardness of an enterprise, the very fact that it is what a soldier would call a forlorn hope, is in itself a call and a claim stronger than any put forth by something easier. The soldier does not give in because the hope is "forlorn." It is a *hope*, be it ever so desperate. He volunteers for it, and win or not, he fights.

There is that in this enterprise which may mark it out as "forlorn." For ages the race has broken one of nature's laws with blind persistency, and the result is a certain lack of moral fibre, grit, "tone." No separate individual is responsible for this, harsh judgments are entirely out of place; but the fact remains that it is so, and it must be taken into account in dealing with the Brahmans and several of the upper Castes of India. Side by side with this element of weakness there is, in apparent contradiction, that stubborn element of strength known as the Caste spirit. This spirit is seen in all I have shown you of what happens when a convert comes. It is as if all the million wills of the million Caste men and women were condensed into one single Will, a concentration of essence of Will not comparable with anything known at home.

Look at this face—it is a photographed fact. Does it not show you an absence of that "something" which nerves to endurance, stimulates to dare? Then listen to this:—A Christian man lies dead. The way to the cemetery lies through the Brahman street, in the chief town of this

Another Brahman, much duller than the last.
These three photographs are perfect as a study
of three types of Brahmanhood as we have it
in Southern India—keen, thoughtful, dull.

District; there is no other way. The Brahman street is
a thoroughfare, it cannot be closed to traffic, but the
Brahmans refuse point blank to allow that dead man to
be carried through. The Bishop expostulates. No; he
was a Christian, he shall not be carried through. Time
is passing. In the Tropics the dead must be buried
quickly. The Bishop appeals to the Collector (Representative of Government here). The Collector gives an order.
The Brahmans refuse to obey. He orders out a company
of soldiers. The Brahmans mass on the housetops and
stone the soldiers. The order is given to fire. Then,
and not till then, the Christians may carry out their
dead; and later on the Brahmans carry out theirs.
This happened some years ago, and outwardly times
have changed since then in that particular town. But
the spirit that it shows is in possession to this day, and
as small things show great, so this street scene shows the
presence of that "something" which intensifies the difficulty of winning the Castes for Christ. Each unit is
weak in itself, but in combination, strong.

"A forlorn hope" we have called the attempt to do what
we are told to do. The word is a misnomer; with our
Captain as our Leader no hope is ever "forlorn"! But
our Leader calls for men, men like the brave of old who
jeopardised their lives unto the death in the high places
of the field, in the day that they came to the help of the
Lord, to the help of the Lord against the mighty. A
jeopardised life may be lost.

Christ our Captain is calling for volunteers; here are
the terms: "Whosoever shall lose his life for My sake
and the Gospel's the same shall find it." The teachers'

life may seem "lost" who lives for his college boys;
the student's life may seem "lost" who spends hour
after hour through the long hot days in quiet talks in
the house. Be it so, for it may mean that. But the
life lost for His Name's sake, the same shall be found
again.

CHAPTER XVII

If it is so very important . . . ?

"Let us for a moment imagine what would have happened on the Galilean hillside, when our Lord fed the five thousand, if the Apostles had acted as some act now. The twelve would be going backwards, helping the first rank over and over again, and leaving the back rows unsupplied. Let us suppose one of them, say Andrew, venturing to say to his brother Simon Peter, 'Ought we all to be feeding the front row? Ought we not to divide, and some of us go to the back rows?' Then suppose Peter replying, 'Oh no; don't you see these front people are so hungry? They have not had half enough yet; besides, they are nearest to us, so we are more responsible for them.' Then, if Andrew resumes his appeal, suppose Peter going on to say, 'Very well; you are quite right. You go and feed all those back rows; but I can't spare anyone else. I and the other ten of us have more than we can do here.'

"Once more, suppose Andrew persuades Philip to go with him; then, perhaps, Matthew will cry out and say, 'Why, they're all going to those farther rows! Is no one to be left to these needy people in front?'

"Let me ask the members of Congress, Do you recognise these sentences at all?"

Eugene Stock, at Shrewsbury Church Congress.

IT was only a common thing. A girl, very ill, and in terrible pain, who turned to us for help. We could do nothing for her. Her people resorted to heathen rites. They prepared her to meet the fierce god they thought was waiting to snatch her away.

We went again and again, but she suffered so that one could not say much, it did not seem any use. The last time we went, the crisis had passed; she would live, they told us with joy. They were eager to listen to us now. "Tell us all about your Way!" clamoured the women, speaking together, and very loud. "Tell us the news from beginning to end!" But, alas! they could take in very little. One whole new Truth was too much for them. "Never mind," they consoled us, "come every day, and then what you say will take hold of our hearts." And I had to tell them we were leaving that evening, and could not come "every day."

The girl turned her patient face towards us. She had smiled at the Name of Jesus, and it seemed as if down in the depths of her weakness she had listened when we spoke before, and tried to understand. Now she looked puzzled and troubled, and the women all asked, "Why?"

There, in that crowded, hot little room, a sense of the unequal distribution of the Bread of Life came over us. The front rows of the Five Thousand are getting the loaves and the fishes over and over again, till it seems as though they have to be bribed and besought to accept them, while the back rows are almost forgotten. *Is it that we are so busy with the front rows, which we can see, that we have no time for the back rows out of sight?* But is it fair? Is it what Jesus our Master intended? *Can it be really called fair?*

The women looked very reproachful. Then one of them said, looking up at me, "You say this is very important. If it is so very important, why did you not come before? You say you will come back again if you can, but how can we be sure that nothing will happen to stop you? We are, some of us, very old; we may die

Is not the contrast good! The old woman so intelligent, the baby so inane. She made a picture sitting there, in her crimson-edged seeley, with her dark old face showing up against the darker wall. She is one of the many we have missed by coming so slowly and so late. "How can I change now!" she says.

before you come back. This going away is not good."
And again and again she repeated, "*If it is so very
important, why did you not come before?*"

Don't think that the question meant more than it did.
It was only a human expression of wonder; it was not
a real desire after God. But the force of the question
was stronger far than the poor old questioner knew; it
appealed to our very hearts.

The people saw we were greatly moved, and they
pressed closer round us to comfort us, and one dear old
grandmother put her arms round me, and stroked my face
with her wrinkled old hand, and said, "Don't be troubled;
we will worship your God. We will worship Him just
as we worship our own. *Now*, will you go away glad?"

The dear old woman was really in earnest, she wanted
so much to comfort us. But her voice seemed to mingle
with voices from the homeland; and another—we heard
another—the Voice I had heard on the precipice-edge—
the voice of our brothers', our sisters' blood calling unto
God from the ground.

Friends, are these women real to you? Look at this
photo of one of them. Surely it was not just a happy
chance which brought out the detail so perfectly. Look
at the thoughtful, fine old face. Can you look at it and
say, "Yes, I am on my way to the Light, and you are
on your way to the Dark. At least, this is what I
profess to believe. And I am sorry for you, but this is
all I can do for you; I can be very sorry for you. I
know that this will not show you the way from the Dark,
where you are, to the Light, where I am. To show you
the way I must go to you, or, perhaps, send you one

whom I want for myself, or do without something I wish
to have; and this, of course, is impossible.   It might be
done if I loved God enough—*but I love myself better than
God or you.*"

You would not say such a thing, I know, but "Whoso
hath this world's good, and seeth his brother have need,
and shutteth up his compassion from him, how dwelleth
the love of God in him?"

A Brahman widow, the only Brahman woman who would let us take her photo. Brahman women wear their seeleys fastened in a peculiar way, and never cut their ears. Brahman widows are always shaven, and wear no jewels. This one is a muscular character, strong and resolute, an ordinary looking woman, but there must be an under-the-surface life which does not show. A widow's fate is described in one word here, "*accursed.*"

CHAPTER XVIII

The Call Intensified

"Sometimes the men and boys will not go away and let us talk to the women; in such cases I find silent prayer the best refuge. In other places the people welcome you, but will listen to anything but the Doctrine of Jesus Christ; and this is harder to bear than anything else I know."
Anna Gordon, China.

"Let the people that are at home not care only to hear about successes; we must train them that they take an interest in the struggle."
Rev. A. Schreiber, Sumatra and India.

"It is a fight making its demands upon physical, mental, and spiritual powers, and there are many adversaries. The dead weight of heathenism, the little appreciation of one's object and purpose, and the actual, vigorous opposition of the powers of darkness, make it a real fight, and only men of grit, of courage, devotion, and infinite patience and perseverance, will win.

"*Have I painted a discouraging picture? Am I frightening good men who might have volunteered and done well? I think not. I think the right sort of men, those who ought to volunteer, will be attracted rather than repelled by the difficulties.*"
Rev. J. Lampard, India.

WE got this photograph that day in December which we spent in the friendly Brahman street.

"There is not another woman in the town who would stand for you like that!" said the men, as she came forward, and, without a thought of posing, stood against the wall for a moment, and looked at the camera straight. Most of the women were afraid even to glance

10

at it, but she was not afraid. She would not stay to talk
to us, however, but marched off with the same resolute
air. For Brahman widows as a whole are by no means
an approachable race. Sometimes we find one who will
open out to us, and let us tell her of the Comfort where-
with we are comforted; but oftener we find them hard,
or hardening rapidly.

It is too soon to write about any of those who have
listened during the past few months, but we put this
photo in to remind you to remember those who are freer
than most women in India to follow the Lord Jesus
Christ, if only they would let His love have a chance of
drawing them. We have been to the various towns in
this and the upper curve of the mountains, but we have
not reached the lower curve towns, or half of the many
villages scattered close under the mountains, and, except
when we went out in camp, we have not of course touched
those farther afield.

There are only five working afternoons in a week,
for Saturday is given up to other things, and Sunday
belongs to the Christians; and when any interest is
shown, we return again to the same village, which
delays us, but is certainly worth while. Then there
are interruptions—sometimes on the Hindu side; festivals,
for instance, when no woman has time to hear; and on
ours, and on the weather's, so to speak, when great heat
or great rain make outdoor work impossible. Theoretically, itinerating is delightfully rapid; but practically, as
every itinerating missionary knows, it is quite slow.
There are other things to be done; those already brought
in have to be taught and trained and mothered, and

There is nothing to say about it except what is said in the chapter. There is nothing much to look at in a Brahman street. But that single simple street scene represents forces which control two hundred and seven million minds.

much time has to be spent in waiting upon God for more; so that, looking back, we seem to have done very little for the thousands about us, and now we must return to the eastern side of the district, for some of the boy converts are there at school, and there may be fruit to gather in after last year's sowing.

But I look up from my writing and see a stretch of mountain range thirty miles long, and this range stretches unbroken for a thousand miles to the North. I know how little is being done on the plains below, and I wonder when God's people will awake, and understand that there is yet very much land to be possessed, and arise and possess it. Look down this mountain strip with me; there are towns where work is being done, but it needs supervision, and the missionaries are too few to do it thoroughly. There are towns and numbers of villages where nothing is even attempted, except that once in two years, if possible, the Men's Itinerant Band comes round; but that does not reach the women well, and even if it did, how much would you know of Jesus if you only heard a parable or a miracle or a few facts from His life or a few points of His doctrine *once in two years*? I do not want to write touching appeals, or to draw one worker from anywhere else,—it would be a joy to know that God used these letters to help to send some-one to China, or anywhere where He has need of His workers,—but I cannot help wondering, as I look round this bit of the field, how it is that the workers are still so few.

We have found the people in the towns and villages willing to let us do what we call "verandah work" when

they will not let us into their houses. Verandah work,
like open-air preaching, is unsatisfactory as regards the
women, but it is better than nothing.

We spent an afternoon in the street this photo shows.
It is a thoroughfare, and so we were not forbidden; but
even so, we always ask permission before we walk down
it. Such an ordinary, commonplace street it looks to
you; there is no architectural grandeur to awe the
beholder, and impress him with the majesty of Brahmanhood; and yet that street, and every street like it, is a
very Petra to us, for it is walled round by walls higher
and stronger than the temple walls round which it is
built; walls built, as it seems, of some crystal rock, im-
perceptible till you come up to it, and even then not
visible, only recognisable as something you cannot get
through.

Our first day there was encouraging. We began at
the far end of the street, and after some persuasion the
men agreed to move to one side, and let us have the
other for any women who would come. Nothing particular happened, but we count a day good if we get a
single good chance to speak in quietness to the women.

Next time we went it was not so good. They had
heard in the meantime all about us, and that we had
girls from the higher Castes with us, and this was terrible
in their eyes. For the Brahman, from his lofty position
of absolute supremacy, holds in very small account the
souls of those he calls low-caste; but if any from the
middle distance (he would not describe them as near
himself, only dangerously nearer than the others) "fall
into the pit of the Christian religion," he thinks it is

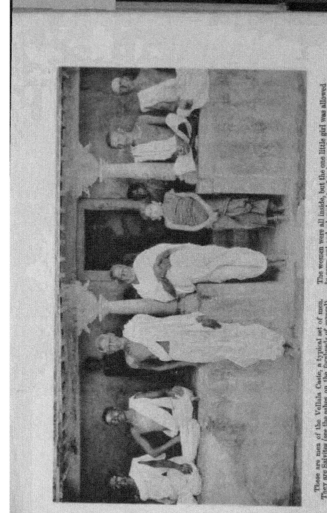

These are men of the Vellala Caste, a typical set of men. They are Saivites (see the ashes on the foreheads of several). The women were all inside, but the one little girl was allowed to come out and solemnly stand to be caught.

time to begin to take care that the Power which took
such effect on them should not have a chance to perform
upon him, and, above all, upon his womankind. So that
day we were politely informed that no one had time to
listen, and, when some women wanted to come, a muscular
widow chased them off. We looked longingly back at
those dear Brahman women, but appeal was useless, so
we went.

In one of the other Castes, the Caste represented by
this row of men, we found more friendliness; they let us
sit on one end of the narrow verandah fronts, and quite
a number of women clustered about on the other. They
were greatly afraid of defilement there, and would not
come too close. And they had the strangest ideas about
us. They were sure we had a powder which, if they
inhaled it, would compel them to be Christians. They
had heard that we went round "calling children," that is,
beckoning them, and drawing them to follow after us,
and that we were paid so much a head for converts. It
takes a whole afternoon sometimes simply to disabuse
their minds of such misconceptions.

I heard this commercial aspect of things explained by
one who apparently knew. A kindly old Brahman
woman had allowed us to sit on her doorstep out of the
sun, and bit by bit we had worked our way to the end of
the verandah, which was a little more shaded, where a
girl was sitting alone who seemed to want to hear. The
old woman sat down behind us, and then an old man
came up, and the two began to talk. Said the old
woman to the old man, "She is trying to make us join
her Way." (I had carefully abstained from any such

expression.) The old man agreed that such was my probable object. "What will she get if we join? Do you know?" "Oh yes; do I not know! For one of us a thousand rupees, and for a Vellalar five hundred. She even gets something for a low-caste child, but she gets a whole thousand for one of us!"

They were both very interested in this conversation, and so indeed was I, and I thought I would further enlighten them, when the old woman got up in a hurry and hobbled into the house. After that, whenever we passed, she used to shake her head at us, and say, "Chee, chee!" No persuasions could ever induce her to let us sit on her doorstep again. We were clearly after that thousand rupees, and she would have none of us.

In the same village there was a little Brahman child who often tried to speak to us, but never was allowed. One day she risked capture and its consequences, and ran across the narrow stream which divides the Brahman street from the village, and spoke to one of our Band in a hurried little whisper. "Oh, I do want to hear about Jesus!" And she told how she had learnt at school in her own town, and then she had been sent to her mother-in-law's house in this jungle village, "that one," pointing to a house where they never had smiles for us; but her mother-in-law objected to the preaching, and had threatened to throw her down the well if she listened to us. Just then a hard voice called her, and she flew. Next time we went to that village she was shut up somewhere inside.

Often as one passes one sees shy faces looking out from behind the little pillars which support the verandahs, and

A Shephard-Caste house of the better sort. We would give a great deal to get into this house, but so far it is closed. You can see straight through to the back courtyard and where the women are, where we may not go. The old man is typical of his class, a thoughtful man of refinement of mind, but wholly indifferent to the teaching.

one longs to get nearer. But it does not do to make any
advance unless one is sure of one's ground. It only
results in a sudden startled scurrying into the house, and
you cannot follow them there. To try to do so would be
more than rude—it would be considered pollution.

Only yesterday we were trying to get to the women
who live in the great house of the village behind the
bungalow. This photo shows you the door we stood
facing for ten minutes or more, first waiting, and then
pleading with the old mother-in-law to let us in to the
little dark room in which you may see a woman's form
hiding behind the door.

But we could not go to them, and they could not come
to us. There were only two narrow rooms between, but
the second of the two had brass water-vessels in it. If
we had gone in, those vessels and the water in them
would have been defiled. The women were not allowed
to come out, the mother-in-law saw well to that; never
was one more vigilant. She stood like a great fat hen
at the door, with her white widow's skirts outspread like
wings, and guarded her chickens effectually. "Go! go by
the way you have come!" was all she had to say to us.

The friendly old man of the house was out. A friendly
young man came in with some rice, and began to measure
it. He invited us to sit down, which we did, and he
measured the rice in little iron tumblers, counting aloud
as he did so in a sing-song chant. He was pleased that
we should watch him, and it was interesting to watch, for
he did it exactly as the verse describes, pressing the rice
down, shaking the iron measure, heaping up the rice till
it was running over, and yet counting this abundant

tumblerful only as one; then he handed the basketful of rice to a child who stood waiting, and asked what he could do for us. We told him how much we wanted to see the women of the house, but he did not relish the idea of tackling the vigorous old mother-in-law, so we gave up the attempt, and went out. As we passed the wall at the back which encloses the women's quarters, we saw a girl look over the wall as if she wanted to speak to us, but she was instantly pulled back by that tyrannical dame, and a dog came jumping over, barking most furiously, which set a dozen more yelping all about us, and so escorted we retired.

This house is in the Village of the Merchant, not five minutes from our gate, but the women in it are far enough from any chance of hearing. The men let us in that day to take the photograph, and we hoped thereby to make friends; but though there are six families living there (for the house is large; the photograph only shows one end of the verandah which runs down its whole length), we have never been once allowed to speak to one of the women; the mother-in-law of all the six takes care we never get the chance. One of the children, a dear little girl, follows us outside sometimes, but she is only seven, and not very courageous; so, though she evidently picks up some of the choruses we sing, she is afraid of being seen listening, and never gets much at a time.

These are some of the practical difficulties in the way of reaching the women. There are others. Suppose you do get in, or, what is more probable in pioneer work, suppose you get a verandah, even then it is not plain sailing by any means. For, first of all, it is dangerously hot. The sun beats down on the street or courtyard to within a foot or two of the stone ledge you are sitting upon, and strikes up. Reflected glare means fever, so you try to edge a little farther out of it without disturbing anyone's feelings, explaining minutely why you are doing it, lest they should think your design is to covertly touch them; and then, their confidence won so far, you begin perhaps with the wordless book, or a lyric set to an Indian tune, or a picture of some parable—never of our Lord—or, oftener still, we find the best way is to open our Bibles, for they all respect a Sacred Book, and read something from it which we know they will understand. We generally find one or two women about the verandahs, and two or three more come within a few minutes, and seeing this, two or three more. But getting them and keeping them are two different things. It is not easy to hold people to hear what they have no special desire to hear. But we are helped; we are not alone. It is always a strength to remember that.

Once fairly launched, interruptions begin. You are in the middle of a miracle, perhaps, and by this time a dozen women have gathered, and rejoice your heart by listening well, when a man from the opposite side of the street saunters over and asks may he put a question, or asks it forthwith. He has heard that our Book says, that if you have faith you can lift a mountain into the sea. Now, there is a mountain, and he points to the pillar out on the plain, standing straight up for five thousand feet, a column of solid rock. There is sea on the other side, he says; cast it in, and we will believe! And the women laugh. But one more intelligent turns to you, "Does your Book really say that?" she asks, "then why can't you do it, and let us see?" And the man strikes in with another remark, and a woman at the edge moves off, and you wish the man would go.

Perhaps he does, or perhaps you are able to detach him from the visible, and get him and those women too to listen to some bit of witnessing to the Power that moves the invisible, and you are in its very heart when another objection is started: "You say there is only one true God, but we have heard that you worship three!" or, "Can your God keep you from sin?" And you try, God helping you, to answer so as to avoid discussion, and perhaps to your joy succeed, and some are listening intently again, when a woman interrupts with a question about your relations which you answered before, but she came late, and wants to hear it all over again. You satisfy her as far as you can, and then, feeling how fast the precious minutes are passing, you try, oh so earnestly, to buy them up and fill them with eternity work, when suddenly the whole community concentrates itself upon your Tamil sister. Who is she? You had waived the question at the outset, knowing what would sequel it, but they renew the charge. If she is a "born Christian," they exclaim, and draw away for fear of defilement—"Low-caste, low-caste!" and the word runs round contemptuously. If she is a convert, they ask questions about her relations (they have probably been guessing among themselves about her Caste for the last ten minutes); if she does not answer them, they let their imagination run riot; if she does, they break out in indignation, "Left your own mother! Broken your Caste!" and they call her by names not sweet to the ear, and perhaps rise up in a body, and refuse to have anything more to do with such a disgraceful person.

Or perhaps you are trying to persuade some of them to learn to read, knowing that, if you can succeed, there will be so much more chance of teaching them, but they assure you it is not the custom for women in that village to read, which unhappily is true; or it may be you are telling them, as you tell those you may never see again, of the Love that is loving them, and in the middle of the telling a baby howls, and all the attention goes off upon it; or somebody wants to go into the house, and a way has to be made for her, with much gathering together and confusion; or a dog comes yelping round the corner, with a stone at its heels, and a pack of small boys in full chase after it; or the men call out it is time to be going; or the women suggest it is time to be cooking; or someone says or does something upsetting, and the group breaks up in a moment, and each unit makes for its separate hole, and stands in it, looking out; and you look up at those dark little doorways, and feel you would give anything they could ask, if only they would let you in, and let you sit down beside them in one of those rooms, and tell them the end of the story they interrupted; but they will not do that. Oh, it makes one sorrowful to be so near to anyone, and yet so very far, as one sometimes is from these women. You look at them, as they stand in their

doorways, within reach, but out of reach, as out of
reach as if they were thousands of miles away. . . .

Just as I wrote those words a Brahman woman came
to the door and looked in. Then she walked in and
sat down, but did not speak. Can you think how
one's heart bounds even at such a little thing as that?
Brahman women do not come to see us every day.
She pulled out a book of palm-leaf slips, and we read
it. It told how she was one of a family of seven, all
born deaf and dumb; how hand in hand they had set
off to walk to Benares to drown themselves in the
Ganges; how a Sepoy had stopped them and taken
them to an English Collector; how he had provided
for the seven for a year, then let them go; how they
had scattered and wandered about, visiting various holy
places, supported by the virtuous wherever they went;
and how the bearer would be glad to receive whatever we
would give her. . . . She has gone, a poor deaf and dumb
and wholly heathen woman; we could not persuade her
to stay and rest. She is married, she told us by signs;
her husband is deaf and dumb, and she has one blind
child. She sat on the floor beside us for a few minutes
and asked questions—the usual ones, about me, all by
signs; but nothing we could sign could in any way
make her understand anything about our God. And
yet she seems to know something at least about her
own. She pointed to her mouth, and then up, and then
down and round, to show the winding of a river, and
signed clearly enough how she went from holy river
to holy river, and worshipped by each, and she pointed
up and clasped her hands. There we were, just as I

had been writing, so near to her, yet so far from
her.

But the greatest difficulty of all in reaching the
women is that they have no desire to be reached.
Sometimes, as on that afternoon when the child came
and wanted to hear, we find one who has desire, but
the greater number have none; and except in the more
advanced towns and villages, where they are allowed
to learn with a Bible-woman, they have hardly a chance
to hear enough to make them want to hear more.

Then, as if to make the case doubly hard (and this
law applies to every woman, of whatever Caste), she is, in
the eyes of the law, the property of her husband; and
though a Christian cannot by law compel his Hindu
wife to live with him, a Hindu husband can compel
his Christian wife to live with him; so that no married
woman is ever legally free to be a Christian, for if the
husband demanded her back, she could not be protected,
but would have to be given up to a life which no English
woman could bear to contemplate. She may say she
is a Christian; he cares nought for what she says. God
help the woman thus forced back!

But, believing a higher Power will step in than the
power of this most unjust law, we would risk any penalty
and receive such a wife should she come. Only, in
dealing with the difficulties and barriers which lie between
an Indian woman and life as a free Christian, it is useless
to shut one's eyes to this last and least comprehensible of
all difficulties, "an English law, imported into India, and
enforced with imprisonment," an obsolete English law!

We have no Brahman women converts in our Tamil

Mission. We hear of a few in Travancore; we know of more in the North, where the Brahmans are more numerous and less exclusive; but there is not a single *bona fide* Brahman convert woman or child in the whole of this District. There was one, a very old woman; but she died two years ago. We may comfort ourselves with the thought that surely some of those who have heard have become secret believers. But will a true believer remain secret always? We may trust that many a dear little child died young, loving Jesus, and went to Him. But what about those who have not died young? I know that a brighter view may be taken, and if the sadder has been emphasised in these letters, it is only because we feel you know less about it.

More has been written about the successes than about the failures, and it seems to us that it is more important that you should know about the reverses than about the successes of the war. We shall have all eternity to celebrate the victories, but we have only the few hours before sunset in which to win them. We are not winning them as we should, because the fact of the reverses is so little realised, and the needed reinforcements are not forthcoming, as they would be if the position were thoroughly understood. Reinforcements of men and women are needed, but, far above all, reinforcements of prayer. And so we have tried to tell you the truth—the uninteresting, unromantic truth —about the heathen as we find them, the work as it is. More workers are needed. No words can tell how much they are needed, how much they are *wanted* here. But we will never try to allure anyone to think of coming

by painting coloured pictures, when the facts are in
black and white. What if black and white will never
attract like colours? We care not for it; our business
is to tell the truth. The work is not a pretty thing, to
be looked at and admired. It is a fight. And battle-
fields are not beautiful.

But if one is truly called of God, all the difficulties
and discouragements only intensify the Call. If things
were easier there would be less need. The greater the
need, the clearer the Call rings through one, the deeper
the conviction grows: *it was God's Call.* And as one
obeys it, there is the joy of obedience, quite apart from
the joy of success. There is joy in being with Jesus
in a place where His friends are few; and sometimes,
when one would least expect it, coming home tired out
and disheartened after a day in an opposing or indifferent
town, suddenly—how, you can hardly tell—such a wave
of the joy of Jesus flows over you and through you, that
you are stilled with the sense of utter joy. Then, when
you see Him winning souls, or hear of your comrades'
victories, oh! all that is within you sings, "I have more
than an overweight of joy!"

CHAPTER XIX

"Attracted by the Influence"

"It seems to have been a mistake to imagine that the Divine Majesty on high was too exalted to take any notice of our mean affairs. The great minds among us are remarkable for the attention they bestow upon minutiæ . . . 'a sparrow cannot fall to the ground without your Father.'"

David Livingstone, Africa.

WE have now left Dohnavur, on the West, and returned to our old battlefield on the East. The evening after our arrival one of those special things happened, though only a little thing some will say—a little child was brought.

There is a temple in the Hindu village near us. We have often tried to reach the temple women, poor slaves of the Brahmans. We have often seen the little girls, some of them bought as infants from their mothers, and trained to the terrible life. In one of the Mission day schools there is a child who was sold by her "Christian" mother to these Servants of the gods; but though this is known it cannot be proved, and the child has no wish to leave the life, and she cannot be taken by force.

Sometimes we see the little girls playing in the courtyards of the houses near the temple, gracious little maidens, winsome in their ways, almost always more refined in manner than ordinary children, and often

This is not Pearl-eyes. Pearl-eyes is tinier, and has more sparkle; but the Castle is the same, and as we have not got Pearl-eyes, we put this small girl here.

beautiful. One longs to help the little things, but no
hand of ours can stretch over the wall and lift even one
child out.

Among the little temple girls in the Great Lake Village
was a tiny girl called Pearl-eyes, of whom we knew nothing; but God must have some purpose for her, for He
sent His Angel to the house one afternoon, and the Angel
found little Pearl-eyes, and he took her by the hand and
led her out, across the stream, and through the wood, to
a Christian woman's house in our village. Next morning
she brought her to us. This is what really happened, I
think; there is no other way to account for it. No one
remembers such a thing happening here before.

I was sitting reading in the verandah when I saw
them come. The woman was looking surprised. She
did not know about the Angel, I expect, and she could
not understand it at all. The little child was chattering
away, lifting up a bright little face as she talked. When
she saw me she ran straight up to me, and climbed on
my knee without the least fear, and told me all about
herself at once. I took her to the Iyer, and he sent for
the Pastor, who sent a messenger to the Village of the
Lake, to say the child was here, and to inquire into the
truth of her story.

"My name is Pearl-eyes," the child began, "and I
want to stay here always. I have come to stay." And
she told us how her mother had sold her when she was a
baby to the Servants of the gods. She was not happy
with them. They did not love her. Nobody loved her.
She wanted to live with us.

But why had she run away now? She hardly seemed

11

to know, and looked puzzled at our questions. The only
thing she was sure about was that she had "run and
come," and that she "wanted to stay." Then the Ammal
came in, and she went through exactly the same story
with her.

We felt, if this proved to be fact, that we could surely
keep her; the Government would be on our side in such
a matter. Only the great difficulty might be to prove it.

Meanwhile we gave her a doll, and her little heart
was at rest. She did not seem to have a fear. With
the prettiest, most confiding little gesture, she sat down
at our feet and began to play with it.

We watched her wonderingly. She was perfectly at
home with us. She ran out, gathered leaves and flowers,
and came back with them. These were carefully arranged
in rows on the floor. Then another expedition, and in
again with three pebbles for hearthstones, a shell for a
cooking pot, bits of straw for firewood, a stick for a
match, and sand for rice.

She went through all the minutiæ of Tamil cookery
with the greatest seriousness. Then we, together with
her doll, were invited to partake. The little thing
walked straight into our hearts, and we felt we would
risk anything to keep her.

Our messenger returned. The story was true. The
women from whose house she had come were certainly
temple women. But would they admit it to us, and, above
all, would they admit they had obtained her illegally?
—a fact easy to deny. Almost upon this they came;
and to the Iyer's question, "Who are you?" one said,
"We are Servants of the gods!" I heard an instructive

aside, "Why did you tell them?"   "Oh, never mind,"
said the one who had answered, "they don't understand!"
But we had understood, and we were thankful for the
first point gained.

They stood and stared and called the child, but she
would not go, and we would not force her. Then they
went away, and we were left for an hour in that curious
quiet which comes before a storm. Our poor little girl
was frightened.   "Oh, if they come again, hide me!" she
begged. One saw it was almost too much for her, high-
spirited child though she is.

The next was worse. A great crowd gathered on the
verandah, and an evil-faced woman, who seemed to have
some sort of power over Pearl-eyes, fiercely demanded
her back. When we refused to make her go, the evil-
faced woman, whose very glance sent a tremble through
the little one, declared that Pearl-eyes must say out
loud that she would not go with her, "Out loud so that
all should hear." But the poor little thing was dumb
with fear. She just stood and looked, and shivered.
We could not persuade her to say a word.

Star was hovering near. She had been through it all
herself before, and her face was anxious, and our hearts
were, I know. It is impossible to describe such a half-
hour's life to you; it has to be lived through to be
understood. The clamour and excitement, and the feeling of how much hangs on the word of a child who does
not properly understand what she is accepting or refusing.
The tension is terrible.

I dared not go near her lest they should think I was
bewitching her. Any movement on my part towards her

would have been the signal for a rush on theirs; but I signed to Star to take her away for a moment. The bewilderment on the poor little face was frightening me. One more look up at that woman, one more pull at the strained cord, and to their question, "Will you come?" she might as likely say yes as no.

Star carried her off. Once out of reach of those eyes, the words came fast enough. Star told me she clung to her and sobbed, "Oh, if I say no, she will catch me and punish me dreadfully afterwards! She will! I know she will!" And she showed cuts in the soft brown skin where she had been punished before; but Star soothed her and brought her back, and she stood—such a little girl—before them all. "I won't! I won't!" she cried, and she turned and ran back with Star. And the crowd went off, and I was glad to see the last of that fearful face, with its evil, cruel eyes.

But they said they would write to the mother, who had given her to them. We noted this—the second point we should have to prove if they lodged a suit against us—and any day the mother may come and complicate matters by working on the child's affections. Also, we have heard of a plot to decoy her away, should we be for a moment off guard; so we are very much on the watch, and we never let her out of our sight.

By this time—it is five days since she came—it seems impossible to think of having ever been without her. Apart from her story, which would touch anyone, there is her little personality, which is very interesting. She plays all day long with her precious dolls, talking to them, telling them everything we tell her. Yesterday it

was a Bible story, to-day a new chorus. She insisted on
her best-beloved infant coming to church with her, and it
had to have its collection too. Everything is most realistic.

Tamil children usually hang their dolls up by their
limbs to a nail in the wall, or stow them away on a shelf,
but this mite has imagination and much sympathy.

In thinking over it, as, bit by bit, her little story came
to light, we have been struck by the touches that tell
how God cares. The time of her coming told of care.
Some months earlier, the temple woman who kept
her had burnt her little fingers across, as a punishment for some childish fault, and Pearl-eyes ran away.
She knew what she wanted—her mother; she knew that
her mother lived in a town twenty miles to the East.
It was a long way for a little girl to walk, "but some
kind people found me on the road, and they were going
to the same town, and they let me go with them, so I
was not afraid, only I was very tired when we got there.
It took three days to walk. I did not know where my
mother lived in the town, and it was a very big town,
but I described my mother to the people in the streets,
and at last I found my mother." For just a little while
there was something of the mother-love, "my mother
cried." But the temple woman had traced her and
followed her, and the mother gave her up.

Then comes a blank in the story; she only remembers
she was lonely, and she "felt a mother-want about the
world," and wandered wearily—

"As restless as a nest-deserted bird
  Grown chill through something being away, though what
  It knows not."

Then comes a bit of life distinct in every detail, and told with terribly unchildish horror. She heard them whisper together about her; they did not know that she understood. She was to be "married to the god," "tied to a stone." Terrified, she flew to the temple, slipped past the Brahmans, crossed the court, stood before the god in the dim half-darkness of the shrine, clasped her hands,—she showed us how,—prayed to it, pleaded, "Let me die! Oh, let me die!" Barely seven years old, and she prayed, "Oh, let me die!"

She tried to run away again; if she had come to our village then, she could not have been saved. We were in Dohnavur, and there was no one here who could have protected her against the temple people. So God kept her from coming then.

About that time, one afternoon one of our Tamil Sisters, whom we had left behind to hold the fort, passed through the Great Lake Village, and the temple women called the child, and said, "See! It is she! The child-stealing Ammal! Run!" It was only said to frighten her, but it did a different work. One day, *the day after we returned*, the thought suddenly came to her, "I will go and look for that child-stealing Ammal"; and she wandered away in the twilight and came to our village, and stood alone in front of the church, and no one knew.

There one of our Christian women, Servant of Jesus by name, found her some time afterwards, a very small and desolate mite, with tumbled hair and troubled eyes, for she could not find the one she sought, that child-stealing Ammal she wanted so much, and she was frightened, all alone in the gathering dark by this big, big church; and very big it must have looked to so tiny a thing as she.

Servant of Jesus thought at first of taking the little one back to her home, but mercifully it was late (another touch of the hand of God), and so instead she took her straight to her own little house, which satisfied Pearl-eyes perfectly. But she would not touch the curry and rice the kind woman offered her. She drew herself up to her full small height and said, with the greatest dignity, "Am I not a Vellala child? May you ask me to break my Caste?"

So Servant of Jesus gave her some sugar, that being ceremonially safe, and Pearl-eyes ate it hungrily, and then went off to sleep.

Next morning, again the woman's first thought was to take her to her own people. But the child was so insistent that she wanted the child-catching Ammal, that Servant of Jesus, thinking I was the Ammal she meant (for this is one of my various names), brought her to me, as I have said, and oh, I am glad she did!

Nothing escapes those clear brown eyes. That morning, in the midst of the confusion, one of the temple women called out that the child was a wicked thief. This is an ordinary charge. They think it will compel submission. "We will make out a case, and send the police to drag you off to gaol!" they yell; and sometimes there is risk of serious trouble, for a case can be made out cheaply in India. But this did not promise to be serious, so we inquired the stolen sum. It came to fourpence half-penny, which we paid for the sake of peace, though she

told them where the money was, and we found out later
that she had told the truth.

I never thought she would remember it—the excite-
ments of the day crowded it out of my mind—but
weeks afterwards, when I was teaching her the text,
" Not redeemed with corruptible things, as silver and
gold," and explaining how much Jesus had paid for us,
she interrupted me with the remark, " Oh yes, I understand ! I know how much you paid for me—fourpence
halfpenny ! "

And now to turn from small-seeming things to large.
Ragland, Tamil missionary, is writing to a friend in 1847.
He is trying to express astronomically the value of a soul.
He asks, " How does the astronomer correct the knowledge of the stars which simple vision brings him ? First,
having discovered that the little dot of light is thousands
of miles distant, and having discerned by the telescope
that it subtends at the eye a sensible angle, and having
measured that angle, a simple calculation shows him the
size of the object to be greater perhaps than that of
the huge ball which he calls his earth." Then, " Take the
soul of one of the poorest, lowest Pariahs of India, and
form it by imagination into, or suppose it represented by,
a sphere.   Place this at the extremity of a line which is
to represent time.   Extend this line and move off your
sphere, farther and farther *ad infinitum*, and what has
become of your sphere ?   Why, there it is, just as before.
. . . It is still what it was, and this even after thousands
of years.   In short, the disc appears undiminished, though
viewed from an almost infinite distance.   *Oh, what an
angle of the mind ought that poor soul to subtend !* "

The letter goes on to suggest another parallel between things astronomical and things spiritual. He supposes an objector admits the size as proved, but demurs as to the importance of these heavenly bodies. "They are, perhaps, only unsubstantial froth, mere puffs of air, vapoury nothings." But the astronomer knows their mass and weight, as well as their size: "Long observation has taught him that planets in the neighbourhood of one given heavenly body have been turned out of their course, how, and by what, he is at first quite at a loss to tell, but he has guessed and reasoned, has found cause for suspecting the planet. He watches, observes, and compares; and after a long sifting of evidence, he brings it in guilty of the disturbance. If it be so, it must have a power to disturb, a power to attract; and if so, it is not a mere shell, much less a mere vapour. It has mass and it has weight, and he calculates and determines from the disturbances what that weight is. Just so with the Pariah's soul. Oh, what a disturbance has it created! What a celestial body has it drawn out from its celestial sphere! Not a star, not the whole visible heavens, not the heaven of heavens itself, but Him Who fills heaven and earth, by Whom all things were created. *Him did that Pariah's soul attract from heaven even to earth to save it. Oh that we would thence learn, and learning, lay to heart the weight and the value of that one soul.*"

And just as the majesty of the glory of the Lord is shown forth nowhere more majestically than in the chapter which tells us how He feeds His flock like a shepherd, and gathers the lambs with His arm, and carries them in His bosom, so nowhere, I think, do we

see the glory of our God more than in chapters of life
which show Him bending down from the circle of the
earth, yea rather, coming down all the way to help it,
" attracted by the influence" of the need of a little
child.

CHAPTER XX

The Elf

"You remember what I said once, that you could not, perhaps, put a whole crown on the head of Jesus—that is, bring a whole country to be His—but you might put one little jewel in His crown." *Bishop French, India and Arabia.*

PEARL-EYES, otherwise the Elf, because it exactly describes her, was very good for the first few weeks, after which we began to know her. She is not a convert in any sense of the term. She is just a very wilful, truthful, exasperating, fascinating little Oriental.

When she is, as she expresses it, "moved to sin," nobody of her own colour can manage her. "You are only *me* grown up," is her attitude towards them all. She is always ready to repent, but, as Pearl sorrowfully says, "before her tears are dry, she goes and sins again," and then, quite unabashed, she will trot up to you as if nothing had happened and expect to be lavishly petted.

I never saw anyone except the Elf look interesting when naughty. She does look interesting. She is a rather light brown, and any emotion makes the brown lighter; her long lashes droop over her eyes in the most pathetic manner, and when she looks up

appealingly she might be an innocent martyr about
to die for her faith.

We have two other small girls with us; the Imp—
but her name is a libel, she reformed some months
ago—and Tangles, who ties herself into knots whenever
she makes a remark. These three have many an argument (for Indian children delight in discussion), and
sometimes the things that are brought to me would shock
the orthodox. This is the last, brought yesterday:
"Obedience is not so important as love. Orpah was
very obedient. Her mother-in-law said, 'Go, return,'
and she did as she was told. But Ruth was not obedient
at all. Four times her mother-in-law said, 'Go,' and yet
she would not go. But God blessed Ruth much more
than Orpah, because she loved her mother-in-law. So
obedience is not so important as love." Only the day
before I had been labouring to explain the absolute necessity for the cultivation of the grace of obedience; but now
it was proved a secondary matter, for Ruth was certainly
disobedient, but good and greatly blessed.

The Elf's chief delinquencies at present, however, spring
from a rooted aversion to her share in the family house-
work (ten minutes' rubbing up of brass water-vessels);
an appetite for slate pencils—she would nibble them by
the inch if we would let her—"they are so nice to eat,"
she says; and, most fruitful of all in sad consequences,
a love of being first.

As regards sin No. 1, I hope it will soon be a thing of
the past, for she has just made a valuable discovery:
"Satan doesn't come very close to me if I sing all the
time I'm rubbing the brasses. He runs away when he

hears me sing, so I sing very loud, and that keeps him
away. Satan doesn't like hymns." And I quite agree,
and strongly advise her to persevere.

Sin No. 2 is likely to pass, as she hates the nasty
medicine we give her to correct her depraved proclivities;
but No. 3 is more serious. It opens the door, or, as she
once expressed it, it "calls so many other sins to come,"
—quarrelling, pride, and several varieties of temper, come
at the "call" of this sin No. 3.

She is a born leader in her very small way, and she
has not learned yet, that before we can lead we must be
willing to be led. "I will choose the game," she remarks,
"and all of you must do as I tell you." Sometimes they
do, for her directions, though decisive, are given with a
certain grace that wins obedience; but sometimes they do
not, and then the Elf is offended, and walks off.

But she is the life of the game, and they chase her and
propitiate her; and she generally condescends to return,
for solitary dignity is dull. If any of the seniors happen
to see it, it is checked as much as possible, but oftener
we hear of it in that very informing prayer, which is to
her quite the event of the evening; for she takes to the
outward forms of religion with great avidity, and the
evening prayer especially is a deep delight to her. She
counts up all her numerous shortcomings carefully and
perfectly truthfully, as they appear to her, and with equal
accuracy her blessings large and small. She sometimes
includes her good deeds in the list, lest, I suppose, they
should be forgotten in the record of the day. All the
self-righteousness latent in human nature comes out, or
used to, in her earlier days, in the evening revelations.

Here is a specimen, taken at random from the first
month's sheaf. She and the Imp had come to my room
for their devotions, preternaturally pious, both of them,
though quite unregenerate. It was the Elf's turn to
begin. She settled herself circumspectly, sighed deeply,
and then began.

First came the day's sins, counted on the fingers of
the right hand, beginning with the fourth finger. "Once,'
and down went the little finger on the palm, "I was
cross with L." (L. being the Imp, nine and a half to the
Elf's seven and a half, but most submissive as a rule)
"I was cross because she did not do as I told her. That
was wrong of me; but it was wrong of her too, so it was
only half a sin. Twice," and the third finger was folded
down, "when I did not do my work well. That was
quite all my fault. Three times," and down went the
middle finger, "when I caught a quarrel with those
naughty little children; they were stupid little children,
and they would not play my game, so I spoiled unity.
But they came running after me, and they said, 'Please
forgive us,' so I forgave them. That was very good of
me, and I also forgave L.; so that is three bad things
and two good things to-day."

I stopped her, and expatiated on the sin of pride, but
her mind was full of the business in hand.

"Then there were four blessings—no, five; but I can't
remember the fifth. The Ammal gave me a box for my
doll, and you gave me some sweets; and I found some
nice rags in your waste-paper basket "—grubbing in rag-
bags and waste-paper baskets is one of the joys of life;
rags are so useful when you have a large family of dolls

who are always wearing out their clothes—"and I have
some cakes in my own box now. Those are four blessings.
But I forget the fifth."

I advised her to leave it, and begin, for the Imp was
patiently waiting her turn. She, good child, suggested
the missing fifth must be the soap—the Ammal had
given each of them a piece the size of a walnut. Yes,
that was it apparently, for the Elf, contented, began—

"O loving Lord Jesus! I have done three wrong
things to-day" (then followed the details and prayer for
forgiveness). "Lord, give L. grace to do what I want her
to do; and when she does not do it, Lord, give me grace
to be patient with her. I thank Thee for causing me to
forgive those little children who would not play the game
I liked. Oh make them good, and make me also good;
and next time we play together give me grace to play
patiently with them. And oh, forgive all the bad things
I have done to-day; and I thank Thee very much for
all the good things I have done, for I did them by Thy
grace." Praise for mercies followed in order: the card-
board box, the lump of sugar-candy, the spoils from the
waste-paper basket, those sticky honey-cakes—which, to
my disquietude, I then understood were secreted in her
seeley box—and that precious bit of soap. Then—and
this is never omitted—a fervently expressed desire for
safe preservation for herself and her friends from "the
bites of snakes and scorpions, and all other noxious
creatures, through the darkness of the night, and when
I wake may I find myself at Thy holy feet. Amen."

No matter how sleepy she is, these last phrases, which
are quite of her own devising, are always included in the

tail-end of her prayer. She would not feel at all safe
on her mat, spread on the ground out of doors in hot
weather, unless she had so fortified herself from all
attacks of the reptile world. And when, one day, we
discovered a nest of some few dozen scorpions within
six yards of her mat, not one of which had ever disturbed
her or any of her "friends," we really did feel that funny
little prayer had power in it after all.

You cannot interrupt in the middle of those rather
confusing confessions, she is far too much engaged to be
disturbed, but when the communication is fairly over,
and she cuddles on your knee for the kissing and caressing
she so much appreciates, you have a chance of explaining
things a little.

She listened seriously that evening, I remember, then,
slipping down off my knee, she added as a sort of post-
script, very reverently, "O Lord Jesus, I prayed it
wrong. I was naughtier than L., much naughtier. But
indeed Thou wilt remember that she was naughty first.
. . . Oh, that's not it! It was not L, it was me! And
I was impatient with those little children. But . . .
but they caused impatience within me." Then getting
hopelessly mixed up between self-condemnation and self-
justification, she gave it up, adding, however, "Next time
we play together, give them grace to play patiently with
me," which was so far satisfactory, as at first she had
scouted the idea that there could be any need of patience
on the other side.

Sometimes she brings me perplexities not new to most
of us. "This morning I prayed with great desire, 'Lord,
keep me to-day from being naughty at all,' and I was

naughty an hour afterwards; I looked at the clock and saw. How was it I was naughty when I wanted to be good? The naughtiness jumped up inside me, so "— (illustrating its supposed action within), "and it came running out. So what is the use of praying?"

Once the difficulty was rather opposite.

"Can you be good without God's grace?"

I told her I certainly could not.

"Well, I can!" she answered delightedly. "I want to pray now."

"Now? It is eight o'clock now. Haven't you had prayer long ago?" (We all get up at six o'clock.)

"No. That's just what I meant. I skipped my prayer this morning, and so of course I got no grace; but I have been helping the elder Sisters. Wasn't that right?"

"Yes, quite right."

"And yet I hadn't got any grace! But I suppose," she added reflectively, "it was the grace over from yesterday that did it."

As a rule she is not distinguished for very deep penitence, but at one time she had what she called "a true sense of sin" which fluctuated rather, but was always hailed, when it appeared in force, as a sign of better things. After a day of mixed goodness and badness the Elf prayed most devoutly, "I thank Thee for giving me a sense of sin to-day. O God, keep me from being at all naughty to-morrow. But if I am naughty, Lord, give me a true sense of sin!"

Professor Drummond speaks of our whole life as a long-drawn breath of mystery, between the two great wonders—the first awakening and the last sleep. I often

12

think of that as I listen to the little children talking to
each other and to us. They are always wondering about
something. One day it was, "Do fishes love Jesus?"
followed by "What is a soul?" The conclusion was, "It's
the thing we love Jesus with." When they first come
to us they invariably think that mountains grow like
trees: "Stones are young mountains, aren't they? and
hills are middle-aged mountains." Later on, every
printed thing on a wall is a text. We were in a railway
station, on our way to the hills: "Look! oh, what
numbers and numbers of texts! But what queer pictures
to have on texts!" One was specially perplexing; it
was a well-known advertisement, and the picture showed
a monkey smoking a cigar. What could that depraved
animal have to do with a *text*? When we got to
the hills the first amazement was the sight of the
fashionable ladies wearing veils. "Don't they like to
look at God's beautiful world? Do they like it better
spotty?"

Tangles has another name; it is the "Ugly Duckling," and it is extremely descriptive; but Ugly Duckling
or not, she is of an inquiring turn of mind, and one
Saturday afternoon, after standing under a tree for fully
five minutes lost in thought, she came to me with a
question: "What are the birds saying to each other?"
I looked at the Ugly Duckling, and she twisted herself
into a note of interrogation, in the ridiculous way she
has, but her face was full of anxiety for enlightenment
about the language of the sparrows. "There," she said,
pointing vigorously to the astonished birds, which instantly flew away, "that little sparrow and this one are

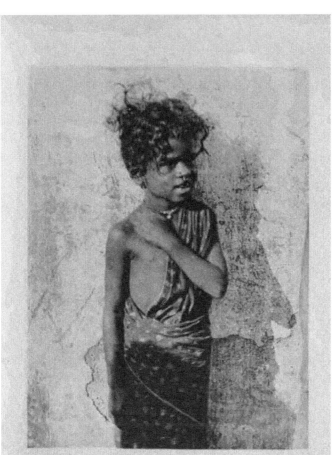

We value this photo exceedingly, it was so hard to get. We were in a big heathen village when we saw this Ugly Duckling, in fact she was one of the most tiresome of the "rabbits" mentioned in chapter I. She saw us, and darted off and climbed a wall and made faces at us in a truly delightful manner. We thought we would take her, and tried. As well try to pick up quicksilver; she would not be caught. The deed was finally done when she had not the least idea of it, and the camera gave a triumphant click as it snapped her unawares. "What do they want her for?" inquired a grown-up by-stander, who had observed our little game. "Look at her hair," said another, "they never saw hair like that in England, that's what they want her for!"

making quite different noises. What are they saying?
I do want to know so much!"

As I imagined the birds in question had just been
having supper, I told her what I thought they were
probably saying. Next day, in the sermon, there was
something about the praise all creation offers to God,
and I saw Tangles knotting her hands together and
going into the queerest contortions in appreciation of
the one bit of the sermon she could understand.

The Imp's questions were various. "What is that?"
—pointing to a busy-bee clock—" is it an English kind of
insect? Don't its legs get tired going round? Oh! is it
dead now?" (when it stopped). "Who made Satan?"
was an early one. "Why doesn't God kill him immediately, and stamp on him?" One day I was trying
to find and touch her heart by telling her how very
sorry Jesus was when we are naughty. She seemed
subdued, then—"Amma, where was the Queen's spirit
after she died and before they buried her, *and what did
they give it to eat?*"

"Did you see Lot's wife?" was a question which
tickled the Bishop when, on his last visitation, he gave
himself up to an hour's catechising upon his tour in the
Holy Land. They were disappointed that he had to
confess he had not. "Oh, I suppose the salt has
melted," was the Elf's comment upon this.

Tangles is distinctly inclined to peace. The Elf, I
grieve to say, is not. Yesterday she announced a
quarrel: "I feel cross!" Tangles objected to quarrel.
"I do feel cross!" and the Elf apparently showed
corroborative symptoms. Then Tangles looked at her

straight: "I'm not going to quarrel. The devil has
arrived in the middle of the afternoon to interrupt
our unity, and I won't let him!" which so touched
the Elf that she embraced her on the spot; and then,
in detailing it all in her prayer in the evening, this in-
corrigible little sinner added, with real emotion, "Lord,
I am not good. I spoiled unity with L." (the Imp), "and
Thou didst feel obliged to remove her to a boarding-
school. Now do help me not to spoil unity with P."
(who is Tangles), "lest Thou shouldst feel obliged to
remove her also to a boarding-school,"—which was a
view of the Imp's promotion which had not struck me
before.

Tangles and she belong to the same Caste, and Tangles
has the character of that Caste as fully developed as the
Elf, and can hold her own effectually. Also she is a
little older and taller, and being the Elf's "elder sister,"
is, therefore, entitled to a certain measure of respect.
All those small things tend to the discipline of the Elf,
who is very small for her age, and who would have
preferred a junior, of a meek and mild disposition, and
whose constant prayer is this: "O Lord, bring another
little girl out of the lion's mouth, but, O Lord, please
let her be a *very little girl!*" Shortly after this prayer
began, a very little girl was brought; but she was a
vulgar infant, and greatly tried the Elf, and she was, for
various reasons, promptly returned to her parents. After
this episode the prayer varied somewhat: "Lord, let her be
a *suitable* child, and give me grace to love her from my
heart when she comes."

The conversation of these young creatures is often

very illuminating, and always most miscellaneous. The
Elf's mind especially is a sort of small curiosity shop, and
displays many assortments. The Elf, Tangles, and little
Delight (Delight is a youthful Christian) are curled up on
the warm red sand with their three little heads close
together. The Elf is telling a story. I listen, and hear
a marvellous muddle of the *Uganda Boys* and *Cyril of
North Africa.* "He was only six years old, and he
stood up and said, 'What you are going to do, do
quickly! I am not afraid. I am going to the Golden
City!' And they showed him the sword and the fire,
and he said, 'Do it quickly!' and they chopped off his
arm, and said, 'Will you deny Jesus?' and he said, 'No!'
and they chopped off his other arm,"—and so on through
all the various limbs in most vivid detail,—"and then they
threw him on the fire, and burnt him till he was ashes;
and he sang praises to Jesus!"

The Elf leans to the tragic. Tangles' mother had a
difference of opinion with a friend. The friend snatched
at her opponent's ear jewels, and tore the ear. Life with
a torn ear was intolerable, so Tangles' mother walked
three times round the well, repeated three times, "My
blood be on your head!" and sprang in. She rose three
times, each time said the same words, and then sank.
All this Tangles confided to the Elf, who concocted
a game based upon the incident—which, however, we
ruthlessly squashed. They are tossing pebbles now
according to rules of their own, and talking vigorously.
"The Ammal told me all the people in England are
white, and I asked her what they did without servants,
and she said they had white servants, *white servants!!*"

and the note of exclamation is intense. The others are
equally astonished. White people as servants! The two
ideas clash. They have never seen a white servant. In
all their extensive acquaintance with white people they
have only seen missionaries (who are truly their servants,
though they hardly realise it yet), and occasionally
Government officials, whose mastership is very much in
evidence. So they are puzzled. They get out of the
difficulty, however. "At the beginning of the beginning
of England, black people must have gone to be the white
people's servants, and they gradually grew white." Yes,
that's it apparently; they faded.

The conversation springs higher. " Do you know what
lightning is? I'll tell you. I watched it one whole
evening, and I think it's just a little bit of heaven's light
coming through and going back again." This sounds
probable, and great interest is aroused. They are discussing the sheet lightning which plays about the sky in
the evening before rain. "Of course it isn't much of
heaven's light, only a little tiny bit getting out and
running down here to show us what it is like inside.
One night I shut my eyes, and it ran in and out, in and
out, oh so fast! Even if I shut my eyes I saw it running
inside my eyes."

" Did you get caned in school to-day?"

" No, not exactly caned," and an explanation follows.
" I was standing beside a very naughty little girl, and the
teacher meant to cane her, but the cane fell on me by
mistake. I wanted to cry, because it hurt, but I thought it
would be silly to cry when it hurt me quite by mistake.
So I didn't cry one tear!"

The Elf hit upon a capital expedient for escaping castigation (which is never very severe). " I found this cane myself. It was lying on the ground in the compound, and I am going to take it to the teacher." Chorus of " Why ?" " Because," and the Elf looked elfish, " if I give it to him with my own hands, how will he cane my hands with it ? His heart will not be hard enough to cane me with the cane I gave him !" and the little scamp looks round for applause. Chorus of admiring " Oh !"

Then they begin again, the Elf as usual chief informant. " I know something !" Chorus, " What ?" " A beautiful doll is waiting for me in a box, and I'm going to have it at Ki-rismas !" " What sort of a doll ?" is the eager inquiry. " I don't know exactly, but God sent it, of course, so I think it must be something like an angel." Chorus, delightedly, " Ah !" " Yes, if it came from God, then of course it came from heaven, and heaven is the place all the angels come from, and they are white and shining, so I think it will be white and shining like an angel." The doll in question is a negress with a woolly head and a scarlet-striped pinafore. It had not struck me as angelic. It is an experiment in dolls. Will it "take"? Ki-rismas came at last, and the heavenly doll with it, but it did not "take." Grievous were the tears and sobs, and the bitterest wail of all was, "I thought God would have sent me a nicer doll !" We changed it for a "nicer doll," for the poor Elf was not wicked, only broken-hearted, and Star, who is supposed to be much too old for dolls, begged for the despised black beauty; because, as the Elf maliciously remarked as she hugged her white

dolly contentedly, "That black thing has a curly head
just like Star's!"

The habit of praying about everything is characteristic
of the Elf, and more than once her uninstructed little soul
has grieved over the strange way our prayers are sometimes answered.   One day she came rushing in full of
excitement.   "Oh, may I go and be examined?   The
Government Missie Ammal is going to examine our
school!   Please let me go!"   The Government Missie
Ammal, a great celebrity who only comes round once a
year, was staying with us, and I asked her if the child
might have the joy of being examined even though she
had not had nearly her year at school.   She agreed, for
the sake of the little one's delight—for an Indian child
likes nothing better than a fuss of any kind—to let her
come into the examination room, and take her examination informally.   We knew she was sure of a pass.   An
hour or two afterwards a scout came flying over to tell
us the awful news.   The Elf had failed, utterly failed,
and she was so ashamed she wouldn't come back,
"wouldn't come back any more."   I went for her, and
found her a little heap of sobs and tears, outside the
schoolroom.   I gathered her up in my arms and carried
her home, and tried to comfort her, but she was crushed.
"I asked God so earnestly to let me pass, and I didn't
pass!   And I thought He had listened, but now I know
He didn't listen at all!"

I was puzzled too, though for a different reason.   I knew
she should easily have passed, and I could only conclude
her wild excitement had made her nervous, for with many
tears she told me, "I did not know one answer! not even

one!" And again she came back to the first and sorest,
"Oh, I did think God was listening, and He wasn't
listening at all!"

At last I got her quieted, and explained, by means of a
rupee and an anna, how sometimes God gives us something better than we ask for; we ask for an anna, and He
gives us a rupee. A rupee holds sixteen annas. She
grew interested: "Then my passing that examination was
the anna. But what is the rupee?" Now the Elf, as
you may have observed, is not weighted with over much
humility, so I told her I thought the rupee must be
humility. She considered a while, then sliding off my
knee, she knelt down and said, with the utmost gravity
and purpose, "O God! I did not want that kind of
answer, but I do want it now. Give me the rupee
of humility!" Then springing up with eyes dancing
with mischief, "Next time I fall into pride you will say,
'Oh, where is that rupee?'"

When the school examinations were over, and the
Missie Ammal came back to rest, I asked her about
the Elf. "She really did very badly, seemed to know
nothing of her subjects; should not have gone in, poor
mite!" It suddenly struck me to ask what class she
had gone into. "The first," said the Missie Ammal.
"But she is in the infants'!" Then we understood.
The Elf had only been at school for a few months, and
had just finished the infant standard book, and had been
moved into the first a day or two before, as the teacher
felt she was well able to clear the first course in the next
six months and take her examination in the following
year, two years' work in one. But it was not intended

she should go in for the Government examination, which
requires a certain time to be spent in preparation; so
when, in the confusion of the arrangement of the classes,
she stood with her little class-fellows of two days only,
the mistake was not noticed. No wonder the poor Elf
failed! We never told her the reason, not desiring
to raise fresh questions upon the mysterious ways of
Providence in her busy little brain; and to this day, when
she is betrayed into pride, she shakes her head solemnly
at herself, and remembers the rupee.

She has lately been staying with the Missie Ammals,
" my very particular friends," as she calls them, at the
C.E.Z. House, Palamcottah. She returned to us full of
matter, and charged with a new idea. " I am no more
going to spend my pocket money upon vanities. I am
going to save it all up, and buy a *Gee-lit Bible*." This gilt-
edged treasure is a fruitful source of conversation. It
will take about six years at the rate of one farthing
a week to save enough to buy exactly the kind she
desires. " I don't want a *common* Bible. It must be
gee-lit, with shining *gee-lit* all down the leaves on the
outside, and the name on the back all *gee-lit* too. That's
the kind of Bible I want!" Just as I wrote that, she
trotted in and poured three half-annas in small change
upon the table. " That's all I've got, and it's six weeks'
savings. Six years is a long, long time!" She confided
to me that she found " the flesh wanted to persuade" her
to spend these three half-annas on cakes. " It is the
flesh, isn't it, that feeling you get inside, that says 'sweets
and cakes! sweets and cakes!' in a very loud voice? I
listened to it for a little, and then I wanted those sweets

and cakes! So I said to myself, If I buy them they will all be gone in an hour, but if I buy that Gee-lit Bible it will last for years and years. So I would not listen any more to my flesh." Then a sudden thought struck her, and she added impressively, "But when *you* give me sweets and cakes, that is different; the feeling that likes them is not 'flesh' then. It is only 'flesh' when I'm tempted to spend my Gee-lit Bible money on them." This was a point I was intended thoroughly to understand. Sweets and cakes were not to be confused with "flesh" except where a Gee-lit Bible was concerned. She seemed relieved when I agreed with her that such things might perhaps sometimes be innocently enjoyed, and with a sudden and rather startling change of subject inquired, "Do they *never* have holidays in hell?"

CHAPTER XXI

Deified Devilry

" Next to the sacrificers, they (the temple women) are the most important persons about the temple. That a temple intended as a place of worship, and attended by hundreds of simple-hearted men and women, should be so polluted, and that in the name of religion, is almost beyond belief; and that Indian boys should grow up to manhood, accustomed to see immorality shielded in these temples with a divine cloak, makes our hearts grow sick and faint."   *Mrs. Fuller, India.*

EXCUSE the title of this chapter. I can write no other. Sometimes the broad smooth levels of life are crossed by a black-edged jagged crack, rent, as it seems, by an outburst of the fiery force below. We find ourselves suddenly close upon it; it opens right at our very feet. We look down and see—hell.

Two girls came to see us to-day; sisters, but tuned to different keys. One was ordinary enough, a bright girl with plenty of jewels and a merry, contented face. The other was finer grained; you looked at her as you would look at the covers of a book, wondering what was inside. Both were married; neither had children. This was the only sorrow the younger had ever had, and it did not seem to weigh heavily.

The elder looked as if she had forgotten how to smile. Sometimes, when the other laughed, her eyes would light for a moment, but the shadow in them deepened almost before the light had come; great soft brown eyes, full of the dumb look that animals have when they are suffering.

I knew her story, and understood. She was betrothed as a baby of four to a lad considerably older; a lovable boy, they say he was, generous and frank. The two of course belonged to the same Caste, the Vellalar, and were thoroughly well brought up.

In South India no ceremony of importance is considered complete without the presence of " the Servants of the gods." These are girls and women belonging to the temple (that is, belonging to the priests of the temple), who, as they are never married, " except to the god who never dies," can never become widows. Hence the auspiciousness of their presence at betrothals, marriages, feasts of all sorts, and even funerals.

But this set of Vellalars had as a clan risen above the popular superstition, and the demoralising presence of these women was not allowed to profane either the betrothal or marriage of any child of the family. So the boy and girl grew up as unsullied as Hindus ever are. They knew of what happened in other homes, but their clan was a large one, and they found their society in it, and did not come across others much.

Shortly before his marriage the boy went to worship in the great temple near the sea. He had heard of its sanctity all his life, and as a little lad had often gone with his parents on pilgrimage there, but now he went to worship. He took his offering and went. He went again and again. All that he saw there was religion, all that he did was religious. Could there be harm in it?

He was married; his little bride went with him trust-fully. She knew more of him than most Indian brides know of their husbands. She had heard he was loving and she thought he would be kind to her.

A year or two passed, and the child's face had a look in it which even the careless saw, but she never spoke about anything to give them the clue to it. She went to stay in her father's house for a few weeks, and they saw the change, but she would not speak even to them.

Then things got worse. The girl grew thin, and the neighbours talked, and the father heard and understood; and, to save a scandal, he took them away from the town where they lived, and made every effort to give them another start in a place where they were not known. But the coils of that snake of deified sin had twisted round the boy, body and soul; he could not escape from it.

They moved again to another town; it followed him there, for a temple was there, and a temple means *that*.

Then the devil of cruelty seized upon him; he would drink, a disgraceful thing in his Caste, and then hold his little wife down on the floor, and stuff a bit of cloth into her mouth, and beat her, and kick her, and trample upon her, and tear the jewels out of her ears. The neighbours saw it, and told.

Then he refused to bring money to her, and she slowly starved, quite silent still, till at last hunger broke down her resolute will, and she begged the neighbours for rice. And he did more, but it cannot be told. How often one stops in writing home-letters. *The whole truth can never be told.*

She is only a girl yet, in years at least; in suffering,
oh, how old she is! Not half is known, for she never
speaks; loyal and true to him through it all. We only
know what the neighbours know, and what her silent
dark eyes tell, and the little thin face and hands.

She was very weary and ill to-day, but she would not
own it, brave little soul! I could see that neuralgia
was racking her head, and every limb trembled when she
stood up; but what made it so pathetic to me was the
silence with which she bore it all. I have only seen her
once before, and now she is going far away with her
husband to another town, and I may not see her again.
She was too tired to listen much, and she knows so little,
not nearly enough to rest her soul upon. She cannot
read, so it is useless to write to her. She is going away
quite out of our reach; thank God, not out of His.

We watched them drive off in the bullock cart, a
servant walking behind. The little pale face of the
elder girl looked out at the open end of the cart; she
salaamed as they drove away. Such a sweet face in its
silent strength, so wondrously gentle, yet so strong,
strong to endure.

Do you wonder I call this sort of thing a look deep
down into hell? Do you wonder we burn as we think
of such things going on in the Name of God? For they
think of their god as God. In His Name the temples
are built and endowed, and provided with "Servants" to
do devil's work. Yes, sin is deified here.

And the shame of shames is that many Englishmen
patronise and in measure support the iniquity. They
attend entertainments at which these girls are present to

sing and dance, and see nothing disgraceful in so doing. As lately as 1893, when the Indian Social Reformers of this Presidency petitioned two notable Englishmen to discountenance " this pernicious practice " (the institution of Slaves of the gods) " by declining to attend any entertainment at which they are invited to be present," these two distinguished men, representatives of our Queen, refused to take action in the matter. Surely this is a strange misuse of our position as rulers of India.[1]

There are so many needs everywhere that I hardly like to speak of our own, but we do need someone to work among these temple women and girls. There is practically nothing being done for them; because it is impossible for any of us to work among them and others at the same time. The nearest Home to which we could send such a one is four hundred miles away. Someone is needed, old enough to have had experience of this kind of work, and yet young enough to learn the language.

Many of these Slaves of the gods were bought, or in some other way obtained, when they were little innocent girls, and they cannot be held responsible for the terrible life to which they are doomed by the law of the Hindu religion. Many of them have hardened past any desire to be other than they are; but sometimes we see the face of a girl who looks as if she might have desire, if only she had a chance to know there is something better for her.

Can it be that, out of the many at home, God has one,

[1] For details, see *The Wrongs of Indian Womanhood*, by Mrs. Fuller.

or better, two, who can come with Him to this South Indian District to do what must always be awful work, along the course of that crack? If she comes, or if they come, let them come in the power of the Holy Ghost, baptised with the love that endures!

This, then, is one look into Hinduism, this ghastly whitened sepulchre, within which are dead men's bones.

CHAPTER XXII

Behind the Door

"When any person is known to be considering the new Religion, all his relations and acquaintances rise en masse; so that to get a new convert is like pulling out the eye-tooth of a live tiger."   Adoniram Judson, Burmah.

EVERY missionary who has despaired of hitting upon an illustration vivid enough to show you what the work is really like among Mohammedans and Caste Hindus will appreciate this simile. After our return from Dohnavur we found that the long-closed villages of this eastern countryside had opened again, and the people were willing to allow us to teach the girls and women. For two months this lasted, and then three boys, belonging to three different Castes, became known as inquirers. Instantly the news spread through all the villages. It was in vain we told them we (women-workers) had never once even seen the boys, had in no way influenced them; the people held to it that, personally responsible or not, the Book we taught to the girls was the same those boys had read (an undeniable fact); that its poison entered through the eyes, ascended to the brain, descended to the heart, and then drew the reader out of his Caste and his religion; and that therefore we could not be tolerated in the

"It took me such a long time to learn to draw nicely," said Victory when she saw this photo; "I used to go to the Brahman street every morning and practise it there." A design is drawn with a piece of chalk on the ground in front of every house each morning during part of December and January, in memory of a goddess who used to amuse herself by drawing these patterns and planting flowers in them. All sorts of geometrical designs are drawn by the women and children, and the regular morning drawing is part of the day's work.

streets or in the houses any more, and so we were turned out.

In one village where many of the relations of one of these three lads live, the tiger growled considerably. One furious old dame called us "Child-snatchers and Powder-mongers," and white snakes of the cobra species, and a particular genus of lizard, which when stamped upon merely wriggles, and cannot be persuaded to die (this applied to our persistence in evil), and a great many other things. The women stood out in the street in defiant groups and would not let us near enough to explain. The men sat on the verandah fronts and smiled, blandly superior to the childish nonsense the women talked, but they did not interfere.

Villages like this—and Old India is made up of such villages—are far removed from the influence of the few enlightened centres which exist. Madras is only a name to them, distant four hundred miles or so, a place where Caste notions are very lax and people are mixed up and jumbled together in a most unbecoming way.

Education, or "Learning," as they call it, they consider an excellent thing for boys who want to come to the front and earn money and grow rich. But for girls, what possible use is it? Can they pass examinations and get into Government employ? If you answered this question you would only disgust them. Then there is a latent feeling common enough in these old Caste families, that it is rather *infra dig.* for their women to know too much. It may be all very well for those who have no pretensions to greatness, they may need a ladder by which to climb up the social scale, but we who are

already at the top, what do we want with it? " Have
not our daughters got their *Caste*?" This feeling is passing away in the towns, but the villages hold out longer.

In that particular village we had some dear little
girls who were getting very keen, and it was so hard to
move out, and leave the field to the devil as undisputed
victor thereon, and I sent one of our workers to try
again. She is a plucky little soul, but even she had
to beat a retreat. They will have none of us.

- We went on that day to a village where they had
listened splendidly only a week before. They had no
time, it was the busy season. Then to a town, farther
on, but it was quite impracticable. So we went to our
friend the dear old Evangelist there, the blind old man.
He and his wife are lights in that dark town. It is
so refreshing to spend half an hour with two genuine
good old Christians after a tug of war with the heathen;
they have no idea they are helping you, but they are,
and you return home ever so much the happier for the
sight of them.

But as we came home we were almost mobbed. In
the old days mobs there were of common occurrence.
It is a rough market town, and the people, after the
first converts came, used to hoot us through the streets,
and throw handfuls of sand at us, and shower ashes
on our hair. In theory I like this very much, but in
practice not at all. The yellings of the crowd, men
chiefly, are not polite; the yelpings of the dogs, set on
by sympathetic spectators; the sickening blaze of the
sun and the reflected glare from the houses; the blinding
dust in your eyes, and the queer feel of ashes down

your neck; above all, the sense that this sort of thing does
no manner of good—for it is not persecution (nothing so
heroic), and it will not end in martyrdom (no such honours
come our way)—all this row, and all these feelings, one
on the top of the other, combine to make mobbing less
interesting than might be expected. You hold on, and
look up for patience and good nature and such like
common graces, and you pray that you may not be down
with fever to-morrow—for fever has a way of stopping
work—and you get out of it all, as quickly as you can,
without showing undue hurry. And then, though little
they know it, you go and get a fresh baptism of love
for them all.

But how delighted one would be to go through such
unromantic trifles every hour of every day, if only at
the end one could get into the hearts and the homes
of the people. As it is, just now, our grief is that we
cannot. We know of several who want us, and we are
shut out from them.

One is a young wife, who saw us one day by the
waterside, and asked us to come and teach her. For
doing this she was publicly beaten that evening in the
open street, by a man, before men; so, for fear of what
they would do to her, we dare not go near the house.
Another is a widow who has spent all her fortune in
building a rest-house for the Brahmans, and who has
not found Rest. She listened once, too earnestly; she has
not been allowed to listen again. Oh, how that tiger bites!

Next door to her is a child we have prayed for for
three years. She was a loving, clinging child when I
knew her then, little Gold, with the earnest eyes. That

last day I saw her, she put her hands into mine, caring
nothing for defilement; "Are we not one Caste?" she
said. I did not know it was the last time I should see
her; that the next time when I spoke to her I should
only see her shadow in the dark; and one wishes now
one had known—how much one would have said! But
the house was open then, and all the houses were. Then
the first girl convert, after bravely witnessing at home,
took her stand as a Christian. Her Caste people burned
down the little Mission school—a boys' school—and
chalked up their sentiments on the charred walls. They
burned down the Bible-woman's house and a school
sixteen miles away; and the countryside closed, every
town and village in it, as if the whole were a single
door, with the devil on the other side of it.

But some of the girls behind the door managed to
send us messages. Gold was one of these. She wanted
so much to see us again, she begged us to come and
try. We tried; we met the mother outside, and asked
her to let us come. She is a hard old woman, with
eyes like bits of black ice, set deep in her head. She
froze us, and refused.

Afterwards we heard what the child's punishment was.
They took her down to the water, and led her in. She
stood trembling, waist deep, not knowing what they
meant to do. Then they held her head under the water
till she made some sign to show she would give in.
They released her then, rubbed ashes on her brow, sign
of recantation, and they led her back sobbing—poor little
girl. She is not made of martyr stuff; she was only
miserable. For some months we saw nothing of her.

We used to go to the next house and persuade the people to let us sing to them. We sang for Gold; but we never knew if she heard.

One evening, as two of us came home late from work, a woman passed us and said hurriedly to me, "Come, come quickly, and alone. It is Gold who calls you! Come!" I followed her in the dark to the house. "I am Gold's married sister," she explained. "Sit down outside in the verandah near the door and wait till the child comes out." Then she went in, and I sat still and waited.

Those minutes were like heart-beats. What was happening inside? But apparently the mother was away, for soon the door opened softly, and a shadow flitted out, and I knew it must be Gold. She dropped on her knees on the little narrow verandah on the other side of the door and crept along to its farther end, and then I could only distinguish a dark shape in the dark. For perhaps five minutes no one came except the sister, who stood at the door and watched. And for those five minutes one was free to speak as freely as one could speak to a shape which one could barely see, and which showed no sign, and spoke no word. Five whole minutes! How one valued every moment of them! Then a man came and sat down on the verandah. He must have been a relative, for he did not mean to go. I wished he would. It was impossible to talk past him to her, without letting him know she was there; so one had to talk to him, but for her, and even this could not last long. Dusk here soon is dark; we had to go. As we went, we looked back and saw him still keeping his unconscious guard over the child in her hiding-place.

There are no secrets in India. It was known that we
had been there, and that stern old mother punished her
child; but how, we never knew.

If any blame us for going at all, let it be remembered
that one of Christ's little ones was thirsty, and she held
out her hand for a cup of cold water. We could not
have left that hand empty, I think.

After that we heard nothing for a year; then an old
man whom we had helped, and who hoped we intended
to help him more, came one evening to tell us he meant
to set Gold free. It was all to be secretly done, and it
was to be done that night. We told him we could have
nothing to do with his plan, and we explained to him
why. "But," he objected, "what folly is this? I thought
you Christians helped poor girls, and this one certainly
wants to come. She is of age. This is the time. If
you wait you will never get her at all." We knew this
was more than probable; to refuse his help was like
turning the key and locking her body and soul into
prison—an awful thought to me, as I remembered
Treasure. But there was nothing else to be done; and
afterwards, when we heard who he was, and what his real
intentions were, we were thankful we had done it. He
looked at us curiously as he went, as if our view of
things struck him as strange; and he begged us never to
breathe a word of what he had said. We never did, but
it somehow oozed out, and soon after that he sickened
and very suddenly died. His body was burnt within
two hours. Post-mortems are rare in India.

Another year passed in silence as to Gold. How often
we went down the street and looked across at her home,

with its door almost always shut, and that icy-eyed
mother on guard. We used to see her going about,
never far from the house. When we saw her we
salaamed; then she would glare at us grimly, and turn
her back on us. Once the whole family went to a
festival; but the girl of course was bundled in and out
of a covered cart, and seen by no one, not even the next-
door neighbours. There was talk of a marriage for her.
Most girls of her Caste are married much younger; but
to our relief this fell through, and once one of us saw her
for a moment, and she still seemed to care to hear, though
she was far too cowed by this time to show it.

Then we heard a rumour that a girl from the Lake
Village had been seen by some of our Christians in a
wood near a village five miles distant. These Christians
are very out-and-out and keen about converts, and they
managed to discover that the girl in the wood had some
thought of being a Christian, and that her being there
had some connection with this, so they told us at once.
The description fitted Gold. But we could not account
for a girl of her Caste being seen in a wood; she was
always kept in seclusion. At last we found out the
truth. She had shown some sign of a lingering love for
Christ, and her mother had taken her to a famous
Brahman ascetic who lived in that wood; and there
together, mother and daughter stayed in a hut near the
hermit's hut, and for three days he had devoted himself
to confuse and confound her, and finally he succeeded,
and reported her convinced.

We heard all this, and sorrowed, and wondered how
it was done. We never heard all, but we heard one

delusion they practised upon her, appealing as they so
often do to the Oriental imagination, which finds such
solid satisfaction in the supernatural. Nothing is so
convincing as a vision or a dream; so a vision appeared
before her, an incarnation, they told her, of Siva, in the
form of Christ. Siva and Christ, then, were one, as they
had so often assured her, one identity under two names.
Hinduism is crammed with incarnations; this presented
no difficulty. Like the old monk, the bewildered child
looked for the print of the nails and the spear. Yes,
they were there, marked in hands and foot and side. It
must be hard to distrust one's own mother. Gold still
trusted her. "Listen!" said the mother, and the vision
spoke. "If the speech of the Christians is true, I will
return within twenty-four days; if the speech of the
Hindus is true, I will not return." Then hour by hour
for those twenty-four days they wove their webs about her,
webs of wonderful sophistry which have entangled keener
brains than hers. She was entangled. The twenty-four
days did their work. She yielded her will on the twenty-
fifth. So the mother and the Brahman won.

These letters are written, as you know, with a definite
purpose. We try to show you what goes on behind the
door, the very door of the photograph, type of all the
doors, that seeing behind you may understand how fiercely
the tiger bites.

This is the tangible brass-bossed door outside of which we so often stand on the stone step and knock, and hear voices from within call, "Everyone is out." The hand-marks are the hand-prints of the Power that keeps the door shut. Once a year, every door and the lintel of every window, and sometimes the walls, are marked like this. That evening, just before dark, the god comes round, they say, and looks for his mark on the door, and, seeing it, blesses all in the house. If there is no mark he leaves a curse. This is the devil's South Indian parody on the Passover.

CHAPTER XXIII

"Pan, Pan is Dead"

"If there is one thing that refreshes my soul above all others, it is that I shall behold the Redeemer gloriously triumphant at the winding up of all things."   *Henry Martyn, N. India.*

"PARTLY founded upon a well-known tradition, mentioned by Plutarch, according to which, at the hour of the Saviour's Agony, a cry of, 'Great Pan is dead,' swept across the waves in the hearing of certain mariners, and the oracles ceased." So reads the head-note to one of Elizabeth Barrett Browning's poems. We look up a classical dictionary, and find the legend there. "This was readily believed by the Emperor, and the astrologers were consulted, but they were unable to explain the meaning of so supernatural a voice."

Pan, and with him all the false gods of the old world, die in the day of the death of our Saviour,—this according to the poem—

> "Gods, we vainly do adjure you,—
> Ye return nor voice nor sign!
> Not a votary could secure you
> Even a grave for your Divine;
> Not a grave, to show thereby,
> Here these grey old gods do lie.
>   Pan, Pan is dead."

And yet—is he dead? quite dead?

Night, moonless and hot. Our camp is pitched on
the west bank of the river; we are asleep. Suddenly
there is what sounds like an explosion just outside.
Then another and another,—such a burstin, bang,—then
a s-s-swish, and I am out of bed, standing out on the
sand; and for a moment I am sure the kitchen tent is
on fire. Then it dawns on me, in the slow way things
dawn in the middle of the night: it is only fireworks
being let off by the festival people—only fireworks!

But I stand and look, and in the darkness everything
seems much bigger than it is and much more awful.
There is the gleaming of water, lit by the fires of the
crowd on the eastern bank of the river. There are
torches waving uncertainly in and out of the vast black
mass—black even in the black of night—where the
people are.   There is the sudden burst and s-s-swish
of the rockets as they rush up into the night, and fall
in showers of colours on the black mass and the water;
and there is the hoarse roar of many voices, mingled
with the bleat of many goats. I stand and look, and
know what is going on. They are killing those goats—
thirty thousand of them—killing them now.

Is Pan dead? . . .

Morning, blazing sun, relentless sun, showing up all
that is going on. We are crossing the river-bed in our
cart. "Don't look!" says my comrade, and I look the
other way. Then we separate. She goes among the
crowds in the river bed, where the sun is hottest and
the air most polluted and the scenes on every side most
sickening, and I go up the bank among the people. We
have each a Tamil Sister with us, and farther down the

stream another little group of three is at work. In all seven, to tens of thousands. But we hope more will come later on.

We have arranged to meet at the cart at about ten o'clock. The bandy-man is directed to work his way up to a big banyan tree near the temple. He struggles up through a tangle of carts, and finds a slanting standing-ground on the edge of the shade of the tree.

All the way up the bank they are killing and skinning their goats. You look to the right, and put your hands over your eyes. You look to the left, and do it again. You look straight in front, and see an extended skinned victim hung from the branch of a tree. Every hanging rootlet of the great banyan tree is hung with horrors—all dead, most mercifully, but horrible still.

We had thought the killing over, or we should hardly have ventured to come; but these who are busy are late arrivals. One tells oneself over and over again that a headless creature cannot possibly feel, but it looks as if it felt . . . it goes on moving. We look away, and we go on, trying to get out of it,—but thirty thousand goats! It takes a long time to get out of it.

We see groups of little children watching the process delightedly. There is no intentional cruelty, for the god will not accept the sacrifice unless the head is severed by a single stroke—a great relief to me. But it is most disgusting and demoralising. And to think that these children are being taught to connect it with religion!

With me is one who used to enjoy it all. She tells me how she twisted the fowls' heads off with her own hands. I look at the fine little brown hands, such loving

little hands, and I can hardly believe it. "You—*you*
do such a thing!" I say. And she says, "Yes; when
the day came round to sacrifice to our family divinity,
my little brother held the goat's head while my father
struck it off, and I twisted the chickens' heads. It was
my pleasure!"

We go up along the bank; still those crowds, and
those goats killed or being killed. We cannot get away
from them.

At last we reach a tree partly unoccupied, but it is
leafless, alas! On one side of it a family party is cheerfully feeding behind a shelter of mats. A little lower
down some Pariahs are haggling over less polite portions
of the goat's economy. They wrap up the stringy things
in leaves and tuck them into a fold of their seeleys. At
our feet a small boy plays with the head. We sit down
in the band of shade cast by the trunk of the tree, and,
grateful for so much shelter, invite the passers-by to
listen while we sing. Some listen. An old hag who
is chaperoning a bright young wife draws the girl
towards us, and sits down. She has never heard a
word of our Doctrine before, and neither has the girl.
Then some boys come, full of mischief and fun, and
threaten an upset. So we pick out the rowdiest of
them and suggest he should keep order, which he does
with great alacrity, swinging a switch most vigorously
at anyone likely to interfere with the welfare of the
meeting.

My little companion speaks to them, as only one who
was once where they are ever can. I listen to her, and
long for the flow at her command. "Do you not do

this and this?" she says, naming the very things they
do; "and don't you say so and so?" They stare, and
then, "Oh, she was once one of us! What is her Caste?
When did she come? Where are her father and mother?
What is her village? Is she not married? Why is she
not? And where are her jewels?" Above all, everyone asks it at once, "What is her Caste?" And they
guess it, and probably guess right.

You can have no idea, unless you have worked among
them, how difficult it is to get a heathen woman to listen
with full attention for ten consecutive minutes. They
are easily distracted, and to-day there are so many things
to distract them, they don't listen very well. They are
tired, too, they say; the wild, rough night has done its
work. Yesterday it was different; we got good listeners.

Being women, and alone in such a crowd of idolaters,
we do not attempt an open-air meeting, but just sit
quietly where we can, and talk to any we can persuade
to sit down beside us. Hindus are safer far than
Mohammedans; they are very seldom rude; but to-day
we know enough of what is going on to make us keep
clear of all men, if we can. They would not say anything much to us, but they might say a good deal to each
other which is better left unsaid.

By the time we have gathered, and held, and then had
to let go, three or four of such little groups, it is breakfast
time, and we want our breakfast badly. So we press
through the crowd, diving under mat sheds and among
unspeakable messes, heaps of skins on either side, and
one hardly knows what under every foot of innocent-look-
ing sand; for the people bury the débris lightly, throwing

a handful of sand on the worst, and the sun does the rest of the sanitation. It is rather horrible.

At last we reach the cart, tilted sideways on the bank, and get through our breakfast somehow, and rest for a few blissful minutes, in most uncomfortable positions, before plunging again into that sea of sun and sand and animals, human and otherwise; and then we part, arranging to meet when we cannot go on any more.

Is Pan dead? . . .

Noon, and hotter, far hotter, than ever. Oh, how the people throng and push, and kill and eat, and bury remains! How can they enjoy it so? What can be the pleasure in it?

We find our way back to that ribbon of shade. It is a narrower ribbon now, because the sun, riding overhead, throws the shadow of a single bough, instead of the broader trunk. But such as it is, we are glad of it, and again we gather little groups, and talk to them, and sing.

Some beautiful girls pass us close, the only girls to be seen anywhere. Only little children and wives come here; no good unmarried girls. One of the group is dressed in white, but most are in vivid purples and crimsons. The girl in white has a weary look, the work of the night again. But most of the sisterhood are indoors; in the evening we shall see more of them, scattered among the people, doing their terrible master's work. These pass us without speaking, and mingle in the crowd.

After an hour in the band of shade, we slowly climb the bank again, and find ourselves among the potters, hundreds and hundreds of them. Every family buys a pot, and perhaps two or three of different sizes; so the potters drive a brisk trade to-day, and have no leisure to listen to us.

It is getting very much hotter now, for the burning sand and the thousands of fires radiate heat-waves up through the air, heated already stiflingly. We think of our comrades down in the river bed, reeking with odours of killing and cooking, a combination of abominations unimagined by me before.

We look down upon a collection of cart boys. The palm-woven mat covers are massed in brown patches all over the sand, and the moving crowds are between. We do not see the others. Have they found it as difficult as we find it, we wonder, to get any disengaged enough to want to listen? At last we reach the long stone aisle leading to the temple. On either side there are lines of booths, open to the air but shaded from the sun, and we persuade a friendly stall-keeper to let us creep into her shelter. She is cooking cakes on the ground. She lets us into an empty corner, facing the passing crowds, and one or two, and then two or three, and so on till we have quite a group, stop as they pass, and squat down in the shade and listen for a little. Then an old lady, with a keen old face, buys a Gospel portion at half price, and folds it carefully in a corner of her seeley. Two or three others buy Gospels, and all of them want tracts. The shop-woman gets a bit restive at this rivalry of wares. We spend our farthings, proceeds of our sales, on her cakes, and she is mollified. But some new attraction in the gallery leading to the temple disperses our little audience,

14

to collect it round itself. The old woman explains that
the Gospel she has bought is for her grandson, a scholar,
she tells us, aged five, and moves off to see the new show,
and we move off with her.

There, in the first stall, between the double row of
pillars, a man is standing on a form, whirling a sort of
crackling rattle high above his head. In the next, another
is yelling to call attention to his clocks. There they are,
ranged tier upon tier, regular "English" busy-bee clocks,
ticking away, as a small child remarks, as if they were
alive. Then come sweet-stalls, clothes-stalls, lamp-stalls,
fruit-stalls, book-stalls, stalls of pottery, and brass vessels,
and jewellery, and basket work, and cutlery, and bangles
in wheelbarrow loads, and medicines, and mats, and money
boxes, and anything and everything of every description
obtainable here. In each stall is a stall-keeper. Occasionally one, like the clock-stall man, exerts himself to sell
his goods; more often he lazes in true Oriental fashion,
and sells or not as fortune decides for him, equally satisfied with either decree. How Indian shopkeepers live at
all is always a puzzle to me. They hardly ever seem to
do anything but *moon*.

On and on, in disorderly but perfectly good-natured
streams, the people are passing up to the temple, or
coming down from worship there. All who come down
have their foreheads smeared with white ashes. Even
here there are goats; they are being pulled, poor reluctant
beasts, right to the steps of the shrine, there to be dedi-
cated to the god within. Then they will be dragged,
still reluctant, round the temple walls outside, then de-
capitated.

I watch a baby tug a goat by a rope tied round its neck. The goat has horns, and I expect every moment to see the baby gored. But it never seems to enter into the goat's head to do anything so aggressive. It tugs, however, and the baby tugs, till a grown-up comes to the baby's assistance, and all three struggle up to the shrine.

We are standing now in an empty stall, just a little out of the crush. Next door is an assortment of small Tamil booklets in marvellous colours, orange and green predominating. There is an empty barrel rolled into the corner, and we sit down on it, and begin to read from our Book. This causes a diversion in the flow of the stream, and we get another chance.

But it grows hotter and hotter, and we get so thirsty, and long for a drink of cocoanut water. It is always safe to drink that. No cocoanuts are available, though, and we have no money. Then a man selling native butter-milk comes working his way in and out of the press, and we become conscious that of all things in the world the thing we yearn for most is a drink of butter-milk. The man stops in front of our stall, pours out a cupful of that precious liquid, and seeing the thirst in our eyes, I suppose, beseeches us to drink. We explain our penniless plight. "Buy our books, and we'll buy your butter-milk," but he does not want our books. Then we wish we had not squandered our farthings on those impossible cakes. The butter-milk man proposes he should trust us for the money; he is sure to come across us again. He is a kind-hearted man; but debt is a sin; it is not likely we shall see him again. The butter-milk man considers.

He is poor, but we are thirsty. To give drink to the thirsty is an act of merit. Acts of merit come in useful, both in this world and the next. He pours out a cupful of butter-milk (he had poured the first one back when we showed our empty hands). We hesitate; he is poor, but we are so very thirsty. The next stall-keeper reads our hearts, throws a halfpenny to the butter-milk man. "There!" he says, "drink to the limit of your capacity!" and we drink. It is a comical feeling, to be beholden to a seller of small Tamil literature of questionable description; but we really are past drawing nice distinctions. Never was butter-milk so good; we get through three brass tumbler-fuls between us, and feel life worth living again. We give the good bookseller plenty of books to cover his halfpenny, and to gratify us he accepts them; but as he does not really require them, doubtless the merit he has acquired is counted as undiminished, and we part most excellent friends.

And now the crowd streaming up to the temple gets denser every moment. Every conceivable phase of devotion is represented here, every conceivable type of worshipper too. Some are reverent, some are rampant, some are earnest, some are careless, awestruck, excited, but more usually perfectly frivolous; on and on they stream.

I leave my Tamil Sister safely with two others at the cart. But the comrade whom I am to meet again at that same cart some time to-day has not turned up. So I go off alone for another try, drawn by the sight of that stream, and I let myself drift along with it, and am caught in it and carried up—up, till I am within the

temple wall, one of a stream of men and women streaming up to the shrine. We reach it at last. It is dark;
I can just see an iron grating set in darkness, with a light
somewhere behind, and there, standing on the very steps
of Satan's seat, there is a single minute's chance to
witness for Christ. The people are all on their faces
in the dust and the crush, and for that single minute
they listen, amazed at hearing any such voice in here;
but it would not do to stay, and, before they have
time to make up their minds what to make of it, I
am caught in another stream flowing round to the
right, and find myself in a quieter place, a sort of
eddy on the outer edge of the whirlpool, where the
worship is less intense, and very many women are
sitting gossiping.

There, sitting on the ground beside one of the smaller
shrines which cluster round the greater, I have such a
chance as I never expected to get; for the women and
children are so astonished to see a white face in here
that they throw all restraint to the winds, and crowd
round me, asking questions about how I got in. For
Indian temples are sacred to Indians; no alien may pass
within the walls to the centre of the shrine; moreover,
we never go to the temples to see the parts that are
open to view, because we know the stumbling-block such
sight-seeing is to the Hindus. All this the women know,
for everything a missionary does or does not do is observed by these observant people, and commented on in
private. Now, as they gather round me, I tell them why
I have come (how I got in I cannot explain, unless it
was, as the women declared, that, being in a seeley, one

was not conspicuous), and they take me into confidence, and tell me the truth about themselves, which is the last thing they usually tell, and strikes me as strange; and they listen splendidly, and would listen as long as I would stay. But it is not wise to stay too long, and I get into the stream again, which all this time has been pouring round the inner block of the temple, and am carried round with it as it pours back and out.

And as I pass out, still in that stream, I notice that the temple area is crowded with all kinds of merchandise, stalls of all sorts, just as outside. Vendors of everything, from mud pots up to jewels, are roaming over the place crying their wares, as if they had been in a market; and right in the middle of them the worship goes on at the different shrines and before the different idols. There it is, market and temple, as in the days of our Lord; neither seems to interfere with the other. No one seems to see anything incongruous in the sight of a man prostrated before a stone set at the back of a heap of glass bangles. And when someone drops suddenly, and sometimes reverently, in front of a stall of coils of oily cakes, no one sees anything extraordinary in it; they know there is a god somewhere on the other side of the cakes.

On and out, through the aisle with its hundred pillars, all stone—stone paving, pillars, roof; on and out, into the glare and the sight of the goats again. But one hardly sees them now, for between them and one's eyes seem to come the things one saw inside—those men and women, hundreds of them, worshipping that which is not God.

Is Pan dead? . . .

Pan is dead! Oh, Pan is dead! For, clearer
than the sight of that idolatrous crowd, I saw this
—I had seen it inside those temple walls:—a pile
of old, dead gods. They were bundled away in a
corner, behind the central shrine—stone gods, mere
headless stumps; wooden gods with limbs lopped off;
clay gods, mere lumps of mud; mutilated and neglected,
worn-out old gods. Oh, the worship once offered to
those broken, battered things! No one worships them
now! For full five minutes I had sat and looked
at them—

> "Gods bereavèd, gods belated,
> With your purples rent asunder!
> Gods discrowned and desecrated,
> Disinherited of thunder!"

There were withered wreaths lying at the feet of some
of the idols near; there were fresh wreaths round the
necks of others. There were no wreaths in this corner
of dead gods. I looked, and looked, and looked again.
Oh, there was prophecy in it!

And as I came out among the living people, the
sight of that graveyard of dead gods was ever with
me, and the triumph-song God's prophetess sang, sang
itself through and through me—Pan is dead! *Quite
dead!*

> "'Twas the hour when One in Sion
> Hung for love's sake on a cross;
> When His brow was chill with dying,
> And His soul was faint with loss;
> When His priestly blood dropped downward,
> And His kingly eyes looked throneward—
> Then, Pan was dead.

"Pan, Pan is Dead"

"By the love He stood alone in,
His sole Godhead rose complete,
And the false gods fell down moaning,
Each from off his golden seat;
All the false gods with a cry
Rendered up their deity—
Pan, Pan was dead."

CHAPTER XXIV

"Married to the God"

"One thing one notices very much as a 'freshman'—that is, the unconscious influence which Christianity has over a nation. Go to the most depraved wretch you can find in England, and he has probably got a conscience, if only one can get at it. *But here the result of heathenism seems to be to destroy men's consciences. They never feel sin as such.*"
Rev. E. S. Carr, India.

"I have heard people say they enjoyed hearing about missions. I often wonder if they would enjoy watching a shipwreck." *Mrs. Robert Stewart, China.*

LEAVE this chapter if you want "something interesting to read"; hold your finger in the flame of a candle if you want to know what it is like to write it. If you do this, then you will know something of the burning at heart every missionary goes through who has to see the sort of thing I have to write about. Such things do not make interesting reading. Fire is an uncompromising thing, its characteristic is that it burns; and one writes with a hot heart sometimes. There are things like flames of fire. But perhaps one cares too much; it is only about a little girl.

I was coming home from work a few evenings ago when I met two men and a child. They were Caste men in flowing white scarves—dignified, educated men. But the child? She glanced up at me, smiled, and

salaamed. Then I remembered her; I had seen her
before in her own home. These men belonged to her
village. What were they doing with her?

Then a sudden fear shot through me, and I looked at
the men, and they laughed. "We are taking her to the
temple there," and they pointed across through the trees,
"to marry her to the god."

It all passed in a moment. One of them caught her
hand, and they went on. I stood looking after them—
just looking. The child turned once and waved her
little hand to me. Then the trees came between.

The men's faces haunted me all night. I slept, and
saw them in my dreams; I woke, and saw them in the
dark. And that little girl—oh, poor little girl!—always
I saw her, one hand in theirs, and the other waving
to me!

And now it is over, the diabolical farce is over, and
she is "tied," as their idiom has it, "tied to the stone."
Oh, she is tied indeed, tied with ropes Satan twisted in
his cruellest hour in hell!

We had to drive through the village a night or two
later, and it was all ablaze. There was a crowd, and it
broke to let our bullock carts pass, then it closed round
two palanquins.

There were many men there, and girls. In the
palanquins were two idols, god and goddess, out on view.
It was their wedding night. We saw it all as we passed:
the gorgeous decorations, gaudy tinsels, flowers fading in
the heat and glare; saw, long after we had passed, the
gleaming of the coloured lights, as they moved among
the trees; heard for a mile and more along the road the

sound of that heathen revelry; and every thud of the
tom-tom was a thud upon one's heart. Our little girl
was there, as one "married" to that god.

I had seen her only once before. She belonged to an
interesting high-caste village, one of those so lately
closed; and because there they have a story about the
magic powder which, say what we will, they imagine I
dust upon children's faces, I had not gone often lest it
should shut the doors. But that last time I went, this
child came up to me, and, with all the confidingness of a
child, asked me to take her home with me. "Do let me
come!" she said.

There were eyes upon me in a moment and heads
shaken knowingly, and there were whispers at once
among the women. The magic dust had been at work!
I had "drawn" the little girl's heart to myself. Who
could doubt it now? And one mother gathered her
child in her arms and disappeared into the house. So I
had to answer carefully, so that everyone could hear. Of
course I knew they would not give her to me, and I
thought no more of it.

I was talking to her grandmother then, a very remarkable old lady. She could repeat page after page from
their beloved classics, and rather than let me sing
Christian stanzas to her and explain them, she preferred
to sing Hindu stanzas to me and explain them. "Consider the age of our great Religion, consider its literature — millions of stanzas! What can you have to
compare with it? These ignorant people about us do
not appreciate things. They know nothing of the classics;
as for the language, the depths of Tamil are beyond

them—is it not a shoreless sea?"   And so she held the conversation.

It was just at this point the child reappeared, and, standing by the verandah upon which we were sitting, her little head on a level with our feet, she joined in the stanza her grandmother was chanting, and, to my astonishment, continued through the next and the next, while I listened wondering. Then jumping up and down, first on one foot, then on the other, with her little face full of delight at my evident surprise, she told me she was learning much poetry now; and then, with the merriest little laugh, she ran off again to play.

And *this* was the child. All that brightness, all that intelligence, "married to a god."

Now I understood the question she had asked me. She was an orphan, as we afterwards heard, living in charge of an old aunt, who had some connection with the temple. She must have heard her future being discussed, and not understanding it, and being frightened, had wondered if she might come to us. But they had taken their own way of reconciling her to it; a few sweets, a cake or two, and a promise of more, a vision of the gay time the magic word marriage conjures up, and the child was content to go with them, to be led to the temple— and left there.

But her people were so thoroughly refined and nice, so educated too,—could it be, *can* it be, possibly true? Yes, it is true; this is Hinduism—not in theory of course, but in practice. Think of it; it is done to-day.

A moment ago I looked up from my writing and saw the little Elf running towards me, charmed to find me all

This is vile enough to look at, but nothing to the reality. If the outer form is this, what must the soul within it be? Yet this is a "holy Brahman;" and if we sat down on that stone verandah he would shuffle past the pillar lest we should defile him. Look at the shadowy shapes behind; they might be spirits of darkness. It is he, and such as he, who have power over little temple flowers.

alone, and quite at leisure for her. And now I watch her as she runs, dancing gleefully down the path, turning again—for she knows I am watching—to throw kisses to me. And I think of her and her childish ways, naughty ways so often, too, but in their very naughtiness only childish and small, and I shiver as I think of her, and a thousand thousand as small as she, being trained to be devil's toys. They brought one here a few days ago to act as decoy to get the Elf back. She was a beautiful child of five. Think of the shame of it!

We are told to modify things, not to write too vividly, never to harrow sensitive hearts. Friends, we cannot modify truth, we cannot write half vividly enough; and as for harrowing hearts, oh that we could do it! That we could tear them up, that they might pour out like water! that we could see hands lifted up towards God for the life of these young children! Oh, to care, and oh for power to make others care, not less but far, far more! care till our eyes do fail with tears for the destruction of the daughters of our people!

This photo is from death in life; a carcass, moving, breathing, sinning—such a one sits by that child to-day.

I saw him once. There is a monastery near the temple. He is "the holiest man in it"; the people worship him. The day I saw him they had wreathed him with fresh-cut flowers; white flowers crowned that hideous head, hung round his neck and down his breast; a servant in front carried flowers. Was there ever such desecration? That vileness crowned with flowers!

I knew something about the man. His life is simply unthinkable. Talk of beasts in human shape! It is slandering the good animals to compare bad men to beasts. Safer far a tiger's den than that man's monastery!

But he is a temple saint, wise in the wisdom of his creed; earthly, sensual, devilish. Look at him till you feel as if you had seen him. Let the photo do its work. It is loathsome—yes, *but true*.

Now, put a flower in his hand—a human flower this time. Now put beside him, if you can, a little girl—your own little girl—and leave her there—*yes, leave her there in his hand.*

CHAPTER XXV

Skirting the Abyss

*"The first thing for us all is to *see* and *feel* the great need, and to create a sentiment among Christian people on this subject. One of the characteristics of this great system is its secrecy—its subtlety. So few *know* of the evils of child-marriage, it is so hidden away in the secluded lives and prison homes of the people. And those of us who enter beyond these veils, and go down into these homes, are so apt to feel that it is a case of the inevitable, and nothing can be done."*　　　　　　　　　　　*Mrs. Lee, India.*

I HAVE been to the Great Lake Village to-day trying again to find out something about our little girl. I went to the Hindu school near the temple. The schoolmaster is a friend of ours, one of the honourable men of the village from which they took that flower. He was drilling the little Brahman boys as they stood in a row chanting the poem they were learning off by heart; but he made them stop when he saw us coming, and called us in.

I asked him about the child. It was true. She was in the temple, "married to the stone." Yes, it was true they had taken her there that day.

I asked if the family were poor; but he said, "Do not for a moment think that poverty was the cause. Certainly not. Our village is not poor!" And he looked quite offended at the thought. I knew the village was rich enough, but had thought perhaps that particular family might be poor, and so tempted to sell the little one; but he exclaimed with great warmth, Certainly not. The child was a relative of his own; there was no question of poverty!

We had left the school, and were talking out in the street facing the temple house. I looked at it, he looked at it. "From hence a passage broad, smooth, easy, inoffensive, down to hell"; he knew it well. "Yes, she is a relative of my own," he continued, and explained minutely the degree of relationship. "Her grandmother, whom you doubtless remember, is not like the ignorant women of these parts. She has learning." And again he repeated, as if desirous of thoroughly convincing me as to the satisfactory nature of the transaction, "Certainly she was not sold. She is a relative of my own."

A relative of his own! And he could teach his school outside those walls, and know what was going on inside, and never raise a finger to stop it, educated Hindu though he is. I could not understand it.

He seemed quite concerned at my concern, but explained that for generations one of that particular household had always been devoted to the gods. The practice could not be defended; it was the custom. That was all. "Our custom."

A stone's-throw from his door is another child who is living a strangely unnatural life, which strikes no one as unnatural because it is "our custom." She is quite a little girl, and as playful as a kitten. Her soft round arms and little dimpled hands looked fit for no harder work than play, but she was pounding rice when I saw her, and looked tired, and as if she wanted her mother.

While I was with her a very old man hobbled in. He was crippled, and leaned full weight with both hands on his stick. He seemed asthmatic too, and coughed and panted woefully. A withered, decrepit old ghoul. The child stood up when he came in and touched her neck where the marriage symbol lay. Then I knew he was her husband.

"What,
No blush at the avowal—you dared to buy
A girl of age beseems your grand-daughter, like ox or ass?
Are flesh and blood ware? are heart and soul a chattel?"

Yes! like chattels they are sold to the highest bidder. In that auction Caste comes first, then wealth and position. And the chattel is bought, the bit of breathing flesh and blood is converted into property; and the living, throbbing heart of the child may be trampled and stamped down under foot in the mire and the mud of that market-place, for all anyone cares.

It is not long since a young wife came for refuge to our house. Three times she had tried to kill herself; at last she fled to us. Her husband came. "Get up, slave," he said, as she crouched on the floor. She would not stir or speak. Then he got her own people to come, and then it was as if a pent-up torrent was bursting out of an over full heart. "You gave me to him. You gave me to him." The words came over and over again; she reminded them in a passion of reproach how, knowing what his character was, they had handed her over to him. But we could hardly follow her, the words poured

15

forth with such fierce emotion, as with streaming eyes,
and hands that showed everything in gestures, she besought them not to force her back. They promised, and
believing them, she returned with them. The other day
when I passed the house someone said, "Beautiful is
there. He keeps her locked up in the back room now."
So they had broken their word to her, and given her
back, body and soul, to the power of a man whose cruelty
is so well known that even the heathen call him a
"demon." What must he be to his wife?

And if that poor wife, nerved by the misery of her
life, dared all, and appealed to the Government, the law
would do as her people did—force her back again to him,
to fulfil a contract she never made. Is it not a shame?
Oh, when will the day come when this merchandise in
children's souls shall cease? We know that many husbands are kind, and many wives perfectly content, but
sometimes we see those who are not, and there is no
redress.

Another of our children sold by auction in the Village
of the Lake is one who used to be such a pretty little
thing, with a tangle of curls, and mischievous, merry
brown eyes. But that was five years ago. Then a fiend
in a man's shape saw her, and offered inducements to her
parents which ended in his marrying her. She was nine
years old.

One year afterwards she was sent to her husband's
home. His motives in marrying her were wholly evil,
but the child knew something of right and wrong,
and she resisted him. Then he dragged her into an
inner room, and he held her down, and smothered her

shrieks, and pressed a plantain into her mouth. It was poisoned. She knew it, and did not swallow it all. But what she was forced to take made her ill, and she lay for days so dizzy and sick that when her husband kicked her as she lay she did not care. At last she escaped, and ran to her mother's house. But the law was on her owner's side; what could she prove of all this, poor child? And she had to go back to him. After that he succeeded in his devil's work, and to-day that child is dead to all sense of sin.

Oh, there are worse things far than seeing a little child die! It is worse to see it change. To see the innocence pass from the eyes, and the childishness grow into wickedness, and to know, without being able to stop it, just what is going on.

I am thinking of one such now. She was four years old when I first began to visit in her grandmother's house. She is six now—only six—but her demoralisation is almost complete. It is as if you saw a hand pull a rosebud off its stem, crumple and crush it, rub the pink loveliness into pulp, drop it then—and you pick it up. But it is not a rosebud now. Oh, these things, the knowledge of them, is as a fire shut up in one's bones! shut up, for one cannot let it all out—it must stay in and burn.

.   .   .   .

Those who know nothing of the facts will be sure to criticise. " It is not an unknown thing for persons to act as critics, even though supremely ignorant of the subject criticised." But those who know the truth of these things well know that we have understated it, carefully toned it down perforce, because it cannot be written in full. It could neither be published nor read.

It cannot be written or published or read, but oh, it has to be lived! *And what you may not even hear, must be endured by little girls.* There are child-wives in India to-day, of twelve, ten, nine, and even eight years old. "Oh, you mean betrothed! Another instance of missionary exaggeration!" We mean married.

"But of course the law interferes!" Perhaps you have heard of the noble law which makes wifehood illegal under twelve. Oh, how the word "law" can blind our eyes, and make us think that all is right when all is utterly wrong! India needs braver laws than that, laws of a surgical character which will cut the cancer out. May God create a conscience upon this subject, and give the courage that is needed to deal in some more drastic fashion with this foul hidden sore.

There are men and women in India to whom many a day is a nightmare, and this fair land an Inferno, because of what they know of the wrong that is going on. For that is the dreadful part of it. It is not like the burning alive of the widows, it is not a horror passed. It is going on steadily day and night. Sunlight, moonlight, and darkness pass, the one changing into the other; but all the time they are passing, this Wrong holds the hours with firm and strong hands, and uses them for its purpose— the murder of little girls. Meanwhile, what can be done by you and by me to hasten the day of its ending? Those who know can tell what they know, or so much as will bear the telling; and those who do not know can believe it is true, and if they have influence anywhere,

use it; and all can care and pray! Praying alone is not
enough, but oh for more real praying! We are playing
at praying, and caring, and coming; playing at doing—
if doing costs—playing at everything but play. We are
earnest enough about that. God open our eyes and
convict us of our insincerity! burn out the superficial
in us, make us intensely in earnest! And may God
quicken our sympathy, and touch our heart, and nerve
our arm for what will prove a desperate fight against
" leaguèd fiends" in bad men's shapes, who do the devil's
work to-day, branding on little innocent souls the very
brand of hell.

I have told of one—that little child who is now as
evil-minded as a little child can be; she is only one of so
many. Let a medical missionary speak.

"A few days ago we had a little child-wife here as a
patient. She was ten or eleven, I think, just a scrap
of a creature, playing with a doll, and yet degraded un-
mentionably in mind. . . . But oh, to think of the
hundreds of little girls! . . . It makes me feel literally
sick. We do what we can. . . . But what can we do?
What a drop in the ocean it is!"

Where the dotted lines come, there was written what
cannot be printed. But it had to be lived through,
every bit of it, by a "scrap of a creature of ten or
eleven."

Another—these are from a friend who, even in writing
a private letter, cannot say one-tenth of the thing she
really means.

"A few days ago the little mother (a child of thirteen)
was crying bitterly in the ward. 'Why are you crying?'

'Because he says I am too old for him now; he will get
another wife, he says.' 'He' was her husband, 'quite a
lad,' who had come to the hospital to see her."

The end of that story which cannot be told is being
lived through this very day by that little wife of thirteen.
And remember that thirteen in India means barely eleven
at home.

"She was fourteen years old," they said, "but such a
tiny thing, she looked about nine years old in size and
development. . . . The little mother was so hurt, she
can never be well again all her life. The husband then
married again . . . as the child was ruined in health . . ."
And, as before, the dots must cover all the long-drawn-out
misery of that little child who "looked about nine."

"There is an old, old man living near here, with a little
wife of ten or eleven. . . . Our present cook's little girl,
nine years old, has lately been married to a man who
already has had two wives." In each of these cases, as
in each I have mentioned, marriage means marriage,
not just betrothal, as so many fondly imagine. Only
to-day I heard of one who died in what the nurse who
attended her described as "simple agony." She had
been married a week before. She was barely twelve
years old.

We do not say this is universal. There are many
exceptions; but we do say the workings of this custom
should be exposed and not suppressed. Question our
facts; we can prove them. To-day as I write it, to-day
as you read it, hundreds and thousands of little wives are
going through what we have described. But "described"
is not the word to use—indicated, I should say, with the

faintest wash of sepia where the thing meant is pitch black.

Think of it, then—do not try to escape from the thought—English women know too little, care too little —too little by far. Think of it. Stop and think of it. If it is "trying" to think of it, and you would prefer to turn the page over, and get to something nicer to read, *what must it be to live through it*? What must it be to those little girls, so little, so pitifully little, and unequal to it all? What must it be to these childish things to live on through it day by day, with, in some cases, nothing to hope for till kindly death comes and opens the door, the one dread door of escape they know, and the tortured little body dies? And someone says, "The girl is dead, take the corpse out to the burying-ground." Then they take it up, gently perhaps. But oh, the relief of remembering it! It does not matter now. Nothing matters any more. Little dead wives cannot feel.

. . . .

I wonder whether it touches you? I know I cannot tell it well. But oh, one lives through it all with them! —I have stopped writing again and again, and felt I could not go on.

Mother, happy mother! When you tuck up your little girl in her cot, and feel her arms cling round your neck and her kisses on your cheek, will you think of these other little girls? Will you try to conceive what you would feel *if your little girl were here*?

Oh, you clasp her tight, so tight in your arms! The thought is a scorpion's sting in your soul. You would

kill her, smother her dead in your arms, before you
would give her to—*that*.

Turn the light down, and come away. Thank God she
is safe in her little cot, she will wake up to-morrow safe.
Now think for a moment steadily of those who are
somebody's little girls, just as dear to them and sweet
needing as much the tenderest care as this your own
little girl.

Think of them. Try to think of them as if they
were your very own. They are just like your own, in
so many ways—only their future is different.

Oh, dear mothers, do you care? Do you care very
much, I ask?

We passed the temple on our way home from the
Village of the Lake. The great gate was open, and the
Brahmans and their friends were lounging in and out,
or sitting in the porch talking and laughing together.
They were talking about us as we passed. They were
quite aware of our object in coming, and were pleased
that we had failed.

Government officials, English-speaking graduates, educated Hindus like our old friend the schoolmaster, all
would admit in private that to take a child to the temple
and "marry her" there was wrong. But very few have
much desire to right the shameful wrong.

There are thousands of recognised Slaves of the gods
in this Presidency. Under other names they exist all
over India. There are thousands of little child-wives;
fewer here than elsewhere, we know, but many everywhere. I do not for a moment suggest that all child-

wives are cruelly handled, any more than I would have it thought that all little girls are available for the service of the gods. Nor would I have it supposed that we see down this hell-crack every day. We may live for years in the country and know very little about it. The medical workers—God help them!—are those who are most frequently forced to look down, and I, not being a medical, know infinitely less of its depths than they. But this I do know, and do mean, and I mean it with an intensity I know not how to express, *that this custom of infant marriage and child marriage, whether to gods or men, is an infamous custom; that it holds possibilities of wrong, such unutterable wrong, that descriptive words concerning it can only " skirt the abyss," and that in the name of all that is just and all that is merciful it should be swept out of the land without a day's delay.*

We look to our Indian brothers. India is so immense that a voice crying in the North is hardly heard in the South. Thank God for the one or two voices crying in the wilderness. But many voices are needed, not only one or two. Let the many voices cry! Every man with a heart and a voice to cry, should cry. Then all the cries crying over the land will force the deaf ears to hear, and force the dull brains to think and the hands of the law to act, and something at last will be done.

But "crying" is not nearly enough. We look to you, brothers of India, to do. Get convictions upon this subject which will compel you to do. Many can talk and many can write, and more will do both, as the years pass, but the crux is contained in the doing.

God alone can strengthen you for it. He who set His face as a flint, can make you steadfast and brave enough to set your faces as flints, till the bands of wickedness are loosed, and the heavy burdens are undone, and every yoke is broken, and the oppressed go free.

It will cost. It is bound to cost. Every battle of the warrior is with confused noise and garments rolled in blood. It is only sham battles that cost something less than blood. Everything worth anything *costs blood.* "Reproach hath broken My heart." A broken heart bleeds. Is it the reproach of the battle you fear? This fear will conquer you until you hear the voice of your God saying, "Fear ye not the reproach of men, neither be afraid of their revilings. . . . Who art thou that thou shouldest be afraid of a man that shall die, and the son of man that shall be made as grass, and forgettest the Lord thy Maker?"

This book is meant for our comrades at home, but it may come back to India, and so we have spoken straight from our hearts to our Indian brothers here. Oh, brothers, rise, and in God's Name fight; in His power fight till you win, for these, your own land's little girls, who never can fight for themselves!

And now we look to you at home. Will all who pity the little wives pray for the men of India? Pray for those who are honestly striving to rid the land of this shameful curse. Pray that they may be nerved for the fight by the power of God's right arm. Pray for all the irresolute. "A sound of battle is in the land, . . . the Lord hath opened His armoury." "Cursed be he that keepeth back his sword from blood." Pray for resolution and the courage of conviction. It is needed.

And to this end pray that the Spirit of Life may come upon our Mission Colleges, and mightily energise the Missionary Educational Movement, that Hindu students may be won to out-and-out allegiance to Christ while they are students, before they become entangled in the social mesh of Hinduism. And pray, we earnestly plead with you, that the Christian students may meet God at college, and come out strong to fight this fiend which trades in "slaves and souls of men"—and in the souls of little girls.

CHAPTER XXVI

From a Hindu Point of View

"The Lord preserve us from innovations foreign to the true principles of the Protestant Church, and foreign to the principles of the C.M.S. Pictures, crosses, and banners, with processions, would do great harm. The Mohammedan natives would say, 'Wah! you worship idols as the Hindus do, and have taziyas (processions) as well as the Mohammedans!' And our Christians would mourn over such things."

Rev. C. B. Leupolt, India.

I AM sitting in the north-west corner of the verandah of a little mission bungalow, on the outskirts of a town sixteen miles south of our Eastern headquarters. This is the town where they set fire to the schoolroom when Victory came. So far does Caste feeling fly. As you sit in the corner of this verandah you see a little temple fitted between two whitewashed pillars, roughly built and rudely decorated, but in this early morning light it looks like a picture set in a frame. It is just outside the compound, so near that you see it in all its detail of colour; the sun striking across it touches the colours and makes them beautiful.

There is the usual striped wall, red and white; the red is a fine terra-cotta, the colour of the sand. The central block, the shrine itself, has inlays of green, red, and blue; there is more terra-cotta in the roof, some yellow too, and white. Beyond on either side there are houses, and beyond the houses, trees and sky.

It is all very pretty and peaceful. Smoke is curling up in the still air from some early lighted fire out of doors; there are voices of people going and coming, softened by distance. There is the musical jingle of bullock bells here in the compound and out on the road, and there is the twitter of birds.

In front of that temple there are three altars, and in front of the altars a pillar. I can see it from where I am sitting now, rough grey stone. Beside it, there is what I thought at first was a sun-dial, and I wondered what it was doing there. Then I saw it had not a dial plate; only a strong cross-bar of wood, and the index finger, so to speak, was longer than one would expect, a sharp wooden spike. As I was wondering what it was a passer-by explained it. It is not a sun-dial, it is an impaling instrument. On that spike they used to impale alive goats and kids and fowls as offerings to the god Siva and his two wives, the deities to whose honour the three altars stand before the little shrine. The pillar on which stands this infernal spike has three circles scored into it, sign of the three divinities.

"The impaling has stopped," say the people, greatly amused at one's horror and distress, for at first I thought perhaps they still did it. "Now we do not impale alive; the Government has stopped it." Thank God for that! But oh, let all lovers of God's creatures pray for and hasten the coming of our Lord Jesus Christ! Government may step in and stop the public clubbing to death of buffaloes, and the impaling of goats and fowls in sacrifice, but it cannot stop the private cruelty, and the still wider-spread indifference on the part of those who are not themselves cruel; only the coming of Christ the Compassionate can do that.

.   .   .   .   .   .

There was the sound of voices just then, as I wrote, many voices, coming nearer, shrill women's voices, cutting through one's thoughts, and I went out to see what was going on.

On the other side of the road, opposite our gate, there is a huge old double tree, the sacred fig tree of India, intertwined with another—a religious symbol to this symbol-loving people. Underneath is a stone platform, and on it the hideous elephant-god. On the same side is a little house. A group of women were gathered under the shade near the house, evidently waiting for something or someone. They were delighted to talk.

We spent half an hour under the tree, and they listened; but we were interrupted by some well-dressed Government officials with their coats, sashes, and badges, and one not strictly Governmental got up in a marvellous fashion, and they joined the group and monopolised the conversation. I waited, hoping they would soon go away, and I listened to what they were saying.

"Yes! she actually appeared! She was a goddess." ("A goddess! Oh!" from the women.) "She came forward, moving without walking, and she stood as a tree stands, and she stretched out her arms and blessed the people, and vanished."

A woman pointed to me. "Like her? Was she like her?"

"Like her!" and the Government official was a little contemptuous. "Did I not say she was a goddess? Is this Missie Ammal a goddess? Is she not a mere woman like yourselves, only white?"

"*She* also came from the bungalow," objected the woman rather feebly, feeling public opinion against her.

"You oyster!" said the official politely, "because a Missie Ammal comes from the bungalow, does it prove that the goddess was a Missie Ammal?" The other women agreed with him, and snubbed the ignoramus, who retired from the controversy.

The story was repeated with variations, such a mixture of the probable with the improbable, not to say impossible, that one got tangled up in it before he had got half through.

Just then an ancient Christian appeared on the scene and quavered in, in the middle of the marvel, with words to the effect that our God was the true God, and they ought to have faith in Him. It was not exactly *à propos* of anything they were discussing, but he seemed to think it the right thing to say, and they accepted it as a customary remark, and went on with their conversation. I asked the old worthy if he knew anything about the story, and at first he denied it indignantly as savouring too much of idolatry to be connected with the bungalow, but finally admitted that once in the dim past he had heard that an Ammal in the bungalow, who was ill and disturbed by the tom-toms at night, got up and went out and tried to speak to the people. And the men, listening now to the old man, threw in a word which illumined the whole, "It was a great festival." I remembered that impaling stake, and understood it all. And in a

240 FROM A HINDU POINT OF VIEW

flash I saw it—the poor live beast—and heard its cries.
They would wring her heart as she heard them in the
pauses of the tom-tom. She was ill, but she got up and
struggled out, and tried to stop it, I am sure—tried, and
failed.

Seven thousand miles away these things may seem
trivial. Here, with that grey stone pillar full in view,
they are real.

I came back to the present. The women were still
there, and more people were gathering. Something was
going to happen. Then a sudden burst of tom-toms, and
a banging and clanging of all manner of noise-producers,
and then a bullock coach drove up, a great gilded thing.
It stopped in front of the little house; someone got out;
the people shouted, "Guru! Great Guru! Lord Guru!"
with wild enthusiasm.

The Guru was not poor. He had two carts laden
with luggage—one item, a green parrot in a cage. Close
to the cage a small boy was thundering away on a tom-
tom, but it did not disturb the parrot. The people
seemed to think this display of wealth demanded an
apology. "It is not his, it belongs to his followers; he,
being what he is, requires none of these things," they
said.

I had to go then, and we started soon afterwards on
our day's round, and I do not know what happened
next; but I had never had the chance of a talk with a
celebrity of this description, and in the evening, on my
homeward way, I stopped before the little house and
asked if I might see him, the famous Guru of one of the
greatest of South Indian Castes.

The Government officials of the morning were there, but the officialism was gone. No coats and sashes and badges now, only the simple national dress, a scarf of white muslin. The one who in the morning had been an illustration of the possible effect of the mixture of East and West, stood in a dignity he had not then, a fine manly form.

The door was open, and they were sentry, for their Guru was resting, they said. "Then he is very human, just like yourselves?" But the strong, sensible faces looked almost frightened at the words. "Hush," they answered all in a breath, "no such thoughts may be even thought here. He is not just like us." And as if to divert us from the expression of such sentiments, they moved a little from the door, and said, "You may look, if you do not speak," and knowing such looks are not often allowed, I looked with interest, and saw all there was to see.

The Guru was in the far corner resting; a rich purple silk, with gold interwoven in borders and bands, was flung over his ascetic's dress. At the far end, too, was a sort of altar, covered with red cloth, and on it were numerous brass candlesticks and vessels, and on a little shelf above, a row of little divinities, some brass ornaments, and flowers.

To the left of this altar there was a high-backed chair, covered by a deer skin; there were pictures of gods and goddesses round the room, especially near the altar, and there were the usual censers, rosaries, and musical instruments, and there was the parrot.

The Government official pointed in, and said, with an

air of pride in the whole, and a certainty of sympathy
too, "There, you see how closely it resembles your
churches; there is not so much difference between you
and us after all!"

Not so much difference! There is a very great difference, I told him; and I asked him where he had seen a
Christian church like this. He mentioned two. One
was a Roman Catholic chapel, the other an English
church.

What could I say? They bear our name; how could
he understand the divisions that rend us asunder?—
Romanists, Ritualists, and Protestants—are we not all
called Christians!

I looked again, and I could not help being struck with
the resemblance. The altar with its brasses and flowers
and candlesticks, and the little shelf above; the pictures
on the walls; the chair, so like a Bishop's chair of
state; the whole air of the place heavy with incense,
was redolent of Rome.

He went on to explain, while I stood there ashamed.
"Look, have you not got that?" and he pointed to the
altar-like erection, with the red cloth and the flowers.

"We have nothing of the sort in our church. Come
and see; we have only a table," I said; but he laughed
and declared he had seen it in other churches, and it
was just like ours, "only yours has a cross above it, and
ours has images; but you bow to your cross, so it must represent a divinity," and, without waiting for any reply, he
pointed next to the pictures.

"They are very like yours, I think," he said, "only
yours show your God on a cross, stretched out and dying

—so "— And he stretched out his arms, and drooped his head, and said something which cannot be translated; and I could not look or listen, but broke in earnestly:

"Indeed, we have no such pictures—at least we here have not; but even if some show such a picture, do they ever call it a picture of God? They only say it is a picture of "— But he interrupted impatiently:

"Do not I know what they say?" And then, with a touch of scorn at what he thought was an empty excuse on my part, he added, "We also say the same" (which is true; no intelligent Hindu admits that he worships idols or pictures; he worships what these things represent). "Your people show your symbols," he continued, in the tone of one who is sure of his ground, "exactly as we show ours. I have seen your God on a great sheet at night; it was shown by means of a magic lamp; and sometimes you make it of wood or brass, as we make ours of stone. The name may change and the manner of making, but the thing's essence is the same."

"The Mohammedans do not show their God's symbol; but we do, and so do the Christians. Therefore between us and the Christians there is more in common than between the Mohammedans and us." This was another Hindu's contribution to the argument.

The chair now served as a text. "When your Bishop comes round your churches, does he not sit in a chair like that, himself apart from the people? And in like manner our Guru sits. There is much similarity. Also do not your Christians stand "—and he imitated the peculiarly deferential attitude adopted on such occasions by some—"just in the fashion that we stand? And do

not your people feel themselves blessed by the presence
of the Great? Oh, there is much similarity!"

I explained that all this, though foolish, was not intended for more than respect, and our Bishops did not
desire it; at which he smiled. Then he went on to
expatiate upon what he had seen in some of our churches
(probably while on duty as Government servant): the
display, as it seemed to him, so like this; the pomp, as
he thought it, so fine, like this; the bowing and pros-
trating, and even on the part of those who did not do
these things, the evident participation in the whole grand
show. And the other men, who apparently had looked in
through the open windows and doors, agreed with him.

He is not the first who has been stumbled in the
same way; and I remembered, as he talked, what a
Mohammedan woman said to a friend of mine about one
of our English churches, seen through her husband's eyes.
"You have idols in your church," she said, "to which
you bow in worship." She referred to the things on or
above the Communion table. My friend explained the
things were not idols. "Then why do your people bow
to them?" Was there nothing in the question?

Often we wonder whether the rapid but insidious
increase of ritual in India is understood at home. In
England it is bad enough, but in a heathen and Mohammedan land it is, if possible, worse; and the worst is, the
spirit of it, or the spirit of tolerance toward it, which is
on the increase even in missionary circles. Some of
our Tamil people attend the English service in these
"advanced" churches after their own service is over, and
thus become familiarised with and gradually acclimatised

to an ecclesiastical atmosphere foreign to them as
members of a Protestant Society.

I remember spending a Sunday afternoon with a
worthy pastor and his wife, stationed in the place where
the church is in which the "idols are worshipped"
according to the Mohammedans. When the bell rang
for evening service he began to shuffle rather as if he
wanted me to go. But he was too polite to say so, and
the reason never struck me till his son came in with an
English Bible and Prayer-Book. The old man put up
his hand to his mouth in the apologetic manner of the
Tamils. "We do not notice the foolish parts of the
service. We like to hear the English. For the sake of
the English we go."

"He did not turn to the East, but he did not keep
quite straight; he just half turned." This from a pastor's
wife, about one whom she had been observing during an
ordination ceremony in the English cathedral. "*He just
half turned.*" It describes the nebulous attitude of mind
of many a one to-day. India has not our historical
background. It has no Foxe's *Book of Martyrs* yet.
Perhaps that is why its people are so indifferent upon
points which seem of importance to us. They have not
had to fight for their freedom, in the sense at least our
forefathers fought; there is no Puritan blood in their
veins; and so they are willing to follow the lead of
almost anyone, provided that lead is given steadily and
persistently; which surely should make those in authority
careful as to those in whose hands that lead is placed.

But the natural instinct of the converted idolater is
dead against complexity in worship, and for simplicity.

He does not want something as like his own old religion
as possible, but as different as possible from it; and so we
have good building material ready to hand, and a foundation ready laid. "But let every man take heed how he
buildeth thereupon."

I hope this does not sound unkind. We give those
who hold different views full credit for sincerity, and a
right to their own opinions; but convictions are convictions, and, without judging others who differ, these are
ours, and we want those at home who are with us in
these things to unite to help to stem the tide that has
already risen in India far higher than perhaps they know.
Brave men are needed, men with a fuller development of
spiritual vertebræ than is common in these easy-going
days, and we need such men in our Native Church. God
create them; they are not the product of theological
colleges. And may God save His Missions in India
from wasting His time, and money, and men, on the
cultivation of what may evolve into something of no
more use to creation than a new genus of jelly-fish.

The Government official and his friends were still
talking among themselves: "Do we not know what
the Christians do? Have we not ears? Have we not
eyes? They do it in their way, we do it in ours. The
thing itself is really the same. Yes, their religion is
just like ours."

They could not see the vital difference between even
the most vitiated forms of Christianity and their own
Hinduism; there were so many resemblances, and these
filled their mental vision at the moment. One could
hardly wonder they could not.

They turned to me again, and with all the vigour of language at my command I told them that neither we nor those with us ever went to any church where we had reason to think there would be an exhibition of ecclesiastical paraphernalia. We did not believe it was in accordance with the simplicity of the Gospel; and I told them how simple the Truth really was, but they would not believe me. Those sights they had seen had struck them much as they struck the convert who described the Confirmation service thus: "We went up and knelt down before a stick" (the Bishop's pastoral staff). They had observed the immense attention paid to all these sacred trifles, and naturally they appeared to them as essential to the whole; part of it, nearly all of it, in fact; and even where the service was in the vernacular, their attention had been entirely diverted from the thing heard by the things seen.

Then I thought of the description of a primitive Christianity service as given in 1 Corinthians. There the idea evidently was that if an outsider came in, or looked in, as Hindus and Mohammedans so often look in here, he should understand what was going on; and being convicted of his sin and need, should be "convinced"; "and so, falling down on his face, he will worship God, and report that God is in you of a truth." Compare the effect produced upon the minds of these Hindu men by what they saw of our services, with the effect intended to be produced by the Holy Ghost. Can we say we have improved upon His pattern?

Oh for a return to the simplicity and power of the

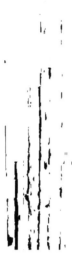

of the signs of Apostleshi
real cross—the reproach
mitre here, but there the

CHAPTER XXVII

Though ye know Him not

"I have known cases of young ministers dissuaded from facing the missionary call by those who posed as friends of Foreign Missions, and yet presumed to argue: 'Your spiritual power and intellectual attainments are needed by the Church at home; they would be wasted in the Foreign Field.' 'Spiritual power wasted' in a land like India! Where is it so sorely needed as in a continent where Satan has constructed his strongest fortresses and displayed the choicest masterpieces of his skill? 'Intellectual ability wasted' among a people whose scholars smile inwardly at the ignorance of the average Western! Brothers, *if God is calling you*, be not deterred by flimsy subterfuges such as these. You will need the power of God the Holy Ghost to make you an efficient missionary. You will find your reputation for scholarship put to the severest test in India. Here is ample scope alike for men of approved spiritual power and for intellectual giants. And so I repeat, *if God is calling you*, buckle on your sword, come to the fight, and win your spurs among the cultured sons of India."

Rev. T. Walker, India.

THE sensation you experience is curious when you rise from the study of Sir Monier Williams' *Brahmanism and Hinduism* and go out to your work, and meet in that work someone who seems to be quoting that same book, not in paragraphs only, but in pages. He is talking Tamil, and the book is written in English; that is all the difference. He was standing by the wayside when I saw him: we got into conversation.

At first he reminded me of a sea anemone, with all its tentacles drawn inside, but gradually one by one they came out, and I saw what he really was; and I think the great Christian scholar, who laboured so hard to understand and translate into words the intricacies and mysteries of Indian thought, would have felt a little repaid had he known how his work would help in the practical business of a missionary's life. Part of our business is to meet the mind with which we are dealing half-way with quick comprehension. It is in this Sir Monier Williams helps.

When once this man felt himself understood, his whole attitude changed. At first, expecting, I suppose, that he was being mistaken for "an ignorant heathen" and worshipper of stocks and stones, he hardly took the trouble to do more than answer, as he thought, a fool according to his folly. The tentacles were all in then.

But that passed soon, and he pointed to the shed behind him, where two or three life-size idol horses stood, and said how childish he knew it was, foolish and vain. But then, what else could be done? Idols are not objects of worship, and never were intended so to be; their only use is to help the uninitiated to worship Something. If nothing were shown them, they would worship nothing; and a non-worshipping human being is an animal, not a man.

He went on to answer the objections to this means of quickening intelligent worship by explaining how, in higher and purer ways, the thinkers of Hinduism had tried to make the unthinking think. "Look at our

temples," he said. " There is a central shrine, with only
one light in it. The darkness of the shrine symbolises
the darkness of the world, of life and death and
being. For life is a darkness, a whirlpool of dark
waters. We stand on its edge, but we do not understand it. It is dark, but light there must be; one
great light. So we show this certainty by the symbol
of the one light in the shrine, in the very heart of our
temples."

This led on to quotations from his own books, question-
ing the validity of such lights, which he finished the
moment one began them, and this again led to our Lord's
words,—how strong they sounded, and how direct—"*I
am the Light of the World.*" But he could not accept
them in their simplicity, and here it was that the book I
had been reading came in so helpfully. He spoke rapidly
and eagerly, and such a mixture of Sanscrit and Tamil
that if I had not had the clue I am not sure I could
have followed him, and to have misunderstood him then
might have driven all the tentacles in, and made it harder
for the next one whom the Spirit may send to win his
confidence.

He told me that, after much study of many religions,
he held the eternal existence of one, Brahma. The human
spirit, he said, is not really distinct from the Divine
Spirit, but identical with it; the apparent distinction
arises from our illusory view of things: there is absolutely
no distinction in spirit. Mind is distinct, he admitted,
and body is distinct, but spirit is identical; so that, " in
a definitely defined sense, I am God, God is I. The so-
called two are one, in all essentials of being." And he

touched himself and said, "I am Brahma.   I myself, my
real I, am God."

It sounds terribly irreverent, but he did not for a
moment mean it so.   Go back to Gen. ii. 7, and try to
define the meaning of the words, "the breath of life," and
you will, if you think enough, find yourself in a position
to understand how the Hindu, without revelation, ends as
he does in delusion.

But, intertwined with this central fibre of his faith,
there were strands of a strange philosophy; he held
strongly the doctrine of Illusion, by which the one im-
personal Spirit, "in the illusion which overspreads it, is
to the external world what yarn is to cloth, what milk is
to curds, what clay is to a jar, but only in that illusion,"
that is, "he is not the actual material cause of the world,
as clay of a jar, but the illusory material cause, as a rope
might be of a snake"; and the spirit of man "is that
Spirit, personalised and limited by the power of illusion;
and the life of every living spirit is nothing but an
infinitesimal arc of the one endless circle of infinite
existence."

Of course there are answers to this sort of reasoning
which are perfectly convincing to the Western, but they
fail to appeal to the Eastern mind.   You suggest a
practical test as to the reality or otherwise of this
"Illusion"—touch something, run a pin into yourself,
do anything to prove to yourself your own actuality,
and he has his answer ready.   Though theoretically
he holds that there is one, and only one, Spirit, he
"virtually believes in three conditions of being—the real,
the practical, and the illusory; for while he affirms

that the one Spirit, Brahma, alone has a real existence, he allows a practical separate existence to human
spirits, to the world, and to the personal God or gods,
as well as an illusory existence. Hence every object is
to be dealt with practically, as if it were really what it
appears to be."

This is only the end of a long and very confusing
argument, which I expect I did not half understand, and
he concluded it by quoting a stanza, thus translated by
Dr. Pope, from an ancient Tamil classic—

> "O Being hard to reach,
> O Splendour infinite, unknown, in sooth
> I know not what to do!"

"He is far away from me," he said, "a distant God to
reach," and when I quoted from St. Augustine, "To Him
who is everywhere, men come not by travelling, but by
loving," and showed him the words, which in Tamil are
splendidly negative, "He is NOT far from every one of
us," he eluded the comfort and went back to the old
question, "What is Truth? How can one prove what is
Truth?"

There is an Indian story of a queen who "proved the
truth by tasting the food." The story tells how her
husband, who dearly loved her, and whom she dearly
loved, lost his kingdom, wandered away with his queen
into the forest, left her there as she slept, hoping she
would fare better without him, and followed her long
afterwards to her father's court, deformed, disguised, a
servant among servants, a *cook*. Then her maidens came
to her, told her of the wonderful cooking, magical in
manner, marvellous in flavour and in fragrance. They are

sure it is the long-lost king come back to her, and they
bid her believe and rejoice. But the queen fears it may
not be true. She must prove it, she must taste the food.
They bring her some. *She tastes, and knows.* And the
story ends in joy. "Oh, taste and see that the Lord is
good." "If any man will do His Will, he shall know."

We got closer in thought after this. For the Oriental,
a story is an illuminating thing. "I have sought for the
way of truth," he said, "and sought for the way of light
and life. Behind me, as I look, there is darkness. Before me there is only the Unknown." And then, with an
earnestness I cannot describe, he said, "I worship Him I
know not, *the Unknown God.*" "Whom, therefore, ye
worship, though ye know Him not, Him declare I unto
you." One could only press home God's own answer to
his words.

One other verse held him in its power before I went:
"I am the Way, the Truth, and the Life." With those
two verses I left him.

It was evening, and he stood in the shadow, looking
into it. There was a tangle of undergrowth, and a heavy
grove of palms. It was all dark as you looked in. Behind was the shrine of the demon steeds, the god and his
wife who ride out at night to chase evil spirits away.
Near by was an old tree, also in shade, with an idol under
it. It was all in shadow, and full of shadowy nothings,
all dark.

But just outside, when I went, there was light; the
soft light of the after-glow, which comes soon after the
sun has set, as a sign that there is a sun somewhere, and
shining. And I thought of his very last words to me,

but I cannot describe the earnestness of them, "*I worship the Unknown God.*"

Friends, who worship a God whom you *know*, whose joy in life is to know Him, will you remember and pray for that one, who to-day is seeking, I think in truth, to find the Unknown God?

CHAPTER XXVIII

How Long?

"I shivered as if standing in the neighbourhood of hell."
Henry Martyn, India.

I HAVE come home from vainly trying to help another child. She had heard of the children's Saviour, and I think she would have come to Him, but they suffered her not. She was, when I first saw her, sweet and innocent, with eyes full of light, great glancing, dancing eyes, which grew wistful for a moment sometimes, and then filled with a laugh again. She told me her mother lived very near, and asked me to come and see her; so I went.

The mother startled me. Such a face, or such a want of a face. One was looking at what had once been a face, but was now a strange spoiled thing, with strange hard eyes, so unlike the child's. There was no other feature fully shaped; it was one dreadful blank. She listened that day, with almost eagerness. She understood so quickly, too, one felt she must have heard before. But she told us nothing about herself, and we only knew that there was something very wrong. Her surroundings told us that.

Before we went again we heard who she was; a
relative of one of our most honoured pastors, himself
a convert years ago.   Then a great longing possessed
us to try to save her from a life for which she had not
been trained, and especially we longed to save her little
girl, and we went to try.   This time the mother welcomed us, and told us how our words had brought back
things she had heard when she was young.   " But now
it is all different, for I am different," and she told us her
story. . . . " So I took poison, but it acted not as I
intended.   *It only destroyed my face,*" and she touched
the poor remnant with her hand, and went on with her
terrible tale.   There were people listening outside, and
she spoke in a hoarse whisper.   We could hardly believe
she meant what she said, as she told of the fate proposed
for her child.   And oh, how we besought her then and
there to give up the life, and let us help her, and that
dear little one.   She seemed moved.   Something awoke
within her and strove.   Tears filled those hard eyes and
rolled down her cheeks as we pleaded with her, in the
name of all that was motherly, not to doom her little
innocent girl, not to push her with her own hands down
to hell.   At last she yielded, promised that if in one
week's time we would come again she would give her up
to us, and as for herself, she would think of it, and perhaps she also would give up the life; she hated it, she
said.

There was another girl there, a fair, quiet girl of
fifteen.   She was ill and very suffering, and we tried for
her too; but there seemed no hope.   " Take the little
one; you are not too late for her," the mother said, and
17

we went with the promise, "One more week and she is yours."

The week passed, and every day we prayed for that little one. Then when the time came, we went. Hope and fear alternated within us. One felt sick with dread lest anything had happened to break the mother's word, and yet one hoped. The house door was open. The people in the street smiled as we stopped our bandy, got out, and went in. I remembered their smiles afterwards, and understood. The mother was there: in a corner, crouching in pain, was the girl; on the floor asleep, *drugged*, lay the child with her little arms stretched out. The mother's eyes were hard.

It was no use. Outside in the street the people sat on their verandahs and laughed. "Offer twenty thousand rupees, and see if her mother will give her to you!" shouted one. Inside we sat beside that mother, not knowing what to say.

The child stirred in her sleep, and turned. "Will you go?" said the mother very roughly in her ear. She opened listless, senseless eyes. She had no wish to go. "She wanted to come last week," we said. The mother hardened, and pushed the child, and rolled her over with her foot. "*She will not go now*," she said.

Oh, it did seem pitiful! One of those pitiful, pitiful things which never grow less pitiful because they are common everywhere. That *little* girl, and this!

We took the mother's hands in ours, and pleaded once again. And then words failed us. They sometimes do. There are things that stifle words.

At last they asked us to go. The girl in the corner

would not speak—could not, perhaps—she only moaned;
we passed her and went out. The mother followed us,
half sorry for us,—there is something of the woman left
in her,—half sullen, with a lowering sullenness. "You
will never see her again," she said, and she named the
town, one of the Sodoms of this Province, to which the
child was soon to be sent; and then, just a little
ashamed of her broken promise, she added, "I would
have let her go, but *he* would not, no, never; and she does
not belong to me now, so what could I do?" We did
not ask her who "he" was. We knew. Nor did we
ask the price he had paid. We knew; fifty rupees,
about three pounds, was the price paid down for a
younger child bought for the same purpose not long
ago. This one's price might be a little higher. That
is all.

We stood by the bullock cart ready to get in. The
people were watching. The mother had gone back into
the house. Then a great wave of longing for that
child swept over us again. We turned and looked
at the little form as it lay on the floor, dead, as it
seemed, to all outward things. Oh that it had been
dead! And we pleaded once more with all our heart,
and once more failed.

We drove away. We could see them crowding to
look after us, and we shut our eyes to shut out the sight
of their smiles. The bullock bells jingled too gladly, it
seemed, and we shut our ears to shut out the sound.
And then we shut ourselves in with God, who knew all
about it, and cared. How long, O God, how long?

And now we have heard that she has gone, and we

know, from watching what happened before, just what will happen now. How day by day they will sear that child's soul with red-hot irons, till it does not feel or care any more. And a child's seared soul is an awful thing.

Forgive us for words which may hurt and shock; we are telling the day's life-story. Hurt or not, shocked or not, should you not know the truth? How can you pray as you ought if you only know fragments of truth? Truth is a loaf; you may cut it up nicely, like thin bread and butter, with all the crusts carefully trimmed. No one objects to it then. Or you can cut it as it comes, crust and all.

Think of that child to-night as you gather your children about you, and look in their innocent faces and their clear, frank eyes. Our very last news of her was that she had been in some way influenced to spread a lie about the place, first sign of the searing begun. I think of her as I saw her that first day, bright as a bird; and then of her as I saw her last, drugged on the floor; I think of her as she must be now, bright again, but with a different brightness—not the little girl I knew— never to be quite that little girl again.

Oh, comrades, do you wonder that we care? Do you wonder that we plead with you to care? Do you wonder that we have no words sometimes, and fall back into silence, or break out into words wrung from one more gifted with expression, who knew what it was to feel!

With such words, then, we close; looking back once more at that child on the floor, with the hands stretched

out and the heavy eyes shut—and we know what it was
they saw when they opened from that sleep—

> "My God! can such things be?
> Hast Thou not said that whatsoe'er is done
> Unto Thy weakest and Thy humblest one,
> Is even done to Thee?
>
> .   .   .   .
>
> Hoarse, horrible, and strong,
> Rises to heaven that agonising cry,
> Filling the arches of the hollow sky,
> How LONG, O GOD, HOW LONG?"

CHAPTER XXIX

What do we count them worth?

"If we are simply to pray to the extent of a simple and pleasant and enjoyable exercise, and know nothing of watching in prayer, and of weariness in prayer, we shall not draw down the blessing that we may. We shall not sustain our missionaries who are overwhelmed with the appalling darkness of heathenism. . . . We must serve God even to the point of suffering, and each one ask himself, In what degree, in what point am I extending, by personal suffering, by personal self-denial, to the point of pain, the kingdom of Christ? . . . It is ever true that what costs little is worth little."

Rev. J. Hudson Taylor, China.

SHE picked up her water-vessel, and stood surveying us somewhat curiously. The ways of Picture-catching Missie Ammals were beyond her. Afterwards she sat down comfortably and talked. That was a year ago.

Then in the evening she and all her neighbours gathered in the market square for the open-air meeting. Shining of Life spoke for the first time. "I was a Hindu a year ago. I worshipped the gods you worship. Did they hear me when I prayed? No! They are dead gods. God is the living God! Come to the living God!"

One after the other the boys all witnessed that evening. Their clear boyish voices rang out round the ring. And some listened, and some laughed.

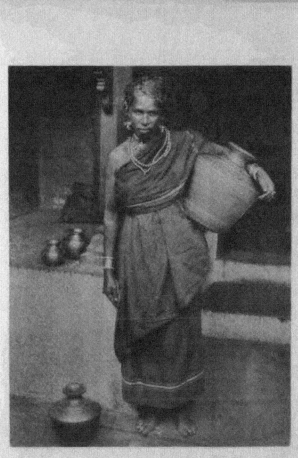

"Do you really think you are like us, do we eat the same kind of curry?" This is a very respectable woman; but look at the face till you understand it, and then try to think how many ideas you and she would have in common.

Behind us there was a little demon temple. It had a verandah barred down with heavy bars. Within these bars you could see the form of an idol. Beside us there was a shrine. Someone had put our lanterns on the top of this pyramid shrine. Before us there was the mass of dark faces. Behind us, then, black walls, black bars, a black shape; before us the black meeting, black losing itself in black. Around us light, light shining into the black. That was as it was a year ago. Now we are back at Dohnavur, and almost the first place we went to was this village, where we had taken the light and set it up in the heart of the dark. An earnest young school-master had been sent to keep that light burning there, and we went expectantly. Had the light spread? We went straight to our old friend's house. She was as friendly as ever in her queer, rough, country way, but her heart had not been set alight. "Tell me what is the good of your Way? Will it fill the cavity within me?" and she struck herself a resounding smack in the region where food is supposed to go. "Will it stock my paddy-pots, or nourish my bulls, or cause my palms to bear good juice? If it will not do all these good things, what is the use of it?"

"If it is so important, why did you not come before?" The dear old woman who asked that lived here, and we searched through the labyrinthic courtyards to find her, but failed. The girl who listened in her pain is well now, but she says the desire she had has cooled. We found two or three who seem lighting up; may God's wind blow the flame to a blaze! But we came back feeling that we must learn more of the power of prayer ourselves if these cold souls are to catch fire. We remembered how, when we were children, we caught the sunlight, and focussed it, and set bits of paper on fire; and we longed that our prayers might be a lens to focus the Love-light of our God, and set their souls on fire.

Just one little bit of encouragement may be told by way of cheer. Blessing went off one day to see if the Village of the Warrior were more friendlily inclined, and Golden went to the Petra where they vowed they would never let us in. Before Blessing entered the village she knelt down under a banyan tree, and, remembering Abraham's servant, prayed for a sign to strengthen her faith that God would work in the place. While she prayed a child came and looked at her; then seeing her pray, she said, "Has that Missie Ammal sent you who came here more than a year ago?" Blessing said "Yes." Then the child repeated the chorus we had taught the children that first day. "None of us forget," she said; and told Blessing how the parents had agreed to allow us to teach if ever we should return. The village had been opened. He goeth before.

Golden's experience was equally strengthening to our faith. In the very street where they held a public demonstration to cleanse the road defiled by our "low-caste" presence, twenty houses have opened, where she is a welcome visitor. But all this is only for Love's sake, they say. They do not yet want Christ; so let us focus the light!

Then there is need for the fire of God to burn the cords that hold souls down. There is one with whom the Spirit strove last year when we were here. But a cord

of sin was twined round her soul. She has a wicked
brother-in-law, and a still more wicked sister, and
together they plotted so evil a plot that, heathen though
she is, she recoiled, and indignantly refused. So they
quietly drugged her food, and did as they chose with her.
And now the knot she did not tie, and which she wholly
detested at first, seems doubly knotted by her own will.
Oh, to know better how to use the burning-glass of
prayer!

There may be a certain amount of sentiment, theoretically at least, in breaking up new ground. The unknown holds possibilities, and it allures one on. But in
retracing the track there is nothing whatever of this.
The broad daylight of bare truth shows you everything
just as it is. Will you look once more at things just as
they are, though it is not an interesting look.

A courtyard where the women have often heard. May
we come in? Oh yes, come in! But with us in comes
an old fakeer of a specially villainous type. His body is
plastered all over with mud; he has nothing on but mud.
His hair is matted and powdered with ashes, his face is
daubed with vermilion and yellow, his wicked old eyes
squint viciously, and he shows all his teeth, crimson with
betel, and snarls his various wants. The women say
"Chee!" Then he rolls in the dust, and squirms, and
wriggles, and howls; and he pours out such unclean vials
of wrath that the women, coerced, give him all he
demands, and he rolls off elsewhere.

Now may we read to the women? No! Many
salaams, but they have no time. Last night there was a
royal row between two friends in adjoining courtyards,

and family histories were laid bare, and pedigrees discovered. They are discussing these things to-day, and having heard it all before, they have no time to read.

Another courtyard, more refined; here the fakeer's opposite, a dignified ascetic, sits in silent meditation. "We know it all! You told us before!" But the women are friendly, and we go in; and after a long and earnest talk the white-haired grandmother touches her rosary. "This is my ladder to heaven." The berries are fine and set in chased gold, but they are only solidified tears, tears shed in wrath by their god, they say, which resolved themselves into these berries. How can tears make ladders to heaven? She does not know. She does not care. And a laugh runs round, but one's heart does not laugh. Such ladders are dangerous.

Another house; here the men have been kind, and freely let us in and out. The Way, they said, is very good; they have heard the Iyer preach. But one day there is a stir in the house. One of the sons is very ill. He has been suffering for some time; now he is suddenly getting worse, and suspicions are aroused. Then the women whisper the truth: the father and he are at daggers drawn, and the father is slowly poisoning him—small doses of strychnine are doing the work. The stir is not very violent, but quite sufficient to make an excuse for not wanting to listen. Well, this sort of thing throws us back upon God. Lord, teach us to pray! Teach us the real secret of fiery fervency in prayer. We know so little of it. Lord, teach us to pray!

" Oh, Amma! Amma! do not pray! Your prayers
are troubling me!"

We all looked up in astonishment. We had just had
our Band Prayer Meeting, when a woman came rushing
into the room, and began to exclaim like this. She was
the mother of one of our girls, of whom I told you once
before. She is still in the Terrible's den. Now the
mother was all excitement, and poured out a curious
story.

"When you went away last year I prayed. I prayed
and prayed, and prayed again to my god to dispel your
work. My daughter's heart was impressed with your
words. I cried to my god to wash the words out. Has
he washed them out? Oh no! And I prayed for a
bridegroom, and one came; and the cart was ready to
take her away, and a hindrance occurred; the marriage
fell through. And I wept till my eyes well - nigh
dissolved. And again another bridegroom came, and again
an obstacle occurred. And yet again did a bridegroom
come, and yet again an obstacle; and I cannot get my
daughter 'tied,' and the neighbours mock, and my Caste
is disgraced "—and the poor old mother cried, just
sobbed in her shame and confusion of face. "Then I
went to my god again, and said, 'What more can I offer
you? Have I not given you all I have? And you
reject my prayer!' Then in a dream my god appeared,
and he said, '*Tell the Christians not to pray. I can do
nothing against their prayers. Their prayers are hindering
me!'* And so, I beseech you, stop your prayers for
fourteen days — only fourteen days — till I get my
daughter tied!"

"And after she is tied?" we asked. "Oh, then she may freely follow your God! I will hinder her no more!"

Poor old mother! All lies are allowed where such things are concerned. We knew the proposed bridegroom came from a place three hundred miles distant, and the idea was to carry the poor girl off by force, as soon as she was "tied." We have been praying night and day to God to hinder this. And He is hindering! But there is need to go on. That mother is a devotee. She has received the afflatus. Sometimes at night it falls upon her, and she dances the wild, wicked dance, and tries to seize the girl, who shrinks into the farthest corner of the little house; and she dances round her, and chants the chant which even in daylight has power in it, but which at night appeals unspeakably. Once the girl almost gave way, and then in her desperation, hardly knowing the sin of it, ran to the place where poison was kept, drank enough to kill two, straight off, then lay down on the floor to die. Better die than do what they wanted her to do, she thought. But they found out what she had done, and drastic means were immediately used, and the poison only made her ill, and caused her days of violent pain. So there is need for the hindering prayer. Lord, teach us how to pray!

Is India crammed with the horrible? "Picturesque," they call it, who have "done it" in a month or two, and written a book to describe it. And the most picturesque part, they agree, is connected with the temples.

India ends off in a pointed rock; you can stand at the very point of the rock, with only ocean before you, and almost all Asia behind. A temple is set at the end of

the point, as if claiming the land for its own. We took
our convert boys and girls to the Cape for the Christmas
holidays, and one morning some of us spent an hour
under an old wall near the temple, which wall, being full
of hermit crabs, is very interesting. We were watching
the entertaining ways of these degenerate creatures when,
through the soft sea sounds, we heard the sound of a
Brahman's voice, and looking up, saw this:

A little group of five, sitting between the rocks and
the sea, giving a touch of life to the scene, and making
the picture perfect. There were two men, a woman, a
child, and the priest. They were all marked with the
V-shaped Vishnu mark. The priest twined the sacred
Kusa grass round the fingers of his right hand, and gave
each a handful of grass, and they did as he had done.
Then they strewed the grass on the sand, to purify it
from taint of earth, and then they began. The priest
chanted names of God, then stopped, and drew signs on
the sand. They followed him exactly. Then they bathed,
bowing to the East between each dip, and worshipping;
then returned and repeated it all. But before repeating
it, they carefully painted the marks on their foreheads,
using white and red pigment, and consulting a small
English hand mirror—the one incongruous bit of West
in this East, but symbolical of the times. The child
followed it all, as a child will, in its pretty way. She
was a dainty little thing in a crimson seeley and many
gold jewels. The elder woman was dressed in dark
green; the colouring was a joy to the eye, crimson and
green, and the brown of the rock, against the blue of
the sea.

It was one of those exquisite mornings we often have
in the Tropics, when everything everywhere shows you
God; shines the word out like a word illumined; sings
it out in the Universe Song; and here in this South
niche of Nature's cathedral, under the sky's transparency,
these five, in the only way they knew, acknowledged the
Presence of one great God, and worshipped Him.   There
was nothing revolting here, no hint of repulsive idolatry.   They worshipped the Unseen.   Very stately the
Sanscrit sounded in which they chanted their adoration.
"King of Immensity! King of Eternity! Boundless,
Endless, Infinite One!"   It might have been the echo
of some ancient Christian hymn. It might have been,
but it was not.

They are not worshipping God the Lord. *They might
be, but they are not.* Whose is the responsibility? Is it
partly yours and mine? The beauty of the scene has
passed from us; the blue of the blue sky is blotted
out—

"Only like souls I see the folk thereunder,
    Bound who should conquer, slaves who should be kings;
Hearing their one hope with an empty wonder,
    Sadly contented with a show of things.

Then with a rush the intolerable craving
    Shivers throughout me like a trumpet call:
Oh to save these! To perish for their saving,
    Die for their life, be offered for them all!"

The picture is made of souls—souls to be saved. "Oh
to save these! To perish for their saving!" That is
what the picture says. Picture! There is no picture.
In the place where it was, there is simply a pain—God's
world, and God dishonoured in it! Oh to see these

people as souls! Refined or vulgar, beautiful or horrible, or just dull, oh to see them "only as souls," and to yearn over them, and pray for them as souls who must live eternally somewhere, and for whom each of us, in our measure, is responsible to God. Do you say we are not responsible for those particular souls? Who said that sort of thing first? " Where we disavow being keeper to our brother we are his Cain." If we are not responsible, why do we take the responsibility of appealing to them in impassioned poetry?

> "Let every kindred, every tribe,
> On this terrestrial ball,
> To Him all majesty ascribe,
> And crown Him Lord of all!"

What is the point of telling people to do a certain thing if we have no concern in whether they do it or not? The angels and the martyrs and the saints, to whom we appealed before, have crowned Him long ago. Our singing to them on the subject will make no difference either way; but when we turn to every kindred and tribe, the case alters. How can they crown Him Lord of all when they do not know about Him? Why do they not know about Him? Because we have not told them. It is true that many whom we have told heard "their one hope with an empty wonder"; but, on the other hand, it is true that the everlasting song rises fuller to-day because of those who, out in this dark heathendom, heard, and responded, and crowned Him King.

But singing hymns from a distance will never save souls. By God's grace, coming and giving and praying will. Are we prepared for this? Or would we rather

sing? Searcher of hearts, turn Thy search-light upon
us! Are we coming, giving, praying *till it hurts*? Are
we praying, yea agonising in prayer? or is prayer but
" a pleasant exercise "—a holy relief for our feelings?

We have sat together under the wall by the Southern
sea. We have looked at the five as they worshipped
Another, and not our God. Now let this little South
window be like a little clear pane of glass, through which
you may look up far to the North, over the border
countries and the mountains to Tibet, over Tibet and
away through the vastness of Central Asia, on to China,
Mongolia, Manchuria; and even then you have only seen
a few of the great dark Northern lands, which wait and
wait—for you.

And this is only Asia, only a part of Asia. God looks
down on all the world; and for every one of the millions
who have never crowned Him King, Christ wore the
crown of thorns. What do we count these millions
worth? Do we count them worth the rearrangement of
our day, that we may have more time to pray? Do we
count them worth the laying down of a single ambition,
the loosening of our hold on a single child or friend?
Do we count them worth the yielding up of anything we
care for very much? Let us be still for a moment and
think. Christ counted souls worth Calvary. *What do
we count them worth?*

CHAPTER XXX

Two Safe

"God has given me the hunger and thirst for souls; will He leave me unsatisfied? No verily."

James Gilmour, Mongolia.

"That one soul has been brought to Christ in the midst of such hostile influences is so entirely and marvellously the Holy Spirit's work, that I am sometimes overjoyed to have been in any degree instrumental in effecting the emancipation of one."

Robert Noble, India.

TWO of our boys are safe. They left us very suddenly. We can hardly realise they are gone. The younger one was our special boy, the first of the boys to come, a very dear lad. I think of him as I saw him the last evening we all spent together, standing out on a wave-washed rock, the wind in his hair and his face wet with spray, rejoicing in it all. Not another boy dare go and stand in the midst of that seething foam, but the spice of danger drew him. He was such a thorough boy!

The call to leave his home for Christ came to him in an open-air meeting held in his village two years ago. Then there was bitterest shame to endure. His father and mother, aghast and distressed, did all they could to prevent the disgrace incurred by his open confession of Christ. He was an only son, heir to considerable

property, so the matter was most serious. The father
loved him dearly; but he nerved himself to flog the boy,
and twice he was tied up and flogged. But they say he
never wavered; only his mother's tears he found hardest
to withstand.

Weeks passed of steadfast confession, and then it came
to the place of choice between Christ and home. He
chose Christ, and early one morning left all to follow
Him. Do you think it was easy? He was a loving
boy. Could it have been easy to stab his mother's
heart?

When the household woke that morning he was on his
way to us. The father gathered his clansmen, and they
came in a crowd to the bungalow.

They sat on the floor in a circle, with the boy in their
midst, and they pleaded. I remember the throb of that
moment now. A single pulse seemed to beat in the
room, so tense was the tension, until he spoke out
bravely. "I will not go back," he said.

They promised everything—a house, lands, his inherit-
ance to be given at once, a wife "with a rich dowry of
jewels"—all a Tamil boy most desires they offered him.
And they promised him freedom to worship God; "only
come back and save your Caste, and do not break your
mother's heart and disgrace your family."

Day after day they came, sometimes singly, sometimes
in groups, but the mother never came. They described
her in heart-moving language. She neither ate nor
slept, they said, but sat with her hair undone, and wept
and wailed the death-wail for her son.

At last they gave up coming, and we were relieved,

for the long-continued strain was severe; and though he
never wavered, we knew the boy felt it. We used to
hear him praying for his people, pouring out his heart
when he thought no one was near, sobbing sometimes as
he named their names. The entreaty in the tone would
make our eyes wet. If only he could have lived at
home and been a Christian there! But we knew what
had happened to others, and we dare not send him back.

Then a year or so afterward we all went to the water
together, and he and three others were baptised. The
first to go down into the water was the elder boy, Shining
of Victory. Shining of Life was second. A few weeks
of bright life—those happy days by the sea—and then
in the same order, and called by the same messenger—
the swift Indian messenger, cholera—they both went
down into the other water, and crossed over to the other
side.

Shining of Life was well in the morning, dead in the
evening. When first the pain seized him he was startled.
Then, understanding, he lay down in peace. The heathen
crowded in. They could not be kept out. They taunted
him as he lay. "This is your reward for breaking your
Caste!" they said. The agony of cholera was on him.
He could not say much, but he pointed up, "Do not
trouble me; this is the way by which I am going to
Jesus," and he tried to sing a line from one of our
choruses, "My Strength and my Redeemer, my Refuge—
Jesus!"

His parents had been sent for as soon as it was known
that he was ill. They hurried over, the poor despairing
mother crying aloud imploringly to the gods who did

not hear.   He pointed up again; he was almost past
speech then, but he tried to say " Jesus" and " Come."

Then, while the heathen stood and mocked, and the
mother beat her breast and wailed, and the father, silent
in his grief, just stood and looked at his son, the boy
passed quietly away.   They hardly believed him dead.

Oh, we miss him so much !   And our hearts ache for
his people, for they mourn as those who have no hope.
But God knows why He took him ; we know it is all
right.

Every memory of him is good.   When the first sharp
strain was over we found what a thorough boy he was,
and in that week by the sea all the life and fun in him
came out, and he revelled in the bathing and boating,
and threw his whole heart into the holiday.   We had
many hopes for him ; he was so full of promise and the
energy of life.

And now it is all over for both.   Was it worth the
pain it cost ?   Such a short time to witness, was it
worth while ?

It is true it was very short.   Most of the little
space between their coming and their going was filled
with preparation for a future of service here.   And yet
in that little time each of the two found one other boy
who, perhaps, would never have been found if the cost
had been counted too great.   And I think, if you could
ask them now, they would tell you Jesus' welcome made
it far more than worth while.

CHAPTER XXXI

Three Objections

"May I have grace to live above every human motive; simply with God and to God, and not swayed, especially in missionary work, by the opinions of people not acquainted with the state of things, whose judgment may be contrary to my own."   *Henry Martyn, India.*

THESE letters have been put together to help our comrades at home to realise something of the nature of the forces ranged against us, that they may bring the Superhuman to bear upon the superhuman, and pray with an intelligence and intensity impossible to uninformed faith. We have long enough under-estimated the might of the Actual. We need more of Abraham's type of faith, which, without being weakened, considered the facts, and then, looking unto the promise, wavered not, but waxed strong. Ignorant faith does not help us much. Some years ago, when the first girl-convert came, friends wrote rejoicing that now the wall of Caste must give way; they expected soon to hear it had. As if a grain of dust falling from one of the bricks in that wall would in anywise shake the wall itself! Such faith is kind, but there it ends. It talks of what it knows not.

Then, as to the people themselves, there are certain fallacies which die hard. We read the other day, in a home paper, that it was a well-known fact that "Indian women never smile." We were surprised to hear it. We had not noticed it. Perhaps, if they were one and all so abnormally depressed, we should find them less unwilling to welcome the Glad Tidings. Again, we read that you can distinguish between heathen and Christian by the wonderful light on the Christians' faces, as compared with "the sad expression on the faces of the poor benighted heathen." It is true that some Christians are really illuminated, but, as a whole, the heathen are so remarkably cheerful that the difference is not so defined as one might think. Then, again, we read in descriptive articles on India that the weary, hopeless longing of the people is most touching. But we find that our chief difficulty is to get them to believe that there is anything to long for. Rather we would describe them as those who think they have need of nothing, knowing not that they have need of everything. And again and again we read thrilling descriptions of India's women standing with their hands stretched out towards God. They may do this in visions; in reality they do not. And it is the utter absence of all this sort of thing which makes your help a necessity to us.

But none of you can pray in the way we want you to pray, unless the mind is convinced that the thing concerning which such prayer is asked is wholly just and right; and it seems to us that many of those who have followed the Story of this War may have doubts about the right of it—the right, for example, of converts leaving their homes for Christ's sake and His Gospel's. All will be in sympathy with us when we try to save

little children, but perhaps some are out of sympathy
when we do what results in sorrow and misunderstanding
—" not peace, but a sword." So we purpose now to
gather up into three, some of the many objections which
are often urged upon those engaged in this sort of
work, because we feel that they ought to be faced and
answered if possible, lest we lose someone's prevailing
prayer.

The first set of objections may be condensed into a
question as to the right or otherwise of our " forcing our
religion" upon those who do not want it. We are
reminded that the work is most discouraging, conversions
are rare, and when they occur they seem to create the
greatest confusion. It is evident enough that neither
we nor our Gospel are desired; and no wonder, when
the conditions of discipleship involve so much. " We
should not like strangers to come and interfere with our
religion," write the friends who object, " and draw our
children away from us; we should greatly resent it. No
wonder the Hindus do!" And one reader of the letters
wrote that she wondered how the girls who came out
ever could be happy for a moment after having done such
a wrong and heartless thing as to disobey their parents.
" They richly deserve all they suffer," she wrote. " It is
a perfect shame and disgrace for a girl to desert her own
people!"

One turns from the reading of the letter, and looks
at the faces of those who have done it; and knowing
how they need every bit of prayer-help one can win for
them, one feels it will be worth while trying to show
those who blame them why they do it, and how it is

they cannot do otherwise if they would be true to Christ.

This objection as to the right or wrong of the work as a whole, leads to another relating to baptism. It is a serious thing to think of families divided upon questions of religion; surely it would be better that a convert should live a consistent Christian life at home, even without baptism, than that she should break up the peace of the household by leaving her home altogether? Or, having been baptised, should she not return home and live there as a Christian?

Lastly—and this comes in letters from those who, more than any, are in sympathy with us—why not devote our energies to work of a more fruitful character? We are reminded of the mass-movement type of work, in which "nations are born in a day"; and often, too, of the nominal Christians who sorely need more enlightenment. Why not work along the line of least resistance, where conversion to God does not of necessity mean fire and sword, and where in a week we could win more souls than in years of this unresultful work?

We frankly admit that these objections and proposals are naturally reasonable, and that what they state is perfectly true. It is true that work among high-caste Hindus all over India (as among Moslems all over the world) is very difficult. It is true that open confession of Christ creates disastrous division in families. It is true there is other work to be done.

Especially we feel the force of the second objection raised. We fully recognise that the right thing is for the convert to live among her own people, and let her

light shine in her own home; and we deplore the terrible
wrench involved in what is known as "coming out." To
a people so tenacious of custom as the Indians are, to a
nature so affectionate as the Indian nature is, this cutting
across of all home ties is a very cruel thing.

And now, only that we may not miss your prayer,
we set ourselves to try to answer you. And, first of all,
let us grasp this fact: it is not fair, nor is it wise, to
compare work, and success in work, between one set of
people and another, because the conditions under which
that work is carried on are different, and the unseen
forces brought to bear against it differ in character and
in power. There is sometimes more "result" written
down in a single column of a religious weekly than is
to be found in the 646 pages of one of the noblest
missionary books of modern days, *On the Threshold of
Central Africa.* Or take two typical opposite lives,
Moody's and Gilmour's. Moody saw more soul-winning
in a day than Gilmour in his twenty-one years. It was
not that the *men* differed. Both knew the Baptism of
Power, both lived in Christ and loved. But these are
extremes in comparison; take two, both missionaries,
twin brothers in spirit, Brainerd of North America and
Henry Martyn of India. Brainerd saw many coming
to Jesus; Martyn hardly one. Each was a pioneer
missionary, each was a flame of fire. "Now let me
burn out for God," wrote Henry Martyn, and he did it.
But the conditions under which each worked varied as
widely spiritually as they varied climatically. Can we
compare their work, or measure it by its visible results?
Did God? Let us leave off comparing this with that—

we do not know enough to compare. Let us leave off
weighing eternal things and balancing souls in earthly
scales. Only God's scales are sufficiently sensitive for
such delicate work as that.

We take up the objections one by one. First, "*Why
do you go where you are not wanted?*"

We go because we believe our Master told us to go.
He said, "all the world," and "every creature." Our
marching orders are very familiar. "Go ye into all the
world and preach the Gospel to every creature." "All
the world" means everywhere in it, "every creature"
means everyone in it. These orders are so explicit that
there is no room to question what they mean.

All missionaries in all ages have so understood these
words "all" and "every." Nearly seven hundred years
ago the first missionary to the Moslems found no welcome,
only a prison; but he never doubted he was sent to
them. "*God wills it,*" he said, and went again. They
stoned him then, and he died—died, but never doubted
he was sent.

Our Master Himself went not only to the common
people, who heard Him gladly, but to the priestly and
political classes, who had no desire for the truth. "Ye
will not come to Me that ye might have life," He
said, and yet He gave them the chance to come by
going to them. The words, "If any man thirst, let him
come unto Me and drink," were spoken to an audience
which was not thirsting for the Gospel.

St. Paul would willingly have spent his strength
preaching the Word in Asia, especially in Galatia, where
the people loved him well; but he was under orders, and

he went to Europe, to Philippi, where he was put in
prison; to Thessalonica, where the opposition was so
strong that he had to flee away by night; to Athens,
where he was the butt of the philosophers. But God
gave souls in each of these places; only a few in comparison to the great indifferent crowd, but he would tell
you those few were worth going for. You would not
have had him miss a Lydia, a Damaris? Above all, you
would not have had him disobey his Lord's command?

So whether our message is welcomed or not, the fact
remains we must go to all; and the worse they are and
the harder they are, the more evident is it that, wanted
or not, it is *needed* by them.

M. Coillard was robbed by the people he had travelled
far to find. "You see we made no mistake," he writes,
"in bringing the Gospel to the Zambesi."

The second objection is, "*Why break up families by
insisting on baptism as a* sine quâ non *of discipleship?*"

And again we answer, Because we believe our Master
tells us to. He said, "Baptising them in the Name of
the Father, and of the Son, and of the Holy Ghost."
What right have we, His servants, to stop short of full
obedience? Did He not know the conditions of high-
caste Hindu life in India when He gave this command?
Was He ignorant of the breaking up of families which
obedience to it would involve? "Suppose ye that I am
come to give peace on earth? I tell you nay, but
rather division." And then come words which we have
seen lived out literally in the case of every high-caste
convert who has come. "For from henceforth there
shall be five in one house divided, three against two,

and two against three. The father shall be divided
against the son, and the son against the father; the
mother against the daughter, and the daughter against
the mother; the mother-in-law against her daughter-in-
law, and the daughter-in-law against her mother-in-law."
These are truly *awful* verses; no one knows better than
the missionary how awful they are. There are times
when we can hardly bear the pain caused by the sight
of this division. But are we more tender than the
Tender One? Is our sympathy truer than His? Can
we look up into His eyes and say, "It costs them too
much, Lord; it costs us too much, to fully obey Thee
in this"?

But granted the command holds, why should not the
baptised convert return home and live there? Because
he is not wanted there, *as a Christian*. Exceptions to
this rule are rare (we are speaking of Caste Hindus),
and can usually be explained by some extenuating cir-
cumstance.

The high-caste woman who said to us, "I cannot live
here and break my Caste; if I break it I must go,"
spoke the truth. Keeping Caste includes within itself
the observance of certain customs which by their very
nature are idolatrous. Breaking Caste means breaking
through these customs; and one who habitually disre-
garded and disobeyed rules, considered binding and
authoritative by all the rest of the household, would not
be tolerated in an orthodox Hindu home. It is not a
question of persecution or death, or of wanting or not
wanting to be there; it is a question *of not being wanted
there,* unless, indeed, she will compromise. Compromise

is the one open door back into the old home, and God only knows what it costs when the choice is made and that one door is shut.

This ever-recurring reiteration of the power and the bondage of Caste may seem almost wearisome, but the word, and what lies behind it, is the one great answer to a thousand questions, and so it comes again and again. In Southern India especially, and still more so in this little fraction of it, and in the adjoining kingdoms of Travancore and Cochin, Caste feeling is so strong that sometimes it is said that Caste is the religion of South India.   But everywhere all over India it is, to every orthodox Hindu, part of his very self.   Get his Caste out of him?   Can you?   You would have to drain him of his life-blood first.

It is the strength of this Caste spirit which in South India causes it to take the form of a determination to get the convert back.   Promises are given that they may live as Christians at home.   " We will send you in a bandy to church every Sunday !"—promises given to be broken.   If the convert is a boy, he may possibly reappear. If a girl—I was going to say *never*; but I remember hearing of one who did reappear, after seventeen years imprisonment—a wreck.   Send them back, do you say? Think of the dotted lines in some chapters you have read; ponder the things they cover; then send them back if you can.

The third objection divides into two halves.   The first half is, " *Why do you not go to the Christians?*"   To which we answer, we do, and for exactly the same reason as that which we have given twice before, because our

Master told us to do so. Our marching orders are three-
fold, one order concerning each form of service touched
by the three objections. The third order touches this,
"Teaching them to observe all things whatsoever I have
commanded you." So we go, and try to teach them the
"all things"; and some of them learn them, and go to
teach others, and so the message of a full Gospel spreads,
and the Bride gets ready for the Bridegroom.

The second half of this last objection is, "*Why not do
easier work?* There are so many who are more accessible, why not go to them?" And there does seem to be
point in the suggestion that if there are open doors,
it might be better to enter into them, rather than keep
on knocking at closed ones.

We do seek to enter the so-called open doors. We
never find they are so very wide open when it is known
that we bring nothing tangible with us. Spiritual things
are not considered anything by most. Still, work among
such is infinitely easier, and many, comparatively speaking, are doing it.

The larger number here are working among the Christians, the next larger number among the Masses, and the
fewest always, everywhere, among the Classes, where
conversion involves such terrible conflicts with the Evil
One, that all that is human in one faints and fails as it
confronts the cost of every victory.

But real conversion anywhere costs. By conversion
we mean something more than reformation; *that* raises
fewer storms. The kind of work, however, which more
than any other seems to fascinate friends at home is what
is known as the "mass movement," and though we have

touched upon it before, perhaps we had better explain
more fully what it really is. This movement, or rather
the visible result thereof, is often dilated upon most
rapturously. I quote from a Winter Visitor: "Christian
churches counted by the thousand, their members by the
million; whole districts are Christian, entire communi-
ties are transformed." And we look at one another, and
ask each other, "Where?"

But to that question certain would answer joyously,
"Here!" There are missions in India where the avowed
policy is to baptise people "at the outset, not on evidence
of what is popularly called conversion. . . . We baptise
them 'unto' the baptism of the Holy Spirit, and not
because we have reason to believe that they have received
the Spirit's baptism,"—we quote a leader in the movement, and he goes on to say, if it is insisted "that we should
wait until this change (conversion) is effected before
baptising them, we reply that in most cases we would
have to wait for a long time, and often see the poor
creatures die without the change."

Of course every effort is made by revival services and
camp meetings to bring these baptised Christians to a
true knowledge of Christ, and it is considered that this
policy yields more fruit than the other, which puts conversion first and baptism second. It is certainly richer
in "results," for among the depressed classes and certain
of the middle Castes, among whom alone the scheme can
be carried out, there is no doubt that many are found
ready to embrace Christianity, as the phrase goes, sometimes genuinely feeling it is the true religion, and desiring
to understand it, sometimes for what they can get.

It must be admitted—for we want to state the case fairly—that a mass movement gives one a splendid chance to preach Christ, and teach His Gospel day by day. And the power in it does lay hold of some; we have earnest men and women working and winning others to-day, fruit of the mass movement of many years ago.

But on the whole, we fear it, and do not encourage it here. The dead weight of heathenism is heavy enough, but when you pile on the top of that the incubus of a dead Christianity—for a nominal thing is dead—then you are terribly weighted down and handicapped, as you try to go forward to break up new ground.

So, though we sympathise with everything that tends towards life and light in India, and rejoice with our brothers who bind sheaves, believing that though all is not genuine corn, some is, yet we feel compelled to give ourselves mainly to work of a character which, by its very nature, can never be popular, and possibly never successful from a statistical point of view, never, till the King comes, Whose Coming is our hope.

CHAPTER XXXII

"Show me Thy Glory!"

"Yesterday I was called to see a patient, a young woman who had been suffering terribly for three days. It was the saddest case I ever saw in my life. . . . I had to leave her to die. . . . The experience was such a terrible one that, old and accustomed surgeon as I am, I have been quite upset by it ever since. As long as I live the memory of that scene will cling to me."
A Chinese Missionary.

"If we refuse to be corns of wheat falling into the ground and dying; if we will neither sacrifice prospects nor risk character and property and health, nor, when we are called, relinquish home and break family ties, for Christ's sake and His Gospel, then we shall abide alone."
Thomas Gajetan Ragland, India.

"Not mere pity for dead souls, but a passion for the Glory of God, is what we need to hold us on to Victory."
Miss Lilias Trotter, Africa.

WE are all familiar with the facts and figures which stand for so much more than we realise. We can repeat glibly enough that there are nearly one thousand five hundred million people in the world, and that of these nearly one thousand million are heathen or Mohammedan. Perhaps we can divide this unthinkable mass into comprehensible figures. We can tell everyone who is interested in hearing it, that of this one thousand million, two hundred million are Mohammedans; two hundred million more are Hindus; four hundred and thirty million are Buddhists and

19

Confucianists; and more than one hundred and fifty million are Pagans.

But have we ever stopped and let the awfulness of these statements bear down upon us? Do we take in, that we are talking about immortal souls?

We quote someone's computation that every day ninety-six thousand people die without Christ. Have we ever for one hour sat and thought about it? Have we thought of it for half an hour, for a quarter of an hour, for five unbroken minutes? I go further, and I ask you, have you ever sat still for one whole minute and counted by the ticking of your watch, while soul after soul passes out alone into eternity?

. . . I have done it. It is awful. At the lowest computation, sixty-six for whom Christ died have died since I wrote "eternity."

"Oh my God! my God! Men are perishing, and I take no heed!" . . .

Sixty-six more have gone. Oh, how can one keep so calm? Death seems racing with the minute hand of my watch. I feel like stopping that terrible run of the minute hand. Round and round it goes, and every time it goes round, sixty-six people die.

I have just heard of the dying of one of the sixty-six. We knew her well. She was a widow; she had no protectors, and an unprotected widow in India stands in a dangerous place. We knew it, and tried to persuade her to take refuge in Jesus. She listened, almost decided then drew back; afterwards we found out why. You have seen the picture of a man sucked under sea by an octopus; it was like that. You have imagined the death-

struggle; it was like that. But it all went on under the
surface of the water, there was nothing seen above, till
perhaps a bubble rose slowly and broke; it was like that.
One day, in the broad noontide, a woman suddenly fell in
the street. Someone carried her into a house, but she
was dead, and those who saw that body saw the marks
of the struggle upon it. The village life flowed on as
before; only a few who knew her knew she had murdered
her body to cover the murder of her soul. We had come
too late for her.

Last week I stood in a house where another of those
sixty-six had passed. Crouching on the floor, with her
knees drawn up and her head on her knees, a woman
began to tell me about it. "She was my younger sister.
My mother gave us to two brothers"— and she stopped.
I knew who the brothers were. I had seen them yesterday—two handsome high-caste Hindus. We had visited
their wives, little knowing. The woman said no more;
she could not. She just shuddered and hid her face
in her hands. A neighbour finished the story. Something went wrong with the girl. They called in the
barber's wife—the only woman's doctor known in these
parts. She did her business ignorantly. The girl died
in fearful pain. Hindu women are inured to sickening
sights, but this girl's death was so terrible that the elder
sister has never recovered from the shock of seeing it.
There she sits, they tell me, all day long, crouching on
the floor, mute.

All do not pass like that; some pass very quietly,
there are no bands in their death; and some are innocent children—thank God for the comfort of that! But

it must never be forgotten that the heathen sin against
the light they have; their lives witness against them.
They know they sin, and they fear death. An Indian
Christian doctor, practising in one of our Hindu towns,
told me that he could not speak of what he had seen
and heard at the deathbeds of some of his patients.

A girl came in a moment ago, and I told her what
I was doing. Then I showed her the diagram of the
Wedge; the great black disc for heathendom, and the
narrow white slit for the converts won. She looked at
it amazed. Then she slowly traced her finger round
the disc, and she pointed to the narrow slit, and her
tears came dropping down on it. " Oh, what must Jesus
feel!" she said. " *Oh, what must Jesus feel!*" She is
only a common village girl, she has been a Christian
only a year; but it touched her to the quick to see that
great black blot.

I know there are those who care at home, but do all
who care, care deeply enough? Do they feel as Jesus
feels? And if they do, are they giving their own?
They are helping to send out others, perhaps; but are
they giving their own?

Oh, are they truly giving themselves? There must be
more giving of ourselves if that wedge is to be widened
in the disc. Some who care are young, and life is all
before them, and the question that presses now is this:
Where is that life to be spent? Some are too old to
come, but they have those whom they might send, if
only they would strip themselves for Jesus' sake.

Mothers and fathers, have you sympathy with Jesus?
Are you willing to be lonely for a few brief years, that

all through eternal ages He may have more over whom
to rejoice, and you with Him? He may be coming very
soon, and the little interval that remains, holds our last
chance certainly to suffer for His sake, and possibly
our last to win jewels for His crown. Oh, the unworked
jewel-mines of heathendom! Oh, the joy His own are
missing if they lose this one last chance!

Sometimes we think that if the need were more clearly
seen, something more would be done. Means would be
devised; two or three like-minded would live together,
so as to save expenses, and set a child free who must
otherwise stay for the sake of one of the three. Workers
abroad can live together, sinking self and its likes and
dislikes for the sake of the Cause that stands first. But
if such an innovation is impossible at home, something
else will be planned, by which more will be spared,
when those who love our God love Him well enough to
put His interests first. "Worthy is the Lamb to receive!" Oh, we say it, and we pray it! Do we act
as if we meant it? Fathers and mothers, is He not
worthy? Givers, who have given your All, have you
not found Him worthy?

"Bare figures overwhelmed me," said one, as he told
how he had been led to come out; "I was fairly
staggered as I read that twenty-eight thousand a day
in India alone, go to their death without Christ. And
I questioned, Do we believe it? Do we really believe
it? What narcotic has Satan injected into our systems
that this awful, woeful, tremendous fact does not startle
us out of our lethargy, our frightful neglect of human
souls?"

mile away.

Out in the m
platforms are b
resting-places wh
a party of labour
one of these platf
due, the river was
rose. It swept tl
whirled them dow:

Suppose that, kr
had begun to fall
to fill, you had ch
were settling down
have passed on con
so ? Would you, co
in perfect tranquillity
you had seen ware ou

If you had, the
wakened you, and for
been cold with a chil
the thought of ii

it not,' doth not He that pondereth the heart consider
it, and He that keepeth thy soul, doth not He know it?
and shall not He render to every man according to his
works?"

Oh, by the thought of the many who are drawn unto
death, and the many that are ready to be slain, by the
thought of the sorrow of Jesus Who loves them, consider
these things!

But all are not called to come! We know it. We
do not forget it. But is it a fact so forgotten at home
that a missionary need press it? What is forgotten
surely is that the field is the world.

You would not denude England! Would England be
denuded? Would a single seat on the Bishop's bench,
or a single parish or mission hall, be left permanently
empty, if the man who fills it now moved out to the
place which no one fills—that gap on the precipice
edge?

But suppose it were left empty, would it be so dreadful after all? Would there not be one true Christian
left to point the way to Christ? And if the worst came
to the worst, would there not still be the Bible, and
ability to read? Need anyone die unsaved, unless set
upon self-destruction? If only Christians in England
knew how to draw supplies direct from God, if only
those who cannot come would take up the responsibility
of the unconverted around them, why should not a parish
here and there be left empty for awhile? Surely
we should not deliberately leave so very many to starve
to death, because those who have the Bread of Life have
a strong desire for sweets. Oh, the spiritual confectionery

consumed every year in England! God open our eyes to
see if we are doing what He meant, and what He means
should continue! But some men are too valuable to be
thrown away on the mission field; they are such successful workers, pastors, evangelists, leaders of thought. They
could not possibly be spared. Think of the waste of
burying brain in unproductive sand! Apparently it is
so, but is it really so? Does God view it like that?
Where should we have been to-day if He had thought
Jesus too valuable to be thrown away upon us? Was
not each hour of those thirty-three years worth more
than a lifetime of ours?

What is God's definition of that golden word "success"?
He looks at Roman Catholic Europe, and Roman and
heathen South America, and Mohammedan and heathen
Africa and Asia, and many a forgotten place in many a
great land. And then He looks at us, and I wonder
what He thinks. Ragland, Fellow of Corpus Christi
College, Cambridge, after years of brain-burying waste,
wrote that He was teaching him that " *of all plans for
securing success the most certain is Christ's own, becoming a
corn of wheat, falling into the ground and dying.*" If
coming abroad means that for anyone, is it too much to
ask? It was what our dear Lord did.

This brings us to another plea. I find it in the verse
that carves out with two strokes the whole result of two
lives. "If any man's work abide. . . . If any man's
work shall be burned." The net result of one man's
work is gold, silver, precious stones; the net result of
another man's work is wood, hay, stubble. Which is
worth the spending of a life?

An earnest worker in her special line of work is looking back at it from the place where things show truest, and she says, "God help us all! What is the good done by any such work as mine? 'If any man build upon this foundation . . . wood, hay, stubble. . . . If any man's work shall be burned he shall suffer loss; but he himself shall be saved, yet so as by fire!' An infinitude of pains and labour, and all to disappear like the stubble and the hay."

Success—what is it worth?

> "I was flushed with praise,
> But pausing just a moment to draw breath,
> I could not choose but murmur to myself,
> 'Is this all? All that's done? and all that's gained?
> If this, then, be success, 'tis dismaller
> Than any failure.'"

So transparent a thing is the glamour of success to clear-seeing poet-eyes, and should it dazzle the Christian to whom nothing is of any worth but the thing that endures? Should arguments based upon comparisons between the apparent success of work at home as distinguished from work abroad influence us in any way? Is it not very solemn, this calm, clear setting forth of a truth which touches each of us? "*Every man's work shall be made manifest, for the Day shall declare it, because it shall be revealed by fire, and the fire shall try every man's work of what sort it is.*" And as we realise the perishableness of all work, however apparently successful, except the one work done in the one way God means, oh, does it not stir us up to seek with an intensity of purpose which will not be denied, to find out what that one work is? The same thought comes out in the verse which tells us that the very things we are to do are prepared before, and we are " created in Christ Jesus" to do them. If this is so, then will the doing of anything else seem worth while, when we look back and see life as God sees it ?

It may be that the things prepared are lying close at our hand at home, but it may be they are abroad. If they are at home there will be settled peace in the doing of them there ; but if they are abroad, and we will not come and do them ?—Oh, then our very prayers will fall as fall the withered leaves, when the wind that stirred them falls, yea more so, for the withered leaves have a work to do, but the prayers which are stirred up by some passing breeze of emotion do nothing, *nothing* for eternity. God will not hear our prayers for the heathen if He means us to be out among them instead of at home praying for them, or if He means us to give up some son or daughter, and we prefer to pray.

Lord save us from hypocrisy and sham ! " Shrivel the falsehood " from us if we say we love Thee but obey Thee not ! Are we staying at home, and praying for missions when Thou hast said to us " Go " ? Are we holding back something of which Thou hast said, " Loose it, and let it go " ? Lord, are we utterly through and through true ? Lord God of truthfulness, save us from sham ! Make us perfectly true !

I turn to you, brothers and sisters at home ! Do you know that if God is calling you, and you refuse to obey, you will hardly know how to bear what will happen afterwards ? Sooner or later you will know, yea burn through every part of your being, with the knowledge

that you disobeyed, and lost your chance, lost it for ever.
For that is the awful part. It is rarely given to one to
go back and pick up the chance he knowingly dropped.
The express of one's life has shot past the points, and one
cannot go back; the lines diverge.

"Some of us almost shudder now to think how nearly
we stayed at home," a missionary writes. "Do not, I
beseech you, let this great matter drift. Do not walk
in uncertainty. Do not be turned aside. You will be
eternally the poorer if you do."

It may be you are not clear as to what is God's will
for you. You are in doubt, you are honest, but a thousand
questions perplex you. Will you go to God about it, and
get the answer direct?

If you are puzzled about things which a straightforward missionary can explain, will you buy a copy
of *Do Not Say*, and read it alone with God? Let me
emphasise that word "alone." "Arise, go forth into the
plain, and I will there talk with thee." "There was a
Voice . . . when they stood and had let down their
wings."

Oh, by the thought of the Day that is coming, when
the fire shall try all we are doing, and only the true
shall stand, I plead for an honest facing of the question
before it is too late!

But this is not our strongest plea. We could pile
them up, plea upon plea, and not exhaust the number
which press and urge one to write. We pass them all,
and go to the place where the strongest waits: God's
Glory is being given to another. This is the most
solemn plea, the supreme imperative call. "Not mere

pity for dead souls, but a passion for the Glory of God,
is what we need to hold us through to victory."

" I am the Lord, that is My Name, and My Glory
will I not give to another, neither My praise to graven
images." But the men He made to glorify Him take
His Glory from Him, give it to another; *that*, the sin
of it, the shame, calls with a low, deep under-call through
all the other calls. God's Glory is being given to another.
Do we love Him enough to care ? Or do we measure
our private cost, if these distant souls are to be won, and,
finding it considerable, cease to think or care ? " Is it
nothing to you, all ye that pass by ? Behold and see "—
" They took Jesus and led Him away. And He,
bearing His cross, went forth into a place called
the place of a skull . . . where they crucified
Him." . . . " Herein is love." . . . " God so loved
the world." . . . Have we petrified past feeling ? Can
we stand and measure now ? " I know that only the
Spirit, Who counted every drop that fell from the torn
brow of Christ as dearer than all the jewelled gates of
Paradise, can lift the Church out of her appreciation of
the world, the world as it appeals to her own selfish
lusts, into an appreciation of the world as it appeals to
the heart of God." O Spirit, come and lift us into this
love, inspire us by this love. Let us look at the vision
of the Glory of our God with eyes that have looked at
His love !

We would not base a single plea on anything weaker
than solid fact. Sentiment will not stand the strain of
the real tug of war; but is it fact, or is it not, that Jesus
counted you and me, and the other people in the world,

actually worth dying for? If it is true, then do we love Him well enough to care with the whole strength of our being, that to-day, almost all over the world, His Glory is being given to another? If this does not move us, is it because we do not love Him very much, or is it that we have never prayed with honest desire, as Moses prayed, "I beseech Thee, show me Thy Glory"? He only saw a little of it. "Behold there is a place by Me, and thou shalt stand upon a rock: and it shall come to pass, while My Glory passeth by, that I will put thee in a clift of the rock, and will cover thee with My hand while I pass by." And the Glory of the Lord passed, and Moses was aware of something of it as it passed, but "My face shall not be seen." And yet that little was enough to mark him out as one who lived for one purpose, shone in the light of it, burned with the fire of it—he was jealous for the Glory of his God.

And we—"We beheld His Glory, the Glory as of the only begotten of the Father, full of grace and truth"; and we—we have seen "the light of the knowledge of the Glory of God in the face of Jesus Christ."

"While My Glory passeth by I will . . . cover thee . . . My face shall not be seen." "But we all with open face, reflecting, as in a mirror, the Glory of the Lord, are changed"—Are we? Do we? Do we know anything at all about it? Have we ever apprehended this for which we are apprehended of Christ Jesus? Have we seen the Heavenly Vision that breaks us down, and humbles us to hear the Voice of the Lord ask, "Who

will go for Us?" and strengthens us to answer, "Here
am I, send me," and holds us on to obey if we hear Him
saying "Go"?

I beseech Thee, show me Thy Glory! Shall we pray
it, meaning it now, to the very uttermost? The uttermost may hold hard things, but, easy or hard, there is no
other way to reach the place where our lives can receive
an impetus which will make them tell for eternity. The
motive power is the love of Christ. Not our love for
Him only, but His very love itself. It was the mighty,
resistless flow of that glorious love that made the first
missionary pour himself forth on the sacrifice and service.
And the joy of it rings through triumphantly, "Yea,
and if I be poured forth . . . . I joy and rejoice with you
all!"

Yes, God's Glory is our plea, highest, strongest, most
impelling and enduring of all pleas. But oh, by the
thought of the myriads who are passing, by the thought
of the Coming of the Lord, by the infinite realities of
life and death, heaven and hell, by our Saviour's cross
and Passion, we plead with all those who love Him,
but who have not considered these things yet, consider
them now!

Let Him show us the vision of the Glory, and
bring us to the very end of self, let Him touch
our lips with the live coal, and set us on fire to
burn for Him, yea, burn with a consuming love for
Him, and a purpose none can turn us from, and a
passion like a pure white flame, "a passion for the
Glory of God!"

Oh, may this passion consume us! burn the self out

of us, burn the love into us—for God's Glory we ask it, Amen.

"Worthy is the Lamb that was slain to receive power, and riches, and wisdom, and strength, and honour, and glory, and blessing . . . Blessing, and honour, and glory, and power be unto Him."

LONDON: MORGAN AND SCOTT.

CPSIA information can be obtained
at www.ICGtesting.com
Printed in the USA
LVHW081115160720
660853LV00015B/107

9 781296 559991